Computer Science and Web Technologies

Computer Science and Web Technologies

Edited by:

Adele Kuzmiakova

ARCLER PRESS

www.arclerpress.com

Computer Science and Web Technologies

Adele Kuzmiakova

Arcler Press
224 Shoreacres Road
Burlington, ON L7L 2H2
Canada
www.arclerpress.com
Email: orders@arclereducation.com

ISBN: 978-1-77407-747-4 (Hardcover)

ABOUT THE EDITOR

Adele Kuzmiakova is a computational engineer focusing on solving problems in machine learning, deep learning, and computer vision. Adele attended Cornell University in New York, United States for her undergraduate studies. She studied engineering with a focus on applied math. While at Cornell, she developed close relationships with professors, which enabled her to get involved in academic research to get hands-on experience with solving computational problems. She was also selected to be Accel Roundtable on Entrepreneurship Education (REE) Fellow at Stanford University and spent 3 months working on entrepreneurship projects to get a taste of entrepreneurship and high-growth ventures in engineering and life sciences. The program culminated in giving a presentation on the startup technology and was judged by Stanford faculty and entrepreneurship experts in Silicon Valley. After graduating from Cornell, Adele worked as a data scientist at Swiss Federal Institute of Technology in Lausanne, Switzerland where she focused on developing algorithms and graphical models to analyze chemical pathways in the atmosphere. Adele also pursued graduate studies at Stanford University in the United States where she entered as a recipient of American Association of University Women International Fellowship. The Fellowship enabled her to focus on tackling important research problems in machine learning and computer vision. Some research problems she worked on at Stanford include detecting air pollution from outdoor public webcam images. Specifically, she modified and set up a variety of pre-trained architectures, such as DehazeNet, VGG, and ResNet, on public webcam images to evaluate their ability to predict air quality based on the degree of haze on pictures. Other deep learning problems Adele worked on include investigating the promise of second-order optimizers in deep learning and using neural networks to predict sequences of data in energy consumption. Adele also places an emphasis on continual education and served as a Student Leader in PyTorch scholarship challenge organized by Udacity. Her roles as the Student Leader were helping students debug their code to train neural networks with PyTorch and providing mentorship on technical and career aspects. Her hobbies include skiing, playing tennis, cooking, and meeting new people.

TABLE OF CONTENTS

LIST OF FIGURES

LIST OF ABBREVIATIONS

AI	Artificial Intelligence
CDN	Content Delivery Networks
DBMS	Database Managing Software
DNS	Domain Naming System
DOM	Document Object Model
EC	European
HTML	Hypertext Markup Language
HTTP	Hypertext Transfer Protocol
IE	Internet Explorer
IS	Information Systems
ISBN	International Standards Book Number
IT	Information-Technology
JSON	JavaScript Entity Notation
ML	Machine Learning
MSA	Micro Services Architecture
MUVE	Multi-User Virtual Environment
MVC	Model Controller View
OS	Operating Systems
OSI Model	Open Structures Interconnection Model
PCs	Personal Computers
RAM	Random-Access Memory
RFID	Radio Frequency Identification Tags
RIA	Rich Internet Application
ROI	Return on Investment
SE	Search Engines
SEO	Search Engine Optimization
SERPs	Search-Engine Result Pages

SMB	Server Messaging Block
SOA	Service Oriented Architecture
SSL	Secure Socket Layer
URI	Uniform Resource Identifier
URL	Uniform Resource Locator
URN	Uniform Resource Name
VoIP	Voice-Over Internet Protocol
VR	Virtual Reality
W3C	Worldwide Web Consortium
WOA	Web-Oriented Architecture
WWW	World Wide Web
XML	Extensible Markup Language

PREFACE

In the modern age, nearly everyone has interacted with computers at some point or another. These machines are versatile and can be applied to almost every aspect of human life, ranging from business, media, and entertainment among others. From a theoretical perspective, Computer Science can be defined as the exploration of a computer's functions or what the computer is capable of doing. In a more practical sense, it involves studying the development of computer programs or the engineering of software programs that make life easier for people.

Basically, computer scientists are focused on software systems, including their theory, design, formulation, and application. Some common fields of study within this discipline are artificial intelligence (AI), human-computer interaction, programming languages, bioinformatics, and software engineering.

While learning how to program forms an essential aspect of computer science studies, it is merely one component of the discipline. Computer scientists develop and examine algorithms in order to solve digital problems; their primary role is finding out what problems are solvable through computers.

You are probably aware that computers don't network with each other in the same way that humans do. Rather, computers depend on codes, or directions to communicate. The way in which computers network with one another through the application of markup languages as well as multimedia packages is called web technology. Within the last few years, web technology as a field has underwent drastic changes, from basic synchronized webpages to the capacity to perform very specific duties on the network without any disruptions.

In this volume, we are going to delve into the growth and evolution of computer science and web-based technologies. Chapter 1 gives a brief review of webpages, sites, and applications, Chapter 2 discusses web-browsers and layout engines, Chapter 3 discusses about the web advancement, Chapter 4 discusses about the web servers, Chapter 5 discusses about the software architectures, Chapter 6 discusses about the emergent web technologies, Chapter 7 discusses about the applications for authentic web technologies, Chapter 8 discusses about the cloud web innovations, Chapter 9 discusses about the how web innovations are transforming marketing, and Chapter 10 discusses about the possible setbacks of web technologies.

Getting computers to perform what you require them to do needs extensive hands-on experience. However, computer science also involves the ability to design digital solutions and affirm that they are accurate. Problem-solving needs precision, creativity, and cautious reasoning. Besides, computer science has solid relations with other disciplines like commerce, science, and education. Meaning computer scientists usually become efficient in other subjects through practice.

Web technologies can be viewed as a gradually evolving field, where some elements are still being used today. Try envisioning a network that lacks web technologies. Even though you may have instant access to personal computers, you still wouldn't have the capacity to run operations in the cloud. Any moment you wanted to check a piece of data, you shall have to perform it through an instant link to the main host computer, which would rather be quite inefficient.

Luckily, web technology removes such inefficiencies by offering computer users efficient ways of interacting with hosted data like websites. Through different markup languages, such as hypertext markup language or HTML, the functions can vary from simply delivering text to generating high capacity graphics and so on.

Chapter 1 Introduction to Web Pages, Sites, and Applications

CONTENTS

1.1. INTRODUCTION

Web technology involves establishing and using mechanisms that make it possible for the computers to communicate with each other. It also makes it possible for us to share building blocks or resources of computer networking systems that are effective.

It is evident in today's world that the internet is very important because it helps us gain access to very many different things. Most of the time, the terms World Wide Web (WWW) and Internet are used with little to no distinction. Regardless of this, they are not the same. The internet refers to a global system of computer networks that are interconnected, and the WWW is one type of services that are transferred through these interconnected computer networks. It is a group of specific resources including text documents, that are linked using URLs and hyperlinks, all which can be accessed from web servers, by using web browsers (Figure 1.1).

Figure 1.1. *Some of the commonly used web technologies include browsers, HTML, and CSS, and web development frameworks.*

Source: https://www.eternalorganizer.com/web-technology-important/ (accessed on 2 April 2020).

The ability to view a webpage on the WWW always starts by either following a hyperlink to the resource or page, or typing the page's URL into a web browser. After this, the web browser is then able to initiate a sequence of background communication messages so as to make sure that the requested page is fetched and displayed.

In the 90s, the use of browsers to view web pages, and also for the movement between different web pages through the use of hyperlinks, was referred to as web surfing, navigating the web, or browsing. We now know that we need the internet for almost everything in the modern world, and this is the importance of web technologies. It might be complex to deal with some web technologies; however, there is no website that would have a good user interface without web technologies.

Some of the web technologies include mark-up languages such as HTTP, HTML, JavaScript, CGI, XML, CSS, and HTML. Other web technologies include databases, business applications, web servers, and programming languages.

Web technologies have a couple of benefits. They make it possible for us to update our content at anytime and anywhere in an easier manner. It is also possible to use the Search Engine Optimization (SEO) to improve our websites on the same pages that are used for editing. In addition to all this, it also lowers the cost, by reducing the amount time it takes to build sites.

There are many different people who use web technologies. Teachers normally use them to ensure that their lesson plans remain on track. They also find it impossible to teach some lessons without web technologies.

It is important to understand what a web server is, how the production of web pages occurs, and how computer communication can help in the visualization of productivity and challenges in any workplace, as well as how to solve these problems.

1.2. WEB PAGES

A webpage refers to a collection of specific information that is found on the WWW and the user is able to see it through a web browser. One can think of it as a group of paper pages that have been linked together into a book. Many web pages that have been bound together in a coherent manner are what make up a website (Puntambekar, 2009).

One or more text files that have been written in a Hypertext Markup Language (HTML) make up the core element of a web page. The elements for most web pages include Cascading Style Sheets for the semantics of a presentation and JavaScript for behavior that is dynamic, either as videos or images.

There are two types of web pages from the perspective of website deployment that is on the side of the server, and these are dynamic and static. Static pages are normally recovered from the file system of the web server without being modified. Dynamic pages have to be created on the fly by the web server, customarily having to draw from a database, so as to ensure that a web template is filled out before it is sent to the browser of the user (Puntambekar, 2009).

1.2.1. How Does a Web Page Work?

So as to understand how a web page works, there are four main terms we need to understand:

1. **Web Page:** This is a simple text file that only accommodates texts, in addition to a group of HYML tags that help in describing the manner in which the text should be formatted when it is displayed on a screen by a browser. The tags are a set of straightforward rules that inform the web browser on the manner in which the page should look when it is being displayed on a screen. These tags provide instructions such as changing of the color or size, or even the arrangement of certain data in the columns. These tags are interpreted by the web browser to decide on the formatting method that will be used to format the text onto the screen (Figure 1.2).

Figure 1.2. *One of the greatest benefits of HTML is that the user is not required to pay any fee to use it*

Source: https://www.lynda.com/HTML-tutorials/HTML-Essential-Training/170427-2.html (accessed on 2 April 2020).

2. **HTML:** In full, this stands for Hyper Text Markup Language. In computer terms, the language that is used to describe the manner

in which a page should be formatted is referred to as the markup language. One does not need the HTML if all they want to do is to display texts in black and white without formatting them. However, if the user wants the fonts changed, addition of colors, embedded graphics, and even to create headlines on the page, the language that is used to achieve this is HTML.

3. **Web Browser:** Common examples of this are the Microsoft Internet Explorer or Netscape Navigator, which are all computer programs or applications that are used for two main purposes: the web browser is able to use the Internet to access the web server, so as to make a request for a page, so that the browser can extract the page into the user's machine, through the network; and the web browser is also able to make interpretations of the sequence of HTML tags that are found on the page, so as to have the ability to display the page as it was intended to be viewed by the creator of the page, on the screen.
4. **Web Server:** This is a part of the computer software that is able to provide responses to the requests that are made by a browser for a page, and use the internet to ensure delivery of the page to the Web browser. One can visualize a web server as an apartment, where each of the apartments are housing the web pages of the users. So as to use the apartment to store a page, the user is required to pay a price for the space. In this complex, the available pages can be viewed by and displayed to any interested person globally. The host can be referred or as the landlord in this situation and the rent can be used to represent the hosting charge. Through the internet, there are very many web servers (millions) that deliver pages to the browsers of even more users.

It is considered quite easy to test out web pages without having to use a server. The browser of the user is able to display the web pages that have been created by the user from the user's personal computer.

1.2.2. HTML and XHTML

There are two main languages used for writing web pages: HTML and XHTML. Let us discuss HTML much further. HTML documents are received by web browsers from either a local storage, or the web server. The web browser then renders the documents into webpages that are in the multimedia form. HTML is able to describe the web page's structure and also the cues that were originally included for the document to appear (Gopalan and Adikesavan, 2014) (Figure 1.3).

Figure 1.3. *Editing HTML is considered quite easy due to the fact that the user does not require a special platform or interface to do so.*

Source: https://time2hack.com/dry-frontend-html-css/amp/ (accessed on 2 April 2020).

The building blocks of the HTML pages are the HTML elements. It is possible to embed images, constructs, and other objects including interactive forms into the page that has been rendered, with the use of HTML. HTML helps in providing a way to create documents that are well structured by ensuring that the structural semantics for texts are denoted, such as quotes, links, lists, paragraphs, headings, etc. Tags are used for the delineating of HTML elements, which are written by using angle brackets. Some of the tags such as, <input/> and <img/> help in the direct introduction of content into the page. Different tags, for example <p> are used for surrounding and providing information on document texts and these may also be inclusive of other tags as subelements. Browsers are not able to display these tags; however, they utilize them for the interpretation of the page's content.

HTML can provide embedded programs that have been written in a language meant for scripting, for example, JavaScript, which can cause an effect on the content and behavior of web pages. Including Cascading Style Sheets helps in defining the layout and look of the content (Puntambekar, 2009).

On the other hand, XHTML which stands for extensible HTML is an extension of the commonly used HTML. HTML was mainly defined as an application of a markup language framework that is flexible, which is the Standard Generalized Markup Language. In contrast, XHTML is an application of a subset of the Standard Generalized Markup Language that is much more restrictive. Documents that use the XHTML language are formed in a proper manner, and therefore can be parsed with the use of standard Extensible Markup Language (XML) parsers, in comparison to HTML which needs a lenient parser that is HTML specific.

The development of XHTML aimed at making HTML much more extensible and also to make it much more interoperable with other formats of data. With HTML, browsers were able to forgive some of the errors, and most of the websites could still be displayed even if the markup had some technical errors. There was stricter handling of errors that was introduced by XHTML (Puntambekar, 2009).

The XML standard, which was approved in 1998, was able to provide a data format that was simpler, and almost as simple as the HTML format. The main aim with shifting to the XML was to ensure that HTML would improve its compatibility to the commonly used XML tools. This possibility would allow for proxies and servers to necessarily transform content for devices that are constrained such as mobile phones. Through the use of namespaces, documents that used the XHRML format can be able to provide extensibility through the inclusion of fragments from other languages that are based on the XML, such as MathMl and Vector Graphics. Finally, the work that is renewed is able to provide an opportunity for the division of HTML into components that are reusable and for the cleaning up of parts of the language that are untidy.

1.2.3. The Relationship between f XHTML and HTML

There are several differences between the two. The tree structure that helps in representing the internal parts of the pages in applications is the Document Object Model (DOM). HTML and XHTML are two separate ways in which the internal parts of the pages in the markup can be represented. Both XHTML and HTML are not as expressive as the DOM, and the XHTML XML syntax is much more expressive than HTML. HTML works by using pseudo-SGML syntax, while XHTML works by using an XML syntax. Due to the fact that the contents of the DOM that are expressible in the syntax differ slightly, the actual behavior of the two models also slightly changes (Sklar, 2011).

Some of the main differences between XHTML and HTML include:

- For the creation of web pages and also other information that can be displayed on a web browser, HTML is the main markup language. XHTML mainly works by providing extensions of the HTML (Figure 1.4).

Figure 1.4. Because XHTML documents contain relatively clean code that is much cleaner, they can be discovered very quickly by search engines

Source: https://networkencyclopedia.com/xhtml/ (accessed on 2 April 2020).

- HTML was developed by both WWW Consortium and Web Hypertext Application Technology Working Group, while XHTML was developed only by the WWW Consortium.
- HTML uses the document file format, while the XHTML uses the Markup language format.
- In HTML, the web pages are written in HTML, while in XHTML, the web pages are written in the extended version of HTML which is much stricter and based on the XML.

1.2.4. Elements of a Web Page

1. **Components:** This is an element that makes it possible to simply add customized and sophisticated content to the user's site without having to code in HTML. They allow the user to display a remote Really Simple Syndication feed, add a path of breadcrumbs, add Luminate Online content, or insert a link that is printer friendly.

2. **Wrappers:** These aid in providing the overall structure that surrounds information that is found on the web page. It is possible for a wrapper to have components within it. It is necessary for all of them to have % page-powered-by% tag, which helps in rendering the logos that are found on each of the pages. This tag points out to a spot at the bottom of the page where an image is located (Sklar, 2011).
3. **Display Templates:** This helps define the formatting of the content items in a continuous manner. Specifically, note the following highlights:
   - The layout or the structure of the web page's body. For example, the template for single display helps in rendering the content of the page by the %page-content% tag that is found in the wrapper.
   - Page level components that are dynamic, such as a list of items that are related.
4. **Page Body:** With the help of the HTML Editor, it is possible for the authors of the site to control the layout and display within the body of the web page.
5. **CSS (Cascading Style Sheets):** These are able to control various dynamic components and element of HTML while being managed from the reports and tools page. It is possible for each component to have style sheets of their own, either those that have been created by the administrator of the website, or those that are out-of-the-box. There are several ways in which the Cascading Style Sheets can be used in the websites:
   - Uploading external Cascading Style Sheets files to Luminate Content Management System, where the HTML references it in the wrapper's <head> segment.
   - Embedding it inline in a <style> block within the wrapper's <head> segment.
   - Defining styles for dynamic components, inclusive of the body, by creating inline styles using the Style Sheets Interface that is found in the Reports and Tools.

It is generally not recommended for the user to implement Cascading Style Sheets through defining <style> tags or inline styles inside the web page's body.

6. **XSLT (Extensible Style Sheet Language Transformation):** These can be used for the styling of the Really Simple Syndication feed (Figure 1.5).

Figure 1.5. In general, the use of cascading style sheets means that the web page has less code behind it, which improves page's download time

Source: https://www.lynda.com/CSS-tutorials/CSS-Essential-Training/5038219-2.html (accessed on 2 April 2020).

1.2.5. Web Style Sheet

Web Style Sheet refers to a way of separating content and presentation for designing webs. Essentially, the HTML or XHTML has the structure and the semantic content of the page. However, the visual layout (style) is not defined. Instead, an external sheet file is used to define the visual layout, which uses a styles sheet language such as XSLT or CSS. This approach of the design is referred to as a separation, due to the fact that it greatly takes the place of the antecedent methodology where the markup of a page was able to define both the structure and style.

Being able to separate content and style is quite advantageous. In this modern time, it has become much more popular due to some developments that have helped in improving the implementation of the Cascading Style Sheets. Some of these benefits include:

- **Speed:** In general, the experiences that users have when using style sheets on a site tend to be much faster in comparison to sites that do not utilize these technologies. Not using these technologies means that the first page loads much slower due to the fact that the content and the style sheet still require to be transferred. The rest of the pages have a faster loading time due to the fact that there is no style information being downloaded. Indeed, the Cascading Style Sheets file will be present in the cache of the browser.

- **Maintainability:** Having to hold all the styles for presentation in a single file can lower the time of maintenance and also lower the possibility of errors occurring. As a result, we see an improvement in the consistency of the presentation. For example, the color of the font that is related with a certain element of the text can be specified, thus making it easy to modify a small section of the characters in a single file. Alternatively, if the user wants to use styles that have been set in the different pages individually, they need an edit of the file, which will end up being error-prone, time consuming, and cumbersome.
- **Accessibility:** It is easier to tweak sites using 1 with either HTML or XHTML in order to make them look similar in a variety of browsers. Sites that use the Cascading Style Sheet normally degrade when they are used on browsers that are not able to exhibit graphics, for example Lynx and other older browsers. Cascading Style Sheets that are not understood by certain browsers are normally ignored. This allows for many different user agents to have access to the site's content, regardless of the fact that they are not able to ensure that the style sheet is rendered, or their design does not include a graphical capability. For example, it is possible for the layout information to be completely disregarded by a browser that uses a Braille display that can be refreshed for the output, and the user will still be able to retrieve all the contents of the page (Figure 1.6).

Figure 1.6. CSS is very easy to use, maintain, and update

Source: https://www.w3schools.com/w3css/w3css_templates.asp (accessed on 2 April 2020).

- **Customization:** If the layout information of a page is externally stored, it is possible for the user to decide to entirely disable the information of the layout, which will still end up leaving the content of the site in a form that is readable. The authors of the site also have the ability to offer multiple style sheets, all which can be utilized for the complete alteration of how the site appears, without causing any changes to the content in the site. Most of the web browsers that are used today provide the opportunity for the users to define their own style sheets, which may be inclusive of instructions that overrule the layout rules of the author.
- **Consistency:** Due to the fact that the semantic file only has the definitions that have intentionally been added by the author, there is a high level of consistency in the styling of the different elements of the content in the document, such as the mathematical expressions, lists, emphasized text and headings all get style properties that have been consistently applied from the external style sheet. During composition, the authors should not stress about the style properties. These details to do with presentation can be procrastinated until the actual time the site is being presented.
- **Portability:** The ability to procrastinate the details to do with the presentation until the presentational moment means that it is possible to easily repurpose a document for a completely different medium of presentation, just by applying a new style sheet that had previously been ready to be used with this new medium, and also one that is compatible with the structural or elemental word stock of the semantic document. It is quite easy to print a document, that has been carefully authored, to a hardcover book that is well equipped with footers and headers, a generated table of contents, and page numbers, all by the simple application of a new style sheet.

1.2.6. Web Scripts

These cannot be visually seen by the user; however, the fact that they are available in the website code provides a definition of how the website is going to behave when responding to a specific click request that the user has sent. In addition to the WWW, in relation to local computers, they also help in automating their processes. In general, scripts have provided a great contribution in ensuring that the web is flexible and easy to use, just as we know it is today.

One individual script plays the role of representing a text document that has a set of commands that require to be executed by either a scripting manager or a specific program, so as to ensure that there is achievement of the desired automated action. This helps in preventing the users from the need to go through many different steps, that are both complicated and time consuming, so as to arrive at a specific result while either working on their personal computers (PCs), or browsing a website. The script provides a text nature that offers the opportunity for the scripts to be opened and edited just by using a simple text editor (Godbole, 2013).

There are five main scripting languages:

- **Shell Scripts:** These are a set of instructions that are meant for the shell. They are also referred to as the command line of an operating system. They are mainly utilized for the manipulation of files, printing of texts, and execution of programs.
- **Macros:** These were next in line. This work by providing the opportunity for mouse movements and repetitive key-strokes to be recorded thus makes it much easier to execute the commands. They were the first phase of the graphical user interface, and as of today, they are utilized in most of the spreadsheet and text editors, such as Open Office, Excel, or Word.
- **Client-Side Scripting:** The internet led to the division of scripting languages into two: server-side scripting and client side scripting. Client-side scripting languages normally undergo execution in the browser of the client. Some of these include: Cascading Style Sheets, HTML, XML, Java Scripts, etc. The main reason why these scripts are important is because everyone can access their source codes. This is a factor that has been very beneficial to beginner programmers, and also for people who are looking to learn more about client-side scripting (Figure 1.7).

Figure 1.7. JavaScript allows developers to create interactive interfaces, which respond to visitors actions, such as hovering their mouse over a link

Source: https://www.scriptplazza.com/100-best-script-resources-sites-for-web-programming/ (accessed on 2 April 2020).

- **Server-Side Scripting:** These scripts are executed on a server and it is only possible for the visitor to have access to the results without being able to access the source codes. They provide a platform for scripts that are much more complicated to be used, due to the fact that the main function of the server is to execute these scripts. With this scripting language, the scripts are able to make a connection to the databases, in addition to utilizing their data as they run. Some of these scripts include Perl, Python, or PHP.
- **Scripts with NTC Hosting:** These provide servers that are fully optimized, therefore having the ability to support the commonly used server-side scripts. A combination of Apache and Linux helps to power the servers so as to ensure the provision of the required stability and speed that will be used to execute the scripts.

1.3. WEBSITE

This is a collection of webpages and other interconnected content that is recognized by a domain name that is common and issues on a minimum of one web server. Some of the commonly used websites are amazon.com, google.com, and wikipedia.org. The WWW is a collection of all the web sites that are publicly accessible. Those that are private, such as those that are created by a company to be used by employees only, are considered to be a part of the intranet. This means that is it possible to access a website through a private local area network or through the internet (Godbole, 2013).

All websites are normally created for a specific purpose, such as education, online shopping and so on. Navigation of the site is normally made possible by hyper-linking between web pages, and most of the time this starts with a home page. There are many devices that the users can use to access websites, such as laptop computers, smartphones, desktops, smart TVs, and tablets. These devices are equipped with a web browser which is a software application that allows the users to access these websites on the previously mentioned devices.

There are many different reasons why a website could be created. These will be discussed later on in this topic. Due to the fact that hyperlinks can be found on any website to another, the ability to distinguish between individual sites may end up being blurred (Godbole, 2013) (Figure 1.8).

Figure 1.8. The main difference between a webpage and a website is that a website refers to a group of webpages that have content on a certain topic. A webpage is a small part of the whole website and usually contains specific information

Source: https://techtrendske.co.ke/website-usefulness-how-much-do-we-need-them/ (accessed on 2 April 2020).

There are some websites that expect the user to register or subscribe so as to log in and have access to the site's content. Web-based emails, business sites, academic journal websites, social networking websites, file-sharing websites, news websites, etc. are all websites that require the user to subscribe or register (Puntambekar, 2009).

1.3.1. Reasons for a Website

Depending on the intended audience, different websites have different purposes. There are some that are made solely to provide information, others are for selling products and/or services, etc. Below are some of the purposes of a website:

- **Informative Websites:** These websites are mainly used for conveying information that is specific and helpful, to either an audience or a user, all aiming at teaching the reader new content, or even for the reader to have a better understanding on a topic that he or she is already aware of. They mainly have information that is actionable such as tips and tricks, guidance, instructions, directions, support information, etc.
- **Entertainment Websites:** In these websites, the visitors are able to see entertainment information that has been showcased. This includes arts, movies, sports coverage, online magazines, humorous websites, gossip oriented websites, etc. So as to make sure that the user will always come back for more information, the sites are designed in a manner that allows them to be easy to navigate, and the information on the site is regularly updated. These sites can also use dynamic content so as to make them much more engaging, such as slideshows, podcasts, videos, etc.
- **E-Commerce Websites:** These sites are created mainly for selling products to users. These websites are optimized in a careful manner, so as to ensure that the purchases are of a high percentage. These websites require for the integration of the latest techniques that are used online for up-selling and closing so as to successfully increase the probability that the user will buy a product every time they visit the site. There are several elements in these websites that help make those websites successful, such as proper payment options or attractive and intuitive mobile design.
- **Service-based Business Websites:** These normally aim to convince the visitors that they should trust the company to effectively provide the services that they need. These websites normally provide articles and information, videos, visual portfolios of the work, testimonials from the customers, etc.
- **Blogs:** These are run by either a group or an individual and are mainly used to provide websites or webpages that are regularly

updated. They are normally written in a conversational or informal format. These sites are much easier to start, and there are many free online services that the users can use, such as wordpress.com. One of the greatest benefits of a blog is that it is very easy to maintain even if the user has very little knowledge on this technology.

- **Social Media Websites:** These are also very easy to use. They are used for sharing and connecting with other users in an easy manner. These websites are fast and easy to use due to their design that is able to build up many different connections that the users can use to share photos, keep in touch, etc. They can be used both commercially and socially (Figure 1.9).

Figure 1.9. Social networking websites provide various services with different features. They utilize different communication tools and run on laptops, desktops, and mobile devices

Source: https://makeawebsitehub.com/social-media-sites/ (accessed on 2 April 2020).

1.3.2. Characteristics of a Good Website

Usability is one of the most important aspects when it comes to creating a website. For any website to succeed, usability is very important. Not only should a website look good to the users for it to be successful, but also provide a user experience that will bring them back. In web design, usability of a website involves designing the website in a manner that the users will find easy to find information easily and fast.

Usability of a website can be improved in many different ways. There are a few characteristics that a website should have so as to make it more appealing to users. These include:

- **They should be compatible with mobile phones:** These days, almost everyone accesses the internet through the mobile phone. This means that it has become necessary to create websites that are mobile optimized. This can be done by checking the appearance of the website on the mobile phone, which can also be checked by the Google Mobile Site Tester. If it is not possible to access the website on the phone, it is also possible to a version that is specifically meant for mobile phones, and this can be done for free through the use of mobile website builders which are based on the web.
- **They need to be accessible to all users:** A website that is considered user friendly needs to be accessible to all users, including the elderly, disabled, and blind. These users normally utilize screen-readers to gain access to the internet. There are simple techniques that can be used during web design that are highlighted by the 508 website accessibility guidelines, and these can be used so as to ensure that the website can easily be accessed on screen-readers, and this will help in making the website accessible to many more people.
- **They should have a well-planned information architecture:** To ensure good usability, the information on the site needs to be organized and presented in a proper manner. These days, websites are being used to provide a lot of information and resources for the attraction of the target user. It is important to carefully plan the sections and categories of the website, in addition to presenting the information in a manner that the users will find easy to access.
- **They have well-formatted and easy-to-scan content:** Most the people who use websites rarely read all the content from the top of the page to the bottom. Most of them just skim through the content. They quickly look for the important parts of the message in the page, so as to find out if the information provided is relevant for what they are looking for. This means that the designer has to make sure they he/she uses headings, paragraphs, bullets, sub-headings, etc. correctly, so that users find it easier to scan through the content.

- **They should have fast loading times:** Websites that normally take too long to load are very annoying. Actually, one of the main reasons why users stop using a website is slow speeds. It is important for the designer to make sure that the loading time for a site is around four to six seconds, so as to improve on the site's usability. Search engines (SE) are normally ranked and a slow site can give a low ranking on a search engine. There are tools that have made it possible for designers to test the speeds of their websites, such as Pingdom, which also provides suggestions on what can be done to improve on the speed. Some of the factors that affect the speed of the website are widgets such as social media and website tracking, and website plug-ins. Limiting the use of these factors can fix this problem. They should only be used when necessary.
- **They should have a consistent display across a variety of browsers:** The compatibility of a browser is one aspect that is overlooked most of the times. Despite the fact that most of the browsers that are used today have become much more efficient due to their evolution, there are still some issues to do with consistency when it comes to different browsers interpreting the website. Websites should be designed to behave in a consistent manner with all the browsers that are commonly used, including Safari, Firefox, Opera, IE, and Chrome.
- **They should be easy to navigate effectively:** This is a very important aspect of web site usability. JavaScript and a simple HTML have proven to provide menus that are able to efficiently and consistently work on all platforms and browsers. The navigation also needs to be free of clutter. The designer should aim to limit the number of items that are found on the menu as much as they can. It may be much easier to work with sub-navigation or a drop-down menu on larger sites that have more pages and sections. The fact that JavaScript and DHTML libraries have advanced greatly, such as Ajax and Motools, has led to the opening of doors for many different possibilities for the creation of navigation systems that are innovative. The menu is not the only aspect that plays a huge role in making the website easier to navigate, there are also some other aspects that need to be

considered. Some of these include: Good Internal Linking; good error handling; good search features; informative footers and headers; multiple ways to explore the content; and a custom 404 page; Description on-screen messages and proper error handling is also key in improving the usability of the website. Being able to correctly handle errors at the code level helps in making sure that the website is free from bugs and is robust. The usability and user experience are improved by displaying the right error messages.

- **They should have clean code and valid mark-up:** Websites are more robust and dependable when they adhere to the specific web design standards and practices. They also help in making the website appear more consistent across devices and browsers and also load faster. In addition, if the situation arises, locating issues on the site and troubleshooting also becomes easier.
- **They should have a color scheme that contrasts:** The content and the background of the site should have the right contrast in color, and this is one of the most important principles in web design. The background and text should have a goon contrast, for example, a white background with black text is much easier to read. Without the proper contrast, the text is hardly legible.
- **It should have forms that are usable:** Forms provide an opportunity for users to interact with the website. They should always be accessible and easy to use.

1.3.3. Static and Dynamic Websites

There are two types of websites: static and dynamic websites. These are discussed below:

1. **Static Websites:** In these websites, the server stores the webpages in the design that is addressed to a client web browser. The main coding language that is used is HTML. The appearance is controlled beyond that of HTML by the Cascading Style Sheets. As part of the main content and for effecting the appearance that is desired, images are normally used. If videos and audios are generally non-interactive or played automatically, they can also be considered as static content (Gosselin, 2010) (Figure 1.10).

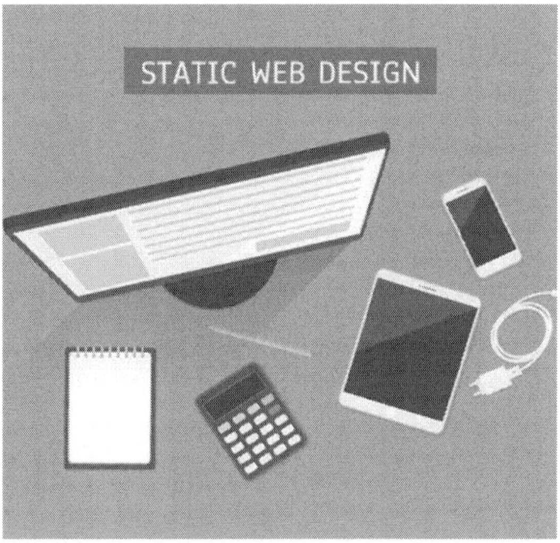

Figure 1.10. *Static web designs are recommended for businesses that are not planning on changing their services and products in the foreseeable future. The storage of these web pages occurs on the server itself and delivery to the user occurs just as the pages were previously stored.*

Source: https://www.seoczar.com/static-website-design/ (accessed on 2 April 2020).

Static websites normally display identical information to all the users. They are able to provide information that is both standard and consistent for a long time period. Despite the fact that is still possible for the owner of the website to periodically update the site, it is a process that is done manually when it comes to editing the text, adding photos, etc. and this needs for one to have basic knowledge in software and web design.

Some of the static websites that are commonly used are a brochure website, a five-page website, or a classic website. They are referred to as static because they provide static information that is pre-defined to the users. The information may be displayed through photos, texts, video/audio, animations, and navigation menus (Gosselin, 2010).

There are four broad categories of software that can be used to edit static websites. These are:

- **Text Editors:** These include TextEdit or Notepad, which work by manipulating HTML and content in a direct manner within the program being used to edit.
- **What You See is What You Get Offline Editors:** These include Adobe Dreamweaver and FrontPage which edit the site with the use of the Graphic User Interface and the final HTML markup is automatically generated by the software of the editor.
- **What You See is What You Get online editors:** These help in creating online presentations that are rich in media such as blogs, intro, widgets, web pages, and other documents.
- **Template-based Editors:** These include iWeb and they provide the opportunity for users to perform the creation and uploading of WebPages to a web-server without having to have detailed knowledge on HTML. This is because they make is possible for the user to pick a template they see suitable from a palette, and they are able to add texts and pictures in the fashion of desktop publishing without having to directly manipulate the HTML code.

Server Side Includes can also be used by static websites for convenient editing, for example, making it possible to share an ordinary menu bar across many pages. This is not considered a dynamic state because the behavior of the site is still static to the reader.

2. **Dynamic Websites:** This is a website that can be automatically and frequently changed and customized. Computer codes that produce the HTML generate server-side dynamic pages. The appearance is sorted out by Cascading Sheets Styles and they are therefore considered as files that are static.

Dynamic sites and Dynamic web systems can be generated by many different available software systems, such as ColdFusion, Active Server Pages, Java Server Pages and Java Servlets, and CGI. For general-use programming languages, there are various web template systems and web application frameworks that are available, such as Ruby, Python, PHP, and Perl which makes it easier and faster to create dynamic websites that are complex (Gosselin, 2010) (Figure 1.11).

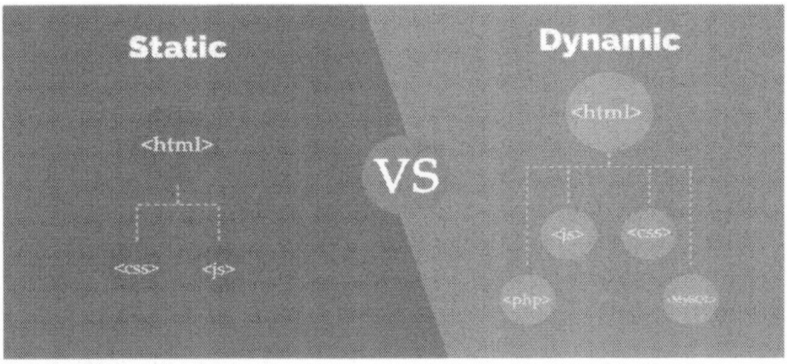

Figure 1.11. *Static websites are normally coded in simple and plain HTML and the dynamic websites are normally coded with the server-side scripting languages, for example, Coldfusion, JSP, ASP, and PHP.*

Source: https://medium.com/@eonian.social/static-vs-dynamic-websites-8e80d231bf86 (accessed on 2 April 2020).

Dynamic sites are able to perform certain actions, such as displaying the present-day state of a user dialogue, monitoring situations that are changing, or providing information in a manner that is personalized to what the individual user requires. For example, requesting the front page of a news site leads to the code that is being used on the web server combining HTML fragments that had initially been stored with news stories that had been gotten from another website or a database through Really Simple Syndication for the production of a page that is inclusive of the latest information (Sklar, 2011).

It is possible for dynamic sites to be interactive when they store and read back browser cookies, use HTML forms, or create a sequence of pages that help in reflecting clicks that were previously done. Dynamic content can also be seen in the ability of the user to input a search request, which is possible through a retail website that has a database of media products. The web page content will respond to this by spontaneously changing the appearance it previously had, and then displaying products of the content that is available.

To instruct the web browser on the manner in which it should interactively modify the contents if the page, the dynamic HTML utilizes JavaScript code. Periodically automatically regenerating a big sequence of pages that are static can help in simulating a dynamic website. This method can help the user avoid the loss in performance that comes with initiation of the dynamic engine on a per-connection or per-user basis (Sklar, 2011).

1.3.4. World Wide Web

This is commonly referred to as the Web, and it is a system of information in which Uniform Resource Locators (URLs) identify documents and other web resources, whereby, the URLs may have hypertexts interlinking them, and they are found in the internet. The Hypertext Transfer Protocol (HTTP) help in transferring the resources of the WWW, and users are able to access them through the web browser, and the web server is used to publish these resources.

The term Web Resources refers to any form of media that has been downloaded, however, webpages are considered to as hypertext media which have undergone formatting through the HTML.

Using this language to format provides the ability to use hyperlinks that have been embedded, containing URLs, and it also allows for the users to navigate other different resources.

Not only do webpages have text, but also video, audio, images, and components of the software which can be displayed as coherent pages of multimedia content on the web browser of the user (Gosselin, 2010) (Figure 1.12).

Figure 1.12 The development of Mosaic, which is a web browser, resulted in a quick acceptance of the world wide web. This browser has interface that is intuitive and reliable, has a Windows port, and is easy to install. These factors ensured its popularity on the web

Source: https://medium.com/@xipetechnology/happy-anniversary-of-the-world-wide-web-a239f957c1 (accessed on 2 April 2020).

Many web resources that either have a theme and domain name that is common, or even both, make up a web site. Web servers are programs that store website as they run on a computer.

They normally respond to appeals that are made by web browsers running on the computer, over the Internet. Publishers are able to provide web site content. This content can also be provided interactively where contributions to the content are made by the users, or the content in largely dependent on the actions of the user, or the users themselves.

1.3.5. Cascading Sheets Style vs. Java Script

Cascading Style Sheets are used to design and format web pages. This application is not able to work on its own; however, it works together with the languages that are used to create websites. It is normally used together with XML and HTML, for giving both the users and the developers of the websites an opportunity to control their layouts, inclusive of designing displays, positioning, and styling.

This application helps in defining how XML and HTML elements should be used and manipulated. CSS is supported by all internet browsers (Gosselin, 2010).

CSS normally styles or formats elements that are provided by XML and HTML, such as tables, boxes, paragraphs, titles, headings, etc. It also helps in providing backgrounds, style of color, fonts, links, lists, outlines, alignments, etc. that are much more defined and improved. When using CSS, there are some specific syntax's that need to be followed.

The syntax and computations are not complex, as it is only a sheet for designing. Therefore, one needs to learn how to use XML or HTML so as to be able to use CSS.

The Java Script design is also meant for webpages that use HTML. All major browsers support JavaScript, for example, Firefox, and Explorer. It is possible to achieve the addition of more interactions and function to the webpage with JavaScript. JavaScript is normally directly embedded into HTML pages. It makes it possible to make reaction to specific elements of HTML when a user clicks them. It is also able to note the browser of a visitor, change or just read the element's content, and it can also be utilized for the retrieval and storage of information that is found on the computer of the visitor (Gosselin, 2010) (Figure 1.13).

Figure 1.13. The main difference between CSS and JavaScript is based on trust and control aspects. While CSS does not guarantee that the applied style will work, JavaScript, enables the user to control the style

Source: https://www.slideshare.net/cheilmann/css-vs-javascript-trust-vs-control (accessed on 2 April 2020).

The insertion of a HTML <script> tag allows for the inclusion of JavaScript functions in a webpage. JavaScript syntax is easy to comprehend and memorize. To find the syntax of a specific required function, the user is able to look at the guidelines of JavaScript. It is also possible to use JavaScript for the validation of forms before sending them to the servers. This means that the server does not have to perform this function.

The major difference between CSS and JavaScript is that JavaScript is much more advanced for web design. It does not limit the user to the sole creation of colors, boxes, tables, and texts. In addition to this, it also allows for the creation of animations, addition of events to images and even setting a timing event for the execution of a certain task that will be accomplished after the set time interval.

Due to the fact that CSS are declarative, there are many more opportunities to optimize it. To accomplish CSS tasks, the browser is able to use the hardware. It is also able to optimize aspects such as running animations and computing elements that are off-screen. JavaScript is not able to achieve this because it does not have access to these Application Programming Interfaces out of the box (Gosselin, 2010).

1.4. WEB APPLICATIONS

A web application refers to a computer program that is specifically meant to serve the client, where the user is able to access it through a web browser. Some of the mainly used web applications include online banking, webmail, online auctions, and online retail sales.

There is not a clear difference between the simple web application and the dynamic web page. When a website is considered a web application, it means that the website has a functionalist that is similar to a mobile application or a desktop software application. There was introduction of support for explicit language by HTML5 that was used to make applications that can be loaded as webpages, however, they have the ability to locally store data and also the ability to continue functioning even when they are not online (Figure 1.14).

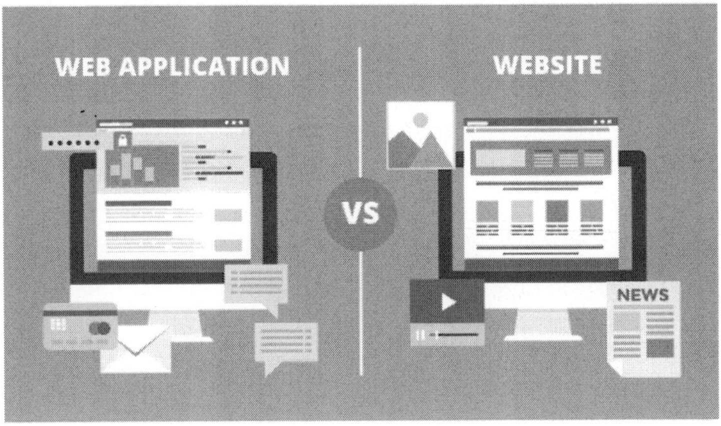

Figure 1.14. One of the major distinctions between a web application and a website is that a website is defined by its content whereas the web application is defined by its interaction with the user

Source: http://www.parallaxdeveloper.com/blogs/uncategorized/what-is-the-difference-between-a-website-and-a-web-application/ (accessed on 2 April 2020).

Applications that have a single page are considered more to be applications due to the fact that they do not accept the commonly used web paradigm that involves the movement between specific pages that have different URLs. These frameworks can be used for increasing the development of the specific web applications for use on the mobile platform (Puntambekar, 2009).

The use of technologies such as JavaScript, Silver light, Flash, Java, DHTML etc., makes it possible to achieve methods that are application specific such as having access to the mouse and keyboard, playing audio, and even drawing on the screen. There are many services that have helped to achieve the combination of all these functions into an interface that is much more familiar, and is also able to adopt the operating system's appearance.

Client-side scripting is often used by web developers for the improvement of functionality, most times for the creation of an experience that is interactive and does not need for the page to reload. These days, there are many different technologies that have been developed with server-side technologies for their coordination with client-side scripting, including PHP, Perl/Plack, J2Ee, and ASP.NET. Ajax is a technology that is able to provide an experience that is much more interactive for the user. It uses a combination of different technologies to create a technique for web development (Puntambekar, 2009).

Web applications are normally divided into certain reasoned chunks that are referred to as tiers. Each tier is normally given a specific task or role to accomplish. The web applications that were traditionally used only had one tier, which was found on the client machine, however, these applications naturally tended to impart themselves to an approach that is n-tiered.

Despite the fact that there were many possible variations, the three-tiered application was the structure that was most commonly used. These three tiers in their most common form are referred in a specific order which is presentation, application, and storage. The first one which is the presentation tier refers to a web browser; the middle tire, application logic, is used to refer to an engine that uses several dynamic web content technologies such as Python, Rails, Ruby, PHO, JSP/Java, Dart, ColdFusion, CGI, or ASP; and the final tier is the storage which refers to the database. In this process, the web browser normally works by sending requests to the application logic, which makes updates and queries against the database so as to service them, leading to the generation of a user interface.

For applications that are much more complicated, it may not be able to efficiently use the three tier solution. In this situation, it is advisable to utilize the n-tiered approach, where is able to achieve a huge benefit of breaking down the business logic, which is commonly found in the application tier, into a model that is more fine-grained. There may be another advantage which involves the addition of an integration tier, which helps in ensuring a separation of the data tier from other tiers, by the provision of an interface that is easy to use for accessing the data. For example, the user would have to call a "list clients" function so as to access the client data, rather than having to directly make a Structured Query Language query on the database against the client table. This helps in providing the ability for the replacing of the underlying database without having to make alterations to the other tiers (Gopalan and Adikesavan, 2014).

Despite the above explanation, there are still some who consider web applications to have two tier architecture. In this situation, the client would have to deal with the presentation tier, the storage tier would be dealt with the server, and the application tier would have to be handled by either both or one of them. Despite the fact that this would be able to raise the level of the application's scalability, and also separate the database and the display, it may not be able to accommodate the specialization of layers, which means that majority of the web applications would not be able to support this application with time.

The use of the web application framework can help in simplifying the writing of web applications. The frameworks help in facilitating the rapid development of applications by providing the opportunity for the team dealing with the development of the app to pay more attention to the exact sections of the app that are specific to their needs, without the need to deal with the commonly occurring issues that have to do with the development of the application, such as user management. Most of these commonly used frameworks are open source software.

Using these frameworks can help in reducing the number of program errors that commonly occur, which can be done by simplifying the code, and by giving time, to part of the team, for paying attention to the framework, while the rest of the team deals with a user case that has been specified. There is a higher probability for problems that are related to security to cause errors in application programs that have constant exposure to attempts from hackers on the Internet. GET after POST is a great practice that can be promoted by the use of frameworks. It is possible to develop apps on the Internet operating systems (OS), however, as of now, there are not enough platforms that are able to incorporate this model (Gopalan and Adikesavan, 2014).

Some of the commonly used simple web applications include presentation tools, online spreadsheets, word processors, etc. There are also some that are much more advanced, such as point-of-sale, video editing, computer-aided design, and project management.

1.4.1. Characteristics of a Web Application

In accordance with the time, web applications have evolved and become much complex, in terms of performance, multimedia use, dynamic nature, etc. The applications that were used traditionally had static content, they were less complex, simple, they had a minimal level of security, and their use was limited. These applications were hardly updated, they had a low level of interactivity, and their functionality was limited. In these modern times, Web Applications have advanced and they come with content that is dynamic, plans, and schedules, and they also contain a large amount of information that can be easily integrated. They also work much better when they have a high level of security (Sklar, 2011) (Figure 1.15).

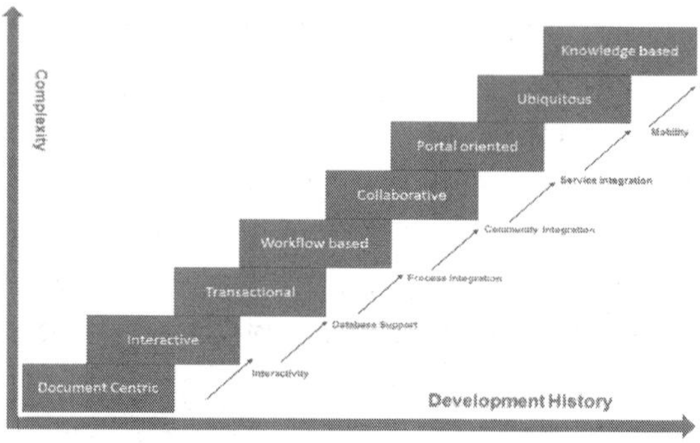

Figure 1.15. Above is a visual representation of the categories of web applications. We can also notice how these categories are affected by an increase in complexity and development history

Source: https://msatechnosoft.in/blog/tech-blogs/categories-of-web-applications-characteristics-of-web-applications (accessed on 2 April 2020).

The characteristics of web applications can be divided into four main categories: Product related characteristics, use related characteristics, development related characteristics, and evolution related characteristics. These are discussed below:

1. **Product Related Characteristics:** This is considered the most important part of web applications. It involves:
   - **Present:** When it comes to the survival and marketing of products, presentation normally plays a role that is very important. In the competitive market, the feel and look of an application can determine the survival and success of an application. Applications need to be in accordance with the trend that is in the market, impressive, and attractive.
   - **Hypertext:** This is considered the web application's base. It includes anchor, node, and link as its basic elements. This helps in providing an application that has an improved performance and

high interactivity, through the implementation of disorientation, cognitive overload, and non-linearity features in the application.

- **Content:** This is the part that deals with the information. Some of the main factors it deals with includes updating, integration, and generation of content. This section involves multimedia, graphics, text, tables, and documents. The content needs to be up-to-date, consistent, reliable, and of high quality. It is also necessary to make sure that the documents are arranged properly.

2. **Use Related Characteristics:** It may not be possible to make predictions on the number of times a web application will be used due to the fact that there may be variations with each user in this situation, as well as in the devices that are being utilized. The characteristics that are related to use of the application may be divided into technical content, social content, and natural content. These will be described below:

- **Natural Content:** This is inclusive of the geographical locations that users are able to access the web applications and also how available they are. Web applications that can be accessed globally and available all day every day have a higher performance level, demand, and stability.
- **Social Content:** This is in relation to the aspects that are user specific. There are so many applications all over the world that compete in the market. They need to have benefits that are both immediate and spontaneous so as to appeal to the user. Some of the important features that need to be considered when developing a web application in this aspect include multiculturalism and scalability.
- **Technical Content:** This is in relation to the devices that are used to access the web applications, and the network of web applications. Some of the important features in this aspect include reliability, stability, connection bandwidth, etc. These features affect how the web application performs. There are specific requirements that are helpful in improving the accessibility and performance of a web application, and these include version, browser configuration, device specification, among others.

3. **Development Related Characteristics:** These include the team, the process the technical infrastructure and the integration process in developing web applications. These are discussed below:

- **Development Team:** The team that is developing the web application needs to be highly knowledgeable in the field of web applications development. The designers, IT experts, application developers, hypertext experts and database developers need to be very proficient. The members need to not only be good at what they do, but also willing to work, interested in the tools and technologies that come up almost daily, and also innovative.
- **The Process of Development:** This process needs to have a high level of flexibility. The processes of development need to be parallel.
- **Technical Infrastructure:** It is important for the app to be free of bugs and there should be a time limit for its development. During the time of development, it is important to consider the browser and the server. Despite the fact that there is no known use of the browser, which is based on the preference of the user, it is important to configure and operate the server as desired.
- **Integration:** It is important to design the app in a way that makes it possible to be integrated by systems and services or external contents that already exist.

4. **Evolution Related Characteristics:** Web applications normally require alterations and upgrades when there are changes in the requirements. All the three characteristics may require to be changed due to the evolutions that may have occurred (development, use, and product). Some of these changes may be due to short time development and market competition (Sklar, 2011).

1.4.2. Categories of Web Applications

Web applications can be categorized in eight main ways: document centric, interactive, transactional, work-flow based, collaborative, portal oriented, ubiquitous, and knowledge based.

1. **Interactive Web Application:** These applications are normally provided by Common Gateway Interface HTML forms. Some of these applications include forms, selection menus, radio buttons, etc. They are normally fast and simple. Creating links and webpages in these types of applications is in accordance with the user input (Sklar, 2011) (Figure 1.16).

Figure 1.16. Interactive applications allow users to interact and communicate with them. This means that users are able to edit, post, and delete information on the application

Source: https://www.xoriant.com/blog/tag/web-application-development (accessed on 2 April 2020).

2. **Document Centric Web Application:** These applications are HTML documents that are static. They are normally directly sent on request to the users, from where they are stored, in the web server. Respective tools are normally used for manually updating these webpages. Document centric web applications have a short response time, they are stable, simple, and static. However, maintaining them is quite expensive, especially when it comes to updating them. Due to the fact that they are static, they have a problem with maintaining consistency, and therefore having no updates of Information that are timely.
3. **Work-Flow based Web Application:** These apps are able to handle workflow in public authorities, private authorities, and companies. They work together with web services so as to ensure that the applications are interoperable. These applications are able to handle workflow in a reliable, robust, and flexible manner while still maintaining the autonomy of the companies they are used in. An example of one of the commonly used applications in this category includes B2B e-commerce solutions.
4. **Transactional Web Application:** These applications make it possible for user to make modifications. Of the other applications,

these are considered to better support queries that are structures from database and they are also much more interactive. Data is handled efficiently and consistently by the database system.

5. **Portal-Oriented Web Application:** There are single access points in these applications that help in making it possible to achieve the separation of services and sources of information that are different. Some of the commonly used portal-oriented web applications include community portals, SE, etc.
6. **Collaborative Web Application:** These are mainly used where the most important aspect is group communications, and it is therefore used as a group application. Some of the examples include e-learning websites, online forums, chat rooms, and other websites that involve the sharing of information such as Wiki.
7. **Knowledge-based Web Application:** Both humans and machines use these types of applications for the provision of knowledge. The knowledge is managed on the basis of semantic web technology. Some of the examples include reusing, linking, and mining the web.
8. **Ubiquitous Web Applications:** These help in providing facilities that are customized at any time and from anywhere for any device. This application however is not able to support many devices; it only has limited support, in addition to having a limited level of interactivity. When the application is being utilized for dynamic adjustments, the user is required to have knowledge of the context that is advanced. An example of this application is services that are based on location.

1.4.3. Rich Internet Applications

These are applications that are based on the web and have some similar characteristics with some of the characteristics of graphical desktop applications. These applications are much more engaging and they can also run much faster due to the fact that they are built with development tools that are powerful. Users get to have a visual experience that is much better with the use of these applications, in addition to having a higher level of interactivity in comparison to the browser applications that were traditionally used, all which only used HTTP and HTML (Godbole, 2013) (Figure 1.17).

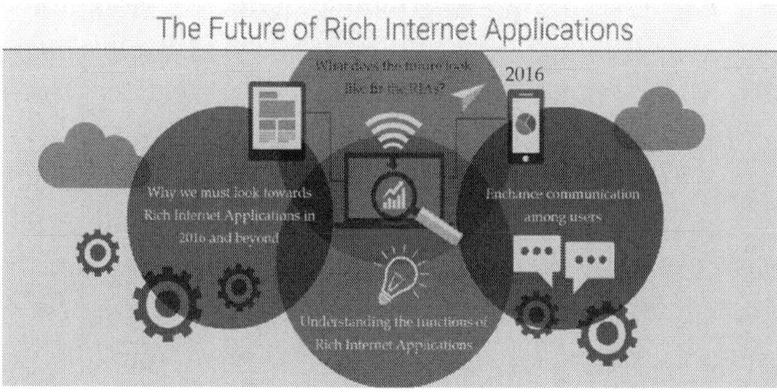

Figure 1.17. . Not only are these applications much cheaper but they are also much more cost efficient in comparison to traditional desktop applications when it comes to maintaining them. They are able to support so many different functions, such as flash, A/V application, and even animation

Source: https://www.indusnet.co.in/future-rich-internet-applications/ (accessed on 2 April 2020).

Most of the early users of the internet were only able to exchange electronic mail messages that were based on texts. However, with introduction to the WWW and HTML, came web pages that were enhanced graphically. Majority of these applications were used to read texts that were displayed on the screen and also deal with information that was static and pre-formatted.

Users required specialized software to deal with the manipulation of data and interaction with sophisticated business logic. Later on, one of the specialists came up with a way to provide applications that users would be able to access through their web browsers through standard Web pages. This became a major breakthrough when it came to the power of the Web; however, there was a huge limitation in the underlying technology. The fact that HTTP is stateless and static meant that there was disconnected and one-sided interaction. In addition, it was used by a green screen mainframe application.

These days, programmers are able to ensure that any functionality that they require in a graphical interface that is based on the web is embedded. This makes it act and look just like software that was traditionally used. Developers are able to use modern tools for the creation of application screens that are complex, with the help of various mixed media, for example video, audio, online conferencing, animations, vector graphic files and bit-map, and multiple fonts. Rich Internet Applications (RIA) provide a level of functionality beyond browsing and reading.

1. **Characteristics of RIA:** There are several major characteristics that differentiate the traditional Web applications from RIA:

- **Direct Interaction:** Interaction is limited to a few standard controls in the traditional web applications that are based on pages, such as form fields, radio buttons, and checkboxes. This makes it very difficult to create applications that are engaging and usable. In contrast, the RIAs are able to utilize many more controls that help in enhancing the experience of the user, and also providing a greater efficiency. For example, RIAs allow the users to directly interact with elements of the page via tools that are used to drag-and-drop, and also those used for editing. These applications are also able to pan across an image or map.
- **Partial-Page Updating:** The standard web pages that are based on HTML are normally loaded once. When an aspect on the page is updated, the server receives the alteration, performs the changes, and then sends back the whole page. With HTML and HTTP, this is the only way it can be done. The traditionally used applications, has many limitations when it came to processing, issues with connectivity, and other issues that required the users to wait for the whole page to reload. It did not matter if there was a broadband connection. The time that the user had to wait was disruptive and long. RIAs however are able to work with the incorporation of additional technologies, for example local caching mechanisms that help in increasing the response level, and in reducing the wait times, high performance client-side virtual machines, and real-time streaming.
- **Improved Feedback:** Due to the fact that RIAs are able to alter sections of a page without having to reload, they are able to provide the user with feedback that is accurate and fast. Additinally, error messages are detailed and informative and actions are confirmed in real-time.
- **Consistent Feel and Look:** RIA tools make it possible to ensure that the user experience and interface is made consistent and properly controlled with different OS and browsers.
- **It Can Be Used Offline:** When there is no connection available, RIA applications can still be used, only if they are designed to ensure the retention of their local state on the machine of the client.

- **Impact on Performance:** RIAs are able to perform much better than the applications that were used traditionally, depending on the characteristics of the network and application. Applications that are able to process locally on the client, instead of having to do round trips to the server, have a higher chance of having an improved server performance. The only disadvantage about this, is that mobile, embedded, and small devices may not be able to use these applications due to lack of the resources they need (Figure 1.18).

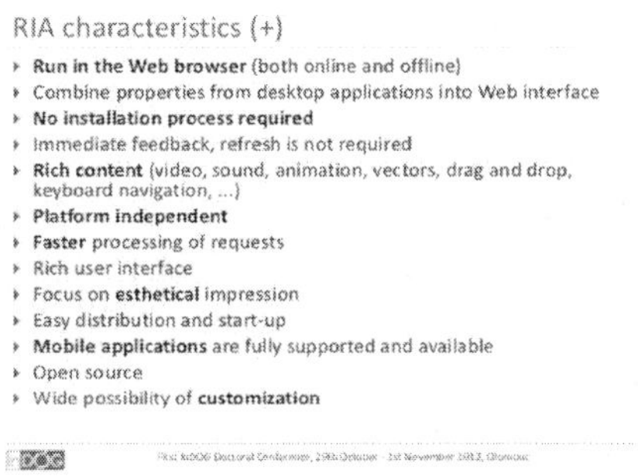

Figure 1.18. *Above is a summary of some of the characteristics of RIA. One of the greatest advantages is that the user does not have to wait for refresh to occur because these applications provide immediate feedback. They also fully support mobile applications.*

Source: https://www.slideshare.net/indogpr/indog-prezentace-netek (accessed on 2 April 2020).

1.4.4. Single-Page Application

This design approach allows for all the content on a new page to be served by dynamically generating it through the ability of JavaScript to manipulate the DOM elements on the page that already exists, without having to load new HTML pages. The architecture of a web page that is traditional, it is possible to have the linking of index.html on the server, with other HTML pages, where the browser then downloads and displays them from scratch.

This design approach provides the user with the opportunity to proceed with interacting with and consuming the page, as the updating or fetching of new elements occurs and this can lead to interactions that are faster as well as faster reloading of content. In addition, it is also possible to alter the URL of the page with the help of the HTML5 History API, without having to load the page again, and therefore, the user is able to ensure the creation of URLs that are separate, for different views (Sklar, 2011).

Single-page applications are considered a necessity if the user requires a rich interaction with the application. So as to provide real-time view changes as the user scrolls or clicks different places, some applications such as Google Maps normally utilize thus approach. In addition, this approach also makes it easier to provide updates in real time. This includes updates on real-time charts, data streaming, and notifications.

This application may also have a few limitations. If the user has static content, the use of this application could make the time the page takes to load worse for the user, and this means one would have to download and execute the payload for JavaScript before the user is able to view any of the content (Sklar, 2011) (Figure 1.19).

Figure 1.19. *Above are some of the benefits that a user can achieve with the use of single-page applications. They are fast, they make the websites unique, they support mobile applications, among others.*

Source: https://www.quora.com/What-are-the-advantages-of-SPA-single-page-application-over-a-normal-web-application (accessed on 2 April 2020).

When it comes to older browsers or the use of internet connections that are slow, it is possible to improve the accessibility by the display of the content of the static HTML upon request. If bots are not able to view any of the content or headers, SEO rankings can be hurt due to not being able to display any HTML content. The situation for loading times can be improved by using the server-side rendering approach. It can also help in providing some improved readability for users that have not enabled JavaScript.

In comparison to multi-page applications, these applications are susceptible to cross-site scripting attacks. This means that hackers are able to client-side scripts into the web applications. One of the main issues to do with security includes sensitive data exposure. When the designers have sensitive data on the initial page load, it is possible to mistakenly send confidential information to malicious users. This is because on the browser, the whole single-page application is not generally visible, and this can provide a pseudo-security aspect. Singe-page applications can also be insecure due to the lack of access control on the functional level. Users can end up gaining access to functions that they should have no permission to use, due to the fact that developers move logic and features to the client after moving them off the server (Gosselin, 2010).

Chapter 2

Web Browsers and Layout Engines

CONTENTS

2.1. INTRODUCTION

The web browser basically is a software program used for accessing data found on the Worldwide Web browsers. Typically, they have a built-in menu that can easily be configured to match the user's needs. The layout engine is referred to as rendering engine or browser engine. It is a primary software element embedded in almost all web browsers. Its main role is to change HTML files and other similar resources found on the website page, into comprehensible visual formant on the user's computing device.

2.2. WEB BROWSER

2.2.1. Web Browsers Visualize Web Content

A web browser rests at the core of how the modern-day society encounters the internet. Each day, several millions of people visit websites through browsers. Some of the five major browsers known today are Internet Explorer (IE), Chrome, Safari, Firefox, and Opera. These which capture about 95% of internet traffic (Figure 2.1).

Figure 2.1. *Web browsers are used to search for information on the internet.*

Source: https://rajalaptop.com/best-web-browsers/ (accessed on 2 April 2020).

One major function of the web browser is accepting a web URL through an address bar, retrieving resources, and showcasing them on the monitor. A browsers operation can be categorized into 4 primary sections, which are Fetch, Process, Display, and Storage. Every category describes a set of functions that browser must execute and consist of subsystems.

- **The Network Layer:** This is a major subsystem that plays a crucial role in fetching information from succeeding web servers through the internet. It receives URLs directly from the browser user-interface, plus it's responsible for producing network calls for fetch resources through HTTP/FTP protocols. The system feeds information to the process substructure, known as the rendering engine, when it becomes accessible and is typically carried in byte size for enhancing performance.

In case the requested website executes a cache, then a copy to the data would be made within the Service Workers or App Cache for subsequent sessions. Caches are ideal for their fast response times, as well as saving network demands for regular visits. A browser originally looks for whichever cache accessibility on local memory slots for requested URLs. Or else, the network level forms an HTTP packet having a domain name that requests a web resource through the internet (Gosselin, 2010).

Network level plays a key role in streamlining the user experience. But it can sometimes be a bottleneck for web performance, considering that browsers normally wait for remote information/content to arrive. Different methods can be used for reducing this effect on the operator's experience nonetheless.

The network stage is followed by processing, which involves accepting information from the network level and feeding the display sub-systems. Programs such as JS engine, UI backend and Render engine form part of this procedure.

2.2.2. Render HTML, Images, CSS, Videos, JavaScript, etc.

The rendering program subsystem is responsible for processing information from the network level, while displaying web material on the screen. On default, it can conveniently process XML, Image, and HTML files. Nevertheless, it can be stretched to accommodate different data types through extensions. There are various render engines which can be used, which are typically written as C++ files. For example: Opera and Chrome make use of Blink whereas IE relies on Trident.

Through rendering engines, it's possible for web resources to be parsed. For instance, the HTML parser translates a HTML system into an item known as the DOM tree. Usually, stylesheets are parsed for producing style protocols for both exterior and inline style components.

The render tree refers to an object which merges parsed HTML together with CSS. It's produced with visual commands and attributes for rendering components on the user's monitor. When the render tree has been developed, it then passes through layout and painting procedures, and shows the results on the screen. Additionally, the layout process comprises of methodologies for calculating dimensions and precise coordinates, showing where every element must show on the viewport (Gosselin, 2010).

Furthermore, the painting process comprises of filing the outline with style attributes such as color, background as well as other crucial CSS properties. Normally, the rendering engine handles data in chunks plus showcases the information within the shortest time imaginable. It won't wait until the whole document content passes through both the structuring and painting procedures (Gosselin, 2010).

- **JavaScript Engine:** Basically, it is a subsystem applied for parsing JavaScript encryption to machine code before implementing it. The JS engines are standard transcribers or just-in-time compilers. Among the most famous engines is Google-V8 engine, which is scripted in form of C++.

The engines consist of two main components: first, there is the memory heap followed by call stack. Normally, memory heap forms the place where memory is allotted for variables, roles, and other JS components.

The call stack just refers to a column of stack frames, or sequential phases implemented by the browser. Moreover, JavaScript refers to a single-threaded procedure and every entry or implementation step is merely a stack frame. The engines have different threads internally used for performing various tasks. Some examples of such duties include:

- Fetching, collecting, and executing code;
- The profiling thread to evaluate functions as well as their time usage;
- Optimizing the implementation work; and
- Garbage collectors.

Moreover, Google's V8 engine utilizes a mark/sweep technique for performing garbage assembly in an incremental manner. It makes use of a browser's idle moments and enhances performance.

When it comes to version 5.9, which was launched in early 2017, both Turbofan and Ignition form the most recent pipelines for the V8 engine. As for NodeJS, it's a server-based JavaScript runtime developed for Google's open-source V8 engine. The program is used to implement JavaScript within the server side.

2.2.3. Software Application for Retrieving, Presenting, and Traversing Information Resources on the World Wide Web

An application program is something that's required to accomplish a specific job on a project or a particular program. Based on the scope of language applied there are various kinds of application software.

- **Internet Browsers:** A web browser (simply known as browser) refers to a software system for accessing data on the Internet. When an operator requests a specific webpage, the browser retrieves all necessary material from the web server before displaying the resultant website on the operator's device. The web browser, however, isn't similar to a search engine, even though these two are typically confused.

For users, search engine is simply a website, same as Google Search or Yahoo, which stores searchable information about other sites. Nevertheless, to link to a site's server and showcase its web pages, the user should have an internet browser installed (Gosselin, 2010).

Internet browsers are utilized on a variety of devices, such as tablets, desktops, smartphones, and laptops. Just recently in 2019, around 4.3 billion individuals used a browser for searching information. The most popular browser currently is Google Chrome, having a 64% universal market share on most devices and is followed by Safari at 17%.

The role of an internet browser is fetching data resources from the Internet and showcase them on the user's machine. This procedure starts when the user adds a Uniform Resource Locator (URL), like www.google.com/into the browser.

Almost all URLs present on the Web begin with either https:/http: meaning the browser shall salvage them through the Hypertext Transfer Protocol (HTTP). As for https, this is the communication that exists between the web browser and server, which is encoded for the reason of security as well as privacy.

When a web page is retrieved, it means that the browser's rendering system exhibits it on the operator's device. It includes photo and video formats which are backed by the browser. Besides, web pages typically contain hyperlinks that are connected to other pages or resources.

Every link features a URL, which whenever clicked on, leads to a new resource. Therefore, the process of pooling content to the operator starts again. Many browsers use the website's internal cache resources for improving loading times, touching on subsequent tours to a similar page. Caches can store several items, such as large photos, so that they don't have to be downloaded directly from the server again. Additionally, cached items are typically only kept for so long as the internet server specifies in the HTTP response texts (Gosselin, 2010).

- **Database Software:** It refers to a software system or utility applied for developing, editing, and preserving database folders and records. This kind of software permits users to keep data in form of organized fields, tables, and rows, which may then be recovered openly and/or via programmatic access. Besides, database software can also be referred to as file management software, even though these phrases aren't actually synonyms.

The database software is mainly applied to store and supervise data/databases, usually in a structured design. It normally offers a graphical interface which allows operators to create, modify, and manage information fields and records within a tabular or structured form. The data kept using this program may be salvaged in either raw or report-style format (Gosselin, 2010).

While database software is same as database managing software (DBMS), a number of database software still lack native language assistance, like SQL and MySQL, or whichever other database that queries language. For instance, MS Access application allows operators to develop, manage, and query any database through its GUI switch and features, without necessarily writing programming queries.

- **Communication Software:** It refers to a program or application developed to pass data from one structure to another. This software offers remote access to structures and transfers files in various formats between computers. Additionally, communication applications form some part of communication structures with software modules classified according to roles found within the (OSI Model) Open Structures Interconnection Model. Among the well-defined examples of communication, applications are file exchange protocol, messaging application and email.

The principle of emailing may be traced up to the early-60s, where it was used a means of communication for different users of time-allotting mainframe computers. By the 70s, message chat system followed emailing and showed up on bulletin board structures and multi-user computer programs. In the 80s, a terminal emulator was developed; it's a software program for logging into mainframes and accessing email. The original decentralized chat structure was known as Bitnet Relay, which was developed in 1985. Another renowned chat system which was introduced during the same period was Minitel (Gosselin, 2010).

Additionally, Instant texting, together with buddy catalog and the online presence idea system, was presented in 1996. Much recently, voice-over internet protocol (VoIP) appears on the small list of common communication software. Besides, VoIP permits operators to make calls via the Web at a convenient rate.

- **Desktop Publishing Software:** Desktop publishing application is a tool used by graphic designers, as well as other professionals to develop visual communications like brochures, web pages, posters, greeting cards and business cards. Programs like Adobe In-Design, QuarkXPress, and MS Publisher are some examples of desktop publication software. A few of these are applied by expert graphic designers and business printing technicians.

Besides, others are applied by office workers, students, small business vendors, teachers, and even non-designers. The word desktop publishing software, when used among professional developers, refers mainly to high-end specialized page layout software programs, such as QuarkXPress and Adobe In-Design.

An explosion of client programs, including the associated promotion hype propelled the usage of "desktop publishing applications" to cover software for creating greeting cards, banners, calendars, and different other creative printing projects.

Ultimately, this caused a wide variety of affordable, low-cost, simple-to-use software which doesn't need conventional design or prepress abilities to use. The main page layout software programs in use by expert graphic developers and business printing prepress specialists are QuarkXPress and Adobe InDesign.

The key players in the arena are Corel, Microsoft, Adobe, Serif, and Quark with products which stay close to the primary use of desktop publication software for specialized page layout. Furthermore, Microsoft, Broderbund, and Nova Development among others have formed consumer or print creativeness as well as home desktop publication software for several years (Gosselin, 2010).

- **Adobe:** It consists of most professional software suites used by developers. Probably you've heard of the words Illustrator and Photoshop, for instance. The firm's other programs aren't page layout software programs for print publishing; instead they comprise of graphics applications, web design apps, and programs for developing and working with PDF files, all which are essential aspects to the publishing procedure. Adobe InDesign controls the sector of expert page layout application.

- **Corel:** This program is widely known for its professional graphics suite which comprise of Corel Photo-Paint and CorelDraw. During the past, the program produced ingenious printing and home publishing systems, also applied for desktop publishing, though the main page layout program from Corel is the CorelDraw.
- Microsoft creates MS Word, PowerPoint, and Excel among other consumer graphics, including other creative printing systems used alone or together with other applications for doing some kind of desktop publishing. Moreover, Microsoft entered into the page layout industry for print with their MS Publisher application.

Apart from the oftentimes fuzzy differentiation of desktop publication into professional, household, and business groups, there are different other kinds of software that are closely tied to desktop publishing. Out of the 4 kinds of software used for desktop publishing, including word processing, graphics, web publishing and page layout, they are all specialized tools for publishing in their unique ways, even though the lines remain blurred. A good part of the ideal design software processes are used for either print or web, plus sometimes double up as page layout, creative print, graphics software and business software among other combinations.

2.2.4. An Information Resource Identified by a URI/URL

Information resource can be defined as both data and information properties of a company, department, or unit. The other name for it is information-technology (IT) or information systems (IS).

The electronic resource is data which is kept in electronic format, which increasingly includes virtual data. Additionally, libraries offer access to a variety of electronic resources. Even though a computer might be applied for play or showing the resource, still other devices like DVD players, gaming stations and mp3 players can also be used. As for electronic databases, these may comprise of complete-text journals, newspapers, photo collections, as well as encyclopedia (Sklar, 2011).

The Uniform Resource Identifier or (URI) refers to a set of characters which unmistakably identifies a given resource. To ensure uniformity, the

URIs follow a preset group of syntax rules, however, it also preserves extensibility through a differently defined hierarchical identification system (e.g., http://). This identification allows for interaction with symbols of the resource through a network, normally the World Wide Web (WWW), through particular protocols.

Schemes that specify a solid syntax and related protocols describe every URI. The most renowned type of URI is Uniform Resource Locator, commonly known informally as just web address. More infrequently seen in application is Uniform Resource Name (URN), which was developed to complement URLs through providing a system for the recognition of resources in specific namespaces.

- **URLs and URNs:** The Uniform Resource Name or (URN) basically is a URI which detects a resource through name in a given namespace. URNs can be applied to reference resources without pinpointing its location, including ways of accessing it. For instance, with regards to (ISBN) International Standards Book Number system, ISBN 0-486-27557-4 describes a particular version of Shakespeare's book Romeo and Juliet. Nevertheless, it offers no information with regards to where they can find the book's copy (Figure 2.2).

Figure 2.2. *URL identifies the location of a website on the vast internet.*

Source: https://www.thebalanceeveryday.com/what-is-internet-browser-892819 (accessed on 2 April 2020).

The URL refers to a URI which stipulates the method of action or gaining the resource representation, meaning, specifying both the primary access system and network location. URN can be compared to an individual's name, whereas a URL can be likened to their home street address.

Otherwise, a URN detects an item while the URL offers a means for discovering it. Technical publications, particularly standards provided by IETF and W3C, typically represent a viewpoint that's defined in the W3C 2001 Recommendation of 2001, acknowledging the term's precedence instead of endorsing whichever formal subdivision into either URN or URL (Stanek, 2014).

URL is a valuable yet informal concept: the URL is a form of URI which identifies a resource through a depiction of its main access mechanism (for instance, its network "location"), instead of some other qualities it might have. Therefore, a URL is basically a URI which seems to point towards a resource through a network.

Still, in non-technical matters and in software used for (WWW) World Wide-Web, the word "URL" continues to be widely used. Moreover, the word "web address" regularly happens in non-technical presentations as a URI synonym which applies the https or http protocols. These assumptions can cause confusion, for instance, when considering the matter of XML namespaces which have a visual resemblance to re-solvable URIs. Some of the specifications presented by the WHATWG choose URL over URI; therefore, newer HTML5 APIs mostly use URL instead of URI.

The shared resource, or networking share, refers to computer resource that is available from a particular host on the computer network. This is an instrument or piece of data on a computer which can be remotely accessed from another processor, typically through a LAN or business intranet.

Generally, network sharing can be made possible through inter-process interaction over the network. A few instances of shareable resources include computer programs, storage devices, printers, and URL. Other examples include shared file access (commonly referred to as folder sharing and disk sharing), mutual printer access, and shared scanner access (Stanek, 2014).

Typically, the shared resource is known as shared disk, shared document, or shared folder. The word file sharing conventionally means mutual file access, particularly in the framework of operating systems (OS), LAN as well as Intranet services, for instance in MS Windows files. Bit-Torrent and other similar software became available during the early 2000s. However, concepts, such as file sharing, increasingly became related with peer-to-peer document sharing through the Internet (Stanek, 2014).

2.2.5. Common File Programs and Protocols

Shared document and printer access need an operating system (OS) on the operator that promotes access to resources through a server, application layer (within the 4/5 level TCP/IP reference system) document sharing protocol, and transport layer protocol for providing shared access.

Then OS promotes access to the client resources. Current OS for personal computers (PCs) consists of distributed filing systems that promote file sharing. However, hand-held computing instruments sometimes require extra software for mutual file access.

The main OS refers to the most frequently used filing share protocol. On MS Windows, the network share is offered through the Windows system module "File and Printer Sending for Microsoft Networks," through MS's SMB (Server Messaging Block) protocol. Similarly, there are other OS which may equally implement that protocol, such as Samba which is an SMB system that runs on the Unix OS as well as other non-Windows/non-MS-DOS OSs like OpenVMS (Godbole, 2013).

The Samba system can be applied to develop network shares that can be accessed, through SMB, from processors that run on Microsoft Windows. Yet another alternative is a mutual disk file system, whereby every computer has easy access to "native" file system within a common disk drive. The shared resource access may also be applied with Web-based Distribution Authoring and Versioning, commonly known as WebDAV.

2.3. LAYOUT ENGINE

Recently, HTML V and CSS3 have been launched, coming with them an entire new quest for the 'most ideal markup' trophy. However, these technologies are just basic tools that are waiting for skilled developers to modify the appropriate project. Being a developer, it is not wise to get into meaningless deliberations to show which markup works the best since they all have their unique points.

In reality, these technologies are just tools that are waiting for practiced developers to modify and apply to the appropriate project.

Even though it's true that both CSS3 and HTML V are works in progress and this will remain so for many years' time, there's really no reason for not starting to use the program it right now.

Meanwhile, time has continuously proven that execution of unfinished specifications will work and may be simply mistaken by the whole W3C recommendation. Which is where systems like Graceful Degradation and Progressive Enhancement come into action (Godbole, 2013).

HTML5 is not an ideal tool for everybody. Thus, you need to be wise and choose how and exactly where to utilize it. Considering all the markup variety you have accessible as tools, it is important to use the correct one for the correct job. Hence, if your site is coded in standards based compliant XHTML, there is actually no cause for changing to HTML5.

Besides, there is also the belief that by utilizing HTML5 code immediately, then your website may become wedged in some type of "limbo" considering that even though the browser shall render HTML5, it still doesn't understand it yet. This might also apply to some other software like search engines (SE) or screen readers.

Finally, you should consider that HTML5 has still been under intense development. Given the massive amount of feedback and ongoing hype surrounding it, the present version is going to change. Therefore, if you are mindful about upcoming changes and are not afraid to adapt your code, then HTML5 is definitely worth trying (Godbole, 2013).

Additionally, Graceful Degradation is an extensively used terminology. It refers to the practice of using the newest technologies first and later fixing anything which needs repair for older browsers. For instance, many developers test their code originally on Firefox before trying it on the older browsers, such as Internet Explorer.

On the contrary, Progressive Enhancement is a practice of building originally for the least capable, outmoded browser and then improving the newest technologies. We, too, apply this model every day. For instance, many at the times people code a particular website starting with the markup, before applying an external CSS folder when including the styling.

This example presents Progressive Enhancement practically. Each of these technologies typically work hand-in-hand, besides it's been how we have been doing things for many years. Besides, both of these exercises must evolve because of the fresh languages which are emerging. In case you intend to go further into each of these terms, then consider reading more about the topic (Jones, 2006).

A simple layout commonly known as Smashing HTML5, covering many of the essential elements that can be coded into HTML5 is possible to achieve. These elements include website name, its slogan, menu, highlighted (featured) zone, and various sub-pages, such as "About Us".

In Header Smashing, the HTML5 Heading block is as easy as it becomes. The header component represents a set of introductory or directional aids Therefore it's more than logical that operators use this for marking up the header. The nav element signifies a part of the page that joins to other sections or to specific parts inside the page: such as a section containing navigation links. It's not all link groups found on the page which must be in the nav element—just the sections which comprise of key navigation blocks are ideal for the nav component. There's quite some buzz concerning the nav element's spec considering that "major navigation blocks" aren't s a very meaningful description.

2.3.1. Formatted Content on the Screen

The layout engine, also known as rendering engine, refers to a software which resembles marked up material (like HTML, Image files and XML, etc.) plus formatting information (like XSL, CSS, etc.), in addition to displaying the formatted content directly on the screen. This "paints" onto the content section of the window that is shown on the printer or monitor. Furthermore, the layout engine is commonly applied in web browsers, mailing clients, and other applications which need the displaying (plus editing) of website contents.

The word "layout engine" only attained popularity when they became effortlessly differentiated from the browser. Case in point, Gecko, which is Mozilla system's open-source layout machine, is applied by a range of products which are resultant from Mozilla's code base, such as Firefox's internet browser, Thunderbird mailing client, and the Sea monkey app program. Oftentimes, Trident, which is the layout machine from IE, gets applied by many programs on the MS Windows platform for rendering HTML, just like Outlook Express, some editions of MS Outlook, including the mini-browsers present in RealPlayer and Winamp (Puntambekar, 2009).

Likewise, Opera Software's patented Presto engine is registered to various other software dealers, apart from being applied in Opera's unique Opera web browser, plus KDE's open-source KHTML machine is commonly used in the KDE's special Konqueror web browser, apart from being utilized in an adapted way, being the framework for the rendering machine in Apple's Safari search browser.

In fact, the word rendering engine may also be used to refer to sentence rendering engines such as Uniscribe or Pango, which make multilingual typescripts available in proper shape, particularly considering bidirectional texts, mergers of "basic characters" together with accents, as well as other complexities of multilingual text. There are roughly 5 main browsers: Firefox, Chrome, IE, Opera, and Safari (Puntambekar, 2009).

On mobile devices the primary browsers are iPhone, Opera Mini, Android Browser, Chrome, and Opera Mobile, which are dependent on WebKit. Based on StatCounter research figures, Firefox, Safari, and Chrome constitute of roughly 71% of universal desktop browser utilization. If we consider mobile devices, then iPhone, Android Browser and Chrome comprise of roughly 54% of usage. These are the main characteristics of functional browsers:

- **The Browser's Key Functionality:** The major role of browsers is to display the web resource by retrieving it from the primary server and showcasing it in the web browser window. Hence, the resource is typically an HTML file, though it may also be a PDF, photo, or some other kind of material. Besides, the resource's location is mentioned by the user through a URL. How a browser deduces and displays HTML documents is shown in both CSS and HTML specifications. The specifications are sustained by W3C (Worldwide Web Consortium) company, which forms the standards protocol for the web (Figure 2.3).

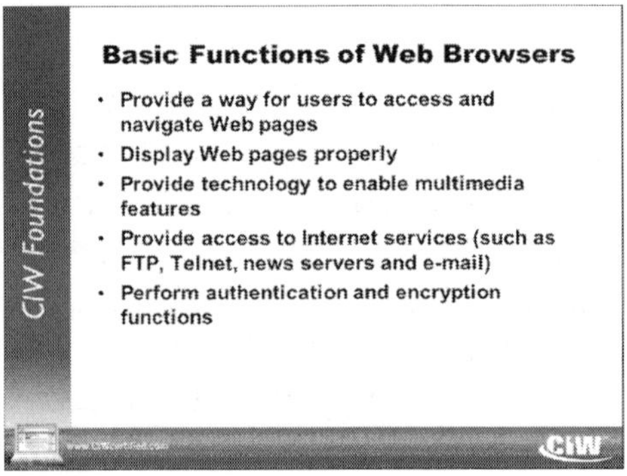

Figure 2.3. *Browsers serve many roles such as displaying webpages correctly.*

Source: https://slideplayer.com/slide/4825725/ (accessed on 2 April 2020).

Over the years browsers simply conformed to a portion of the specifications then developed their unique extensions. This initiated some serious compatibility matters for web authors. Nowadays, majority of the web browsers adapt to these specifications. The Browser user interfaces share a lot of features with one another. A few of these shared user interface features are: address-bar for, back and forward controls, bookmarking commands, refresh button or home button which takes the user back to the home page.

What is even more interesting, the web browser's user interface isn't indicated in any formal description, but instead comes from positive practices shaped through years of experience, including by browsers that resemble one another. Additionally, HTML5 specification doesn't describe UI components a browser should have, though it mentions a few common features. Out of these, there is the address bar, tool bar and status bar. Plus, of course, other features exclusive to a particular browser such as Firefox's downloads supervisor (Sklar, 2011).

- **The Browser's Top-Level Framework:** The browser's core elements include the user interface which comprises of the address-bar, bookmarking menu and back/forward button. Each component of the browser has a control display, apart from the window in which you can check up the page requested.
- **The Browser Engine:** It marshals activities between the rendering engine and UI. The rendering machine is responsible for showcasing the requested material. For instance, in case the requested material is HTML, then the rendering engine will parse both HTML and CSS before displaying the parsed material directly on the screen. Networking is useful for network calls, such as the HTTP requests, making use of varying implementations for varying platforms behind the platform-independent user-face. In addition, there's the UI backend which is commonly applied for drawing simple widgets such as combo boxes as well as windows. The backend exposes a general-purpose interface which isn't platform specific. Beneath that, it utilizes (OS) operating system utility interface technologies. Furthermore, all browsers have some form of data storage present at the persistence level. This browser may have to save all kinds of data regionally, like cookies. Besides, browsers also promote storage mechanisms like the local Indexed DB, WebSQL Cache Storage, and File System.
- **Parsing:** Since parsing forms a significant portion of the rendering

engine, it is important to delve a bit more into it for better understanding. First, it is important to start with the introduction of parsing. It is a document that converts a specific input into a program. The final outcome of parsing is typically a nodes tree that signifies the model of the file and this is known as syntax tree or parse tree. As an example, parsing the command 2 + 3 – 1 may return the user to a particular selected tree.

On the other hand, Grammars Parsing relies on the syntax policies that the document obeys: including the type of language/format that it was scripted in. Each format that you can parse should have some deterministic grammar elements, comprising of vocabulary as well as syntax rules. It's known as context-free grammar. The standard human languages don't fall under these groups, and hence can't be parsed using common parsing methods (Silva, 2012).

Likewise, parsing may be differentiated into two main sub-processes, which include either syntax or lexical analyses. In particular, lexical analysis refers to the process of subdividing the input into manageable tokens. Tokens comprise of the primary language vocabulary or the assembly of useful building blocks. For human language, this will comprise of all words which are found in the dictionary plus for that particular language. Syntax analyzing involves the application of language syntax policies.

Usually, parsers subdivide the task between two modules. First, the lexer (often called tokenizer) is needed for subdividing the input into various valid tokens, including the parser which is responsible for fashioning the parse tree through evaluating the document structure depending on the language syntax guidelines. Additionally, the lexer recognizes how to strip inappropriate characters such as white spaces or line breaks.

The parsing procedure is largely iterative. The parser shall typically request the lexer for some fresh token and attempt to match it with a couple of the syntax policies. In case a rule is successfully matched, then the node that corresponds to this token shall be included to the parsing tree, plus the parser shall request for yet another token where possible (Silva, 2012).

In case there are no rule matching, then the parser shall store up the token internally, while continuing to bid for tokens up to the point where a rule that matches every internally kept token is detected. If there's no rule that found, then it means the parser shall propose an exception. Basically, the document processed wasn't valid and featured various syntax errors.

For some cases, the parse tree isn't the ultimate product and parsing is typically used in translation, where it transforms the input file to another different format. An example is in compilation. A compiler that assembles source code into the machine code will first parse it within a parse tree, before translating this tree into the machine code file (Silva, 2012).

Let's consider a basic mathematical language format to understand the parse process. First, Vocabulary as a language may include integers, plus, and minus signs. While language syntax building mechanisms are expressions, operations, and terminologies. Language can further include a wide variety of expressions. The expression is described as a "term" and followed by the "operation" and then another term.

The operation is basically a plus or minus token, whereas a term refers to an integer, expression or even token. By analyzing the command 2 + 3 – 1. Basically, the primary substring matching a defined rule is 2, in accordance to rule No.5 of the parsing sequence. The secondary match is 2 + 3 which conforms to the third policy: a term that's followed by some operation and another term altogether. The subsequent match shall essentially be hit by the final part of the input. The input 2 + 3 – 1 can be considered an expression since it's already known that 2 + 3 resembles a term, therefore this term can be followed closely by an operation and another different term. But 2 + 1 won't match any policy and thus is considered an invalid entry (Silva, 2012).

- **Official Descriptions for Syntax and Vocabulary:** Vocabulary is typically expressed through regular expressions. Case in point, a language can be described as either: INTEGER: 0| [1–9] or [0–9] * as a PLUS: or MINUS. As shown, integers are mostly defined through a regular expression while Syntax is commonly defined in the format known as BNF. In addition, a language may be parsed with regular parsers in case its grammatical aspect is in form of a context-free grammar. The intuitive description of a context-free grammar refers to a grammar which can be wholly defined in BNF form (Figure 2.4).

```
<skos:Concept rdf:about="urn:example#spiralGalaxy">
  <skos:altLabel xml:lang="en">spiral nebula</skos:altLabel>
  <skos:broader rdf:resource="urn:example#galaxy"/>
  <skos:definition xml:lang="en"> A spiral galaxy is defined here
    following the definition in ...</skos:definition>
  <skos:hiddenLabel xml:lang="en">spiral glaxy</skos:hiddenLabel>
  <skos:narrower rdf:resource="urn:example#barredSpiralGalaxy"/>
  <skos:notation rdf:datatype="urn:example#_notation">5.1.1</skos:notation>
  <skos:prefLabel xml:lang="de">Spiralgalaxie</skos:prefLabel>
  <skos:prefLabel xml:lang="en">spiral galaxy</skos:prefLabel>
  <skos:related rdf:resource="urn:example#spiralArm"/>
  <skos:scopeNote xml:lang="en">The Sa/Sc/Sd subtypes of Spiral
    galaxies are not represented here,
    and should be noted in image comments.</skos:scopeNote>
</skos:Concept>
<rdf:Description rdf:about="urn:example#_notation">
  <dc:description>Notation described in foo.pdf</dc:description>
</rdf:Description>
```

Figure 2.4. *Syntax is the language that computers use to process information into comprehensible format.*

Source: https://www.researchgate.net/figure/Figure-examples-of-a-SKOS-vocabulary-Concept-the-skos-namespace-is-presumed-to-have_fig1_51942733 (accessed on 2 April 2020).

There are two kinds of parsers which include: the top/down and bottom/up parsers. The intuitive description is that top/down parsers inspect the high-level configuration of the syntax, apart from trying to establish a rule match. As for bottom/up parsers, they begin with the input and progressively convert it into a set of syntax rules, beginning from the low range rules, up to the much higher-level rules.

Normally, the top/down parser starts from the higher rank rule: where it identifies $2 + 3$ as the main expression. It shall then detect $2 + 3 - 1$ in form of an expression (a procedure involving identification of the expression develops, blending the other rules, though the starting point forms the highest rank rule). The bottom/up parser is capable of scanning the input up to the point where a rule is corresponding. It shall then replace this matching command with the rule. Something that will proceed on until the final part of the input. Next, a party matched expression would be added onto the parser' stack (Silva, 2012).

2.3.2. A Layout Engine Embedded in Web Browsers, E-Mail Clients, E-Book Readers, On-Line Help Systems

Web browsers are designed to visualize Web material, where they render HTML, photos, CSS, JavaScript, and videos. Meanwhile, software applications are meant for retrieving, offering, and navigating information resources through the Worldwide Web. The information resource can be recognized through a URI/URL, plus it could be in form of a web page, video, and just about any other set of content. Moreover, it may be applied to access data offered by web-servers within private networks, or files found in a file system (Godbole, 2013).

The Layout Engine gathers marked up details (available as HTML, XML, photos, and files, it's equally responsible for formatting information in form of CSS and XSL, then later displaying the formatted material on the screen. Furthermore, the layout engine is normally embedded within web browsers, e-book readers, e-mail clients, and virtual assistance systems. To showcase Web content, various devices run diverse layout engines thus rendering HTML and CSS separately.

Nowadays, a new type of networking web known as 2.0 has come up. It's a writing and participatory web that produces (user-generated content). Fresh applications might allow each user to interact or collaborate with one another through a social network dialogue box as inventors of content. Besides, the Rich Internet Applications or (RIA) represents a Social Web and Web-Structure Architecture that makes up a good part of web programs. As for "Semantic Web," it's sometimes applied as a synonym term for "Web3.0," which is a powerful browser that can assess your response, examine the Internet for any likely answers, and finally organize the outcome for you.

There's also a higher version of Web being developed, known as Web4.0, it combines Artificial intelligence (AI), Semantic Web, Personalization, and Mobility features. Besides, the super-intelligent electronic agent system can also be found embedded within the machine. It can instantly recognize users when you stand directly in front of the machine, since it integrates the device's inbuilt camera system into its intelligent framework. Besides, through facial recognition, they machine can know that it's you who's using it. As for Web 4.0, it's typically characterized in form of a Web OS. And the whole web forms a single (OS) operating system whereby information passes from one particular point to another (Godbole, 2013).

2.3.3. Displaying Web Content

Most layout engines have display pages which offer a fresh level of control across the look and texture of your content. This ultimately empowers marketers and developers to create striking designs for internet content. Display pages utilize both page elements and web content for providing a simple method to create attractive layouts for showcasing articles. One effective way of using display pages is creating standardized editions for articles. In case you examine the material on various writing platforms, you'll notice that every article follows quite a distinct format (Figure 2.5).

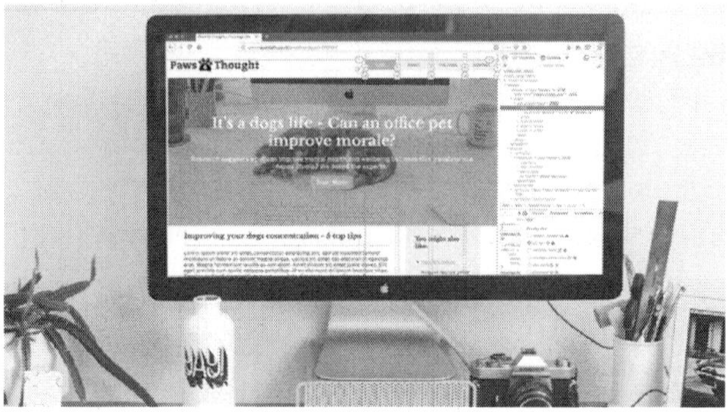

Figure 2.5. *Web content is usually displayed in HTML format that's readable to humans.*

Source: https://www.creativebloq.com/how-to/build-a-blog-with-grid-and-flex-box (accessed on 2 April 2020).

Even though there are various millions of pages which are principally comprised of HTML, or any variation, generally we perceive data, applications, graphics, audio, e-services, and individual web pages among other factors. Considering that there are several hundreds of methods for delivering data on a site, there's a standard amount of knowledge with regards to (SEO) search engine optimization (SEO) which must be read in form of an advisory showing how anything apart from the text ought to be delivered.

Presently, SE exist in the form of text-based scripts and are among the most common ways that people utilizing a browser can identify sites of interest. Whenever you're discussing SEO, the web content should be subdivided into certain basic formats considering the format of modern-day websites (Godbole, 2013).

For Non-Template Website Content, the website gives a blank space in which web content is scripted in form of bullets and paragraphs. Besides, information shown in these pages can embellish both the services as well as amenities offered by a company. The non-template material is mainly used since it has a reduced amount of info graphics entailed and can be personalized. It also reduces page load speeds. The template web content consists of information that's captured in form of specific formats availed on the web page. Every aspect of website content is scripted within fixed spaces. The web content comprises of graphics and structural frameworks, equally template web material is more pre-dominant among newer websites.

Responsive Website Design is a technique that submits that design as well as development must respond to the operator's behavior and environment depending on screen size, orientation, and platform. This practice comprises of a blend of elastic grids and layouts, photos, and an intelligent application of CSS media enquiries (Godbole, 2013).

When the user shifts from laptop use to iPad, ultimately the website must automatically be adjusted to allow for resolution, photo size, and scripting functions. One should also consider the general settings found on their devices; in case they own an iOS VPN for instance, the website shouldn't block the operator's access to the webpage. Otherwise, the website must have the necessary technology for automatically responding to the operator's preferences. Ultimately, this shall remove the need for having a different design as well as development phase for every new appliance on the market.

2.3.4. Different Devices Run Different Layout Engines

Getting a website to appear the same on varying browsers has for long been an ongoing matter for web designers throughout the globe. The logic is simple-basically the visualization of sites depends on various unique variables like, for instance, how the browser is capable of interpreting the page. Any website is simply a group of instructions defining how a website ought to look like. It entirely depends on the internet browser to provide rendering by reading the whole code of your site, apart from producing a particular output.

Still, there are some differences with regards to code interpretation. This is why you must check how your website appears like on varying OS and internet browsers during the web development stage. It's also advisable to use online resources such as http://browsershots.org, to check how your webpages appear on different browsers (Godbole, 2013).

A great website should appear standard and have all the essential features it requires to work in any particular browser. Regrettably, there's no simple solution for that. It's crucial to check the specifications of every browser which fails to showcase your website appropriately and make the essential modifications to your code. These compatibility matters may arise not just in different browsers, though also due to old browser editions that doesn't support entirely the modern standards.

If your site uses submit buttons, check boxes or edit fields, then they must be properly visualized based on the user's OS as well as its design. Normally, browser fonts have the tendency to appear slightly unique when rendered in form of a Linux computer, PC, and Mac. Among the areas where websites almost always appear distinct is on form pages (Stanek, 2014).

Various OS as well as browsers adequately render the buttons through forms and texting boxes that are completely differently. Through the PC, default submission buttons are rather square as well as flat looking, plus on a Mac system, the default submission buttons are well shaded ovals with some form of gradient.

Case in point, the submit button may seem as if it's a gray rectangle shown on your Windows Original theme, plus like an oval in case you apply the XP style. Being a workaround, it's possible to develop custom buttons that can be used for your site. The program of an ordinary submission button sounds like '1<input type=submit/>.'

Furthermore, it is possible to replace the program with another code so as to categorize the submit button photo. For instance, if you fashion your pages at a pixel level of 1024×768, then they won't easily fit inside the visitor's screen having a screen resolution level of 800×600. To solve this, you must not apply stationary dimensions for your site, that is, rather than setting the width at = 1024px you may consider using a width of = 100% instead. While this may not fix every issue, generally it ensures that the page precisely fits within the screen (Stanek, 2014).

2.3.5. Render HTML and CSS Differently

While it's possible to embed various protocols inside web pages, a "web page" comprising of "HTML" (or whichever variation) material is still the leading way in which content is shared. Whereas there are various web pages consisting of localized proprietary frameworks (most typically, business sites), several millions of websites are still in existence which are organized around a common central idea. Most blogs basically are a form of website containing largely web pages structured in HTML format, even though a blogger might be totally oblivious that the webpages consist of HTML because of the blogging tool which might be in use) (Sklar, 2011).

Many millions of individuals use blogs online; the blog is presently the new "Homepage," which is, a venue whereby an individual can disclose personal information, or create a concept regarding who this particular individual is or their brand content. While a blog can be written for different other purposes, like promoting a company, the essential part of blogging is the notion that it's authored by a "person" plus that person reveals details from their unique perspective.

Nowadays, blogs have grown to become a powerful weapon often used by content promoters, who wish to grow their website's traffic, and, rank well in (SERPs) search-engine result pages. New research from Technorati reveals that blogs currently outrank social networks in terms of visitor influence. Search engine websites are comprised mostly of HTML material, but also features a typically structured system for displaying information (Sklar, 2011).

The (SERP) Search-Engine Results Page shows a heading; normally the search engine's (SE) name itself, followed by a group of websites as well as their web addresses. These web addresses are often listed based on their degree of relevance, based on the overall search query. Usually, searchers key in keywords or search word phrases to locate or search exactly what they're delving for on the internet.

Discussion boards comprise of "textual" material structured by HTML or any other variation which may be seen in a website browser. The driving system of a discussions board lies in the fact that operators are registered then upon registration can immediately write posts. Usually, a discussion board consists of posts that ask some question concerning which other users might offer answers to those particular questions.

The ecommerce websites are mostly composed of text-based material and implanted with graphics exhibiting an image of the product(s) for sale. Nevertheless, there are very few websites that are organized page-by-page through some version of HTML. Typically, webpages are designed as they are getting served from the database onto the customer through a web browser. Nevertheless, the user views the mostly text document showing as a webpage that's to be displayed within a web browser. E-commerce websites are normally structured by the software known as "shopping cart" (Sklar, 2011).

2.4. LAYOUT ENGINES AND WEB BROWSERS

2.4.1. Blink

Blink is a powerful browser engine often integrated into the Chrome browser, including various other projects. It was established as part of Chromium's signature project with help from Google, Microsoft, Facebook, Adobe Systems, Intel, Opera, Samsung, and IBM. It was originally launched in April 2013. The Blink app is an element of the WebCore aspect of WebKit that was initially a fork for KHTML and KJS files from KDE. It's embedded in Chrome systems beginning with the version 28. Besides, MS Edge beginning at edition 79, Opera (15+), Amazon Silk, Vivaldi, and different other Chromium-model browsers and frameworks (Figure 2.6).

Figure 2.6. *Majority of Linux browsers run on the blink engine.*

Source: https://www.pngfuel.com/free-png/dufba (accessed on 2 April 2020).

Most of Web Core's programming code was applied for features which Google Chrome utilized differently like sandboxing, as well as the multi-process system. These components were transformed to accommodate the Blink fork, plus although somewhat bulkier, it permitted for greater flexibility by prompting room for fresh features in the coming future.

Additionally, the fork helps to lessen vendor prefixes; whereby existing prefixes are phased out while new experimental functionalities are allowed on an opt-in context. Apart from these pre-arranged changes, the Blink initially stays relatively the same as Web Core. Through commit count, Google in itself has been among the greatest contributors to the Web Kit program base, as from the late 2009.

2.4.2. Chrome, Opera 15+

Google Chrome represents a cross-platform internet browser created by Google. The system was first launched in 2008 for MS Windows and then later distributed on iOS, Android, Linux, and macOS platforms. This browser is the primary module of Chrome OS, whereby it acts as the main platform for internet apps. Majority of Google Chrome's source code originates from Google's clear-source Chromium project, though Chrome is registered as a proprietary freeware.

The Web Kit in particular formed the first rendering engine to be invented, however Google ultimately forked it to develop the Blink engine; besides all Chrome variations apart from iOS currently use Blink. From July 2019, it's believed that Chrome commands approximately 71% of the international browser market-share for traditional PCs, including 63% across every possible platform. Due to this, Google has significantly grown the "Chrome" name to now include other items: such as Chrome OS, Chromebit, Chromebox, Chromecast, Chromebase, and Chromebook.

As for OPERA 15, it's an exceptional browser that integrates a special acoustic design with cutting-edge performance, so as to create a vigorous but precise audio performance, effectively adapted to capture both acoustic playback and live song applications. However, with the modern OPERA series, dBTechnologies have succeeded once more in packing cutting-edge DSP processing, modern design functions and user-friendliness in an unmatched fashion in its price category. Exceeding power and an exclusive acoustic framework combine together to deliver a defined yet pristine sound, especially adaptable to accommodate both playback and live sound applications.

Moreover, Opera's asymmetrical horn feature has totally been redesigned so as to attain asymmetrical-vertical dispersion, as well as double horizontal dispersion and guaranteeing an optimized throw sequence. The program is fitted with a high capacity Class D 600 Watts amplifier with advanced DSP processing, whereby FIR filters permit the systems to effortlessly deliver a clear audio performance, standard, and very clear from all listening positions.

2.4.3. Gecko

It's the ultimate rendering engine utilized by Mozilla Co.'s web browser items like Firefox and Sea monkey. There were different other browsers previously, like Flock and Galeon, which used Gecko as a rendering machine. A great majority fell into irrelevancy then disappeared. There are some few applications still in use nonetheless. There isn't a lot left with regards to actively established gecko-based browsers, though there are some few choices to consider:

- **K-Meleon:** This is a Microsoft Windows browser based on Gecko although it is still undergoing major developments. While there hasn't been any solid release since 2015, there was a prior preview release date back in 2018. Generally, the Gecko-oriented rendering engine that it applies has diverged from Gecko to what it is known as "Goanna."
- **TenFourFox:** This is a Gecko-based web browser used by Power-focused Macintosh computers-which is still getting actively developed. The TenFourFox program is an ideal choice particularly if you own an older computer.
- **Pale Moon:** This is a Firefox fork that has differed quite a lot since the period of its inception, a short while ago. Pale moon has continually been multithreaded and providing multi-core performance, besides it's presently running on Open MP. A single browser tab might slow down another (that is, all browsers have this matter which they share mutually.

The process of opening more tabs needs additional processing as well as resources. It's feasible to enjoy greater performance without having to experience taxing system resources. Besides, you can't possible download extra RAM). This is a Gecko-style browser though it has some other unique aspects to it, the variations existing between its rendering engine as well as modern Gecko are considerable. Furthermore, Pale Moon is accessible for both Linux and Windows systems. The application's homepage can be found at http://www.palemoon.org/.

- **GNU IceCat:** This is a regular Firefox durable release with general default configuration adjustments and some bundled privacy-based extensions; this isn't a totally different browser. Instead, its whole "codebase" is really just a couple of bash-scripts that modifies the graphics, includes extensions, and alters configuration options. On the other hand, IceCatMobile is, same as the Ice cat PC version, only a plain portable Firefox Extension Support Release with varying configuration factors and branding. It's accessible from the open software that is F-Droid app store.
- **Water Fox:** This is a watered-down edition of the active Firefox version. It is available for Linux, macOS, and Windows systems. Plus, the changes are significant enough to possibly refer to it as the fork. However the changes are generally elimination of Firefox code without including original code. It is basically a stripped-down remake of the app.

2.4.4. Firefox, Netscape, and Sea Monkey

Mozilla Firefox, also known basically as Firefox, operates as a no cost and open-source internet browser formed by the Mozilla Group and its affiliate, the Mozilla Corporation. Firefox utilizes the Gecko layout machine to render online pages, which executes current and expected web standards. By 2017, Firefox had started to integrate new technologies within the code phrase Quantum, for promoting parallelism as well as an intuitive operator interface.

The Firefox system is formally accessible for the Windows 7 version, including the newer Linux and macOS systems. Some of its unofficial ports may also be used for different Unix and Unix-based OS such as FreeBSD, illumos, Solaris Unix, OpenBSD, and NetBSD. Similarly, Firefox is accessible for both Android and iOS; even though, the iOS edition utilizes a WebKit layout engine rather than Gecko because of platform limitations, just like with most other iOS internet browsers.

Originally, Firefox was developed in 2002 within the codename "Phoenix" borrowing from the Mozilla community network that wanted a standalone browser, instead of the Mozilla App Suite bundle. In its beta stage, Firefox grew to become very popular among testers, who praised the program for its speed, high security levels, and add-ons in comparison to Microsoft's originally-dominant IE VI. Since its release in 2004, Firefox has challenged the IE's domination with more than 60 million downloads in just 9 months. Firefox also is the successor to Netscape Navigator, since the Mozilla community originally was developed by Netscape during 1998 before its acquirement by AOL.

Firefox's use increased to a rate of 32.21% by the finish of 2009, with edition 3.5 surpassing Internet Explorer 7, even though not all editions of IE entirely. Usage then decreased in contrast to Google Chrome. By January 2020, Firefox already has a usage ratio of 9.87% as a "desktop" browser, based on statistics from StatCounter, therefore making it the 2nd most popular browser in comparison to Google Chrome. Based on Mozilla statistics, it's estimated that there existed more than half-a-billion Firefox users globally in 2014, even though a majority of nations have Google Chrome installed as their key web browser, Firefox remains to control more than 50% desktop use in Eritrea and Cuba.

In addition, Netscape web browser forms the general name covering a series of internet browsers formerly created by Netscape Communications Company, which is a previous subsidiary of AOL. While the original browser originally was the dominant browser with regards to usage share, however due to early browser wars, the system lost almost each individual share market to IE. Besides, Netscape was discontinued plus support over all Netscape browsers including client products were ended on March 1st, 2008 (Puntambekar, 2009).

The Netscape Navigator application was a name given to Netscape's internet browser from editions 1.0 up to 4.8. The original variety of the browser got launched in 1994, referred to as Mosaic then later Mosaic Netscape up to when a legal challenge was made coming from NCSA foundation or National Center for Supercomputer Applications, where the name got transformed to Netscape Navigator. Additionally, the company's name got transformed from Mosaic Communications Company to Netscape Communications Group.

This browser became the most advanced accessible and was a major success, turning into a market leader when still operating in beta. Furthermore, Netscape's feature-count as well as market share continued growing immensely following the release of version 1.0. Later, version 2.0 was added to include a whole mail reader known as Netscape Mail, therefore changing Netscape from a simple internet browser to a Web site. In this time, both the suite and browser were called Netscape Navigator. Within the same period, AOL began bundling their program with Microsoft's IE.

The Edition 3.0 of Netscape became the first to encounter some severe competition coming from MS IE 3.0, though Netscape withheld Microsoft's challenge and continued to be the leading browser for the period. Version 3.0 further became available in the "Gold" edition that comprised of a WYSIWYG-HTML editor, later included to Netscape Communicator being the standard feature. Besides, it was sold in form of retail app for profit.

Netscape 3.0 introduced different new features like fresh plug-ins, background shades for tables, the catalog attribute, as well as the applet feature. Netscape Navigator 3 became the undisputed internet browser bigwig in its period with over 90% share, though it was later corroded by the open IE that came with Windows 95.

The SeaMonkey works as a liberal and open-source Web suite. It's the extension of the previous Mozilla Application Suite, depending on the similar source code, which by itself developed from Netscape Communicator and constituted the root of both Netscape 6 and 7 applications. Originally, SeaMonkey was formed in 2005 after the Mozilla Foundation considered focusing its systems on standalone projects like Thunderbird and Firefox.

The creation of SeaMonkey app is mostly community-driven, as opposed to Mozilla Application Suite that until its last launched version (1.7.13) mostly was managed by the Mozilla Group.

The new project-managing team is known as SeaMonkey Council. In comparison to Firefox, SeaMonkey's internet browser preserves the rather traditional-looking framework of Netscape as well as the Mozilla Suite, particularly the XUL architecture. Consequently, this allows operators to expand SeaMonkey by revising Thunderbird add-ons, or even add-ons which were previously attuned to Firefox browser before the latter was converted to WebExtensions.

2.4.5. Trident

Trident, commonly referred to as MSHTML, refers to a proprietary browsing machine for the MS Windows edition of IE that was developed by Microsoft. Trident was originally introduced through the launch of (version 4.0) IE during the year October 1997. It's been steadily improved and remains to be popular today. For the versions 7 to 8 of IE, Microsoft instituted some major changes to Trident layout's engine for purposes of improving compliance with internet standards and adding support for fresh technologies (Puntambekar, 2009).

Originally, Trident was developed as a software application to allow software programmers to effortlessly add web browsing features to their individual applications. This provides a COM interface that's useful for accessing as well as editing internet pages in whichever COM-supported setting, such as NET or C++. For example, the web browser control may be included to the C++ program, plus Trident be applied to adequately access the page presently displayed within the web browser while retrieving element values as well. Activities from the internet browser control may equally be captured. The Trident functionality turns to be available through linking the folder mshtml.dll onto the software program.

All IE editions for Windows newer than 4.0 use Trident. Furthermore, Trident is used by other internet browsers and software modules. In Windows 98, Me, and 2000 Trident is also applied for the Windows folder manager/shell and Explorer. Additionally, the Add/Remove Projects instrument in Windows 2000 utilizes Trident to officially render the collection of installed programs, besides in Windows XP it's further applied for User Accounts Control Management Panel that works as an HTML Application. Furthermore, Trident wasn't used by IE in MacOS.

2.4.6. Maxthon

Maxthon, formerly referred to as MyIE2, functions as a freeware internet browser created by the firm Maxthon Ltd., from Beijing, China. It's available for macOS, Linux, Windows, and Maxthon Smartphone for IOS, Android, and Windows 8 device. With regards to version 3, the Maxthon app supports a pair of web browser engines which are Trident and WebKit. Besides, Maxthon won the CNET (WebWare 100) Awards in the years 2008 and 2009, as well as #97 in the PC World's group of the top 100 Brands of 2011 (Figure 2.7).

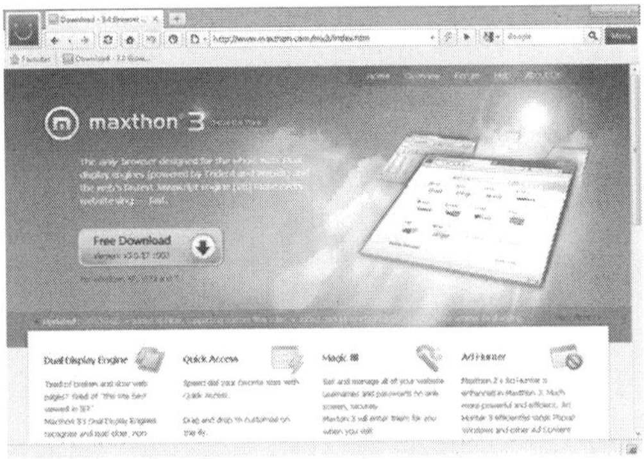

Figure 2.7. *Maxthon is a popular freeware application that's compatible with IOS, Android, and other devices.*

Source: https://www.afterdawn.com/software/network/browsers/maxthon_browser_portable.cfm (accessed on 2 April 2020).

Maxthon has offices all over the world in places like Shanghai and San Francisco in America. However, majority of Maxthon's mechanics are found in the business headquarters in Beijing that develops and preserves various editions of Maxthon web browser, for use by Windows, IOS, macOS, and Android Phones. Furthermore, Maxthon has developed other products such as the Chinese language broadcast and information portal commonly referred to as i.maxthon.cn, as well as Mandarin language's casual game program and humor site known as 'Kid Safe,' which is an internet browser that's ideal for iOS and Android systems (Puntambekar, 2009).

2.4.7. Web Kit

This is a browsing engine established by Apple and is mostly applied in its Safari internet browser, including the iOS internet browsers as well. Web

Kit is equally utilized by BlackBerry Browsers, Tizen mobile OS, as well as a browser meant for Amazon eBook Kindle reader. The Web Kit's C++ app coding interface offers a group of classes for displaying Web material in windows, apart from implementing browser features like following links once clicked upon by the user, supervising a back-forward inventory, and even managing the history of pages newly visited.

The Web Kit's HTML as well as JavaScript engines began as fork components of both KJS and KHTML libraries from KDE, plus have since been increasingly developed by Apple, KDE contributors, Google, Bit stream, BlackBerry, Nokia, and different other OS. Additionally, on April 3rd, 2013, Google pronounced that it had officially forked Web Core, a module of Web Kit, for use in future editions of Google Chrome including the Opera internet browser, covering the moniker Blink.

Currently, Web Kit is available within the BSD-form license, but with an exception of Java Script Core and Web Core elements, which are accessible under the (GNU) Lesser General Public Licensure. By March 7th, 2013, the Web Kit brand became Apple's trademark, officially registered under the American Patent and Trademark Agency.

2.4.8. Safari

The Safari browser was originally established by Apple, depending on the WebKit machine. Originally launched on desktop during the year 2003 alongside Mac (OS) X Panther, a smartphone version has also been launched with iOS appliances since the iPhone's launch in 2007. Generally, Safari serves as the primary browser for Apple devices. The Windows edition was available starting from 2007 up to 2012.

Up to 1997, Apple's Macintosh processors shipped together with Netscape Navigator as well as Cyberdog web browsers. Additionally, Mac's web explorer was henceforth incorporated as the default internet browser for the Mac OS 8.1 appliance and later, integrated as part of the 5 year agreement alongside Apple and Microsoft.

Within that period, Microsoft managed to release 3 different editions of IE for the Mac system, which were bundled together Mac OS 9 and Mac OS 8, even though Apple still continued to use Netscape Navigator serving as an alternative. Eventually, launched the Mac OS X version of IE which served Mac devices, and was featured as a default browser for every Mac OS X launch, going from the Mac OS X DP4 version up to Mac (OS) X v10.2 (Puntambekar, 2009).

- **Safari 1:** This is the original version of Safari browser that was launched on January 7th, 2003, under the supervision of Steve Job at the Macworld Center in San Francisco. He announced that the tech giant had invented its own unique web browser, commonly referred to as Safari. The program is based on Apple's inner fork of KHTML rendering machine, known as Web Kit. This company launched the original beta version, which is accessible just for Mac (OS) X, later on during that same day.

Thereafter, a large number of both official and unofficial Safari 1 beta versions came up, until ultimately version 1.0 was launched on 23 June 2003. Originally only accessible as a different download for the Mac (OS) X 10.2, the Safari browser was later bundled together with Mac (OS) X v10.3 during the month of October 24th. Where Mac's IE was included just as a regular alternative browser. The Version 1.0.3, which was launched on August 13th, 2004 became the final version to officially support Mac (OS) X 10.2, whereas 1.3.2 which was launched on Jan 12th, 2006 became the last edition to officially support the Mac OS (X) 10.3 system. Nevertheless, 10.3 received some security updates that will last up to 2007.

- **Safari 2:** By April 2005, a promising Safari developer called Dave Hyatt prepared his findings by fixing certain specific bugs found in Safari, therefore allowing it to successfully pass the Acid2 exam established by the Website Standards Project. Within the same month, he further announced that his unique development edition of Safari fully passed the test, therefore making it the first ever browsing app in history to achieve this feat.

The Safari 2.0 application was launched on April 29th of the same year, being the only internet browser covered by Mac (OS) X 10.4. This edition was advertised by Apple as having a 1.8x speed booster over edition 1.2.4, though it didn't yet have the Acid2 bug repairs.

Some necessary changes were originally unavailable to final users, unless the user downloaded and assembled the WebKit sourcing code themselves, or operated through the coded builds accessible at OpenDarwin. org. Besides, Apple eventually launched module 2.0.2 of Safari that incorporated the modifications needed to pass Acid2, which was later launched on October 31st of 2005.

By June 2005, following some disapproval from KHTML developers concerning the lack of access for change logs, Apple transferred the development sourcing code and bug-tracking of JavaScript Core and

Web Core to the Open Darwin.org portal. The WebKit itself was equally released in form of an open source. However, the source code applied for non-renderer features of the browser, like its GUI components, remains proprietary (Carleton, 2013).

For the final stable edition of Safari 2, a version known as Safari 2.0.4 got launched on January 10th, 2006 for the Mac (OS) X system. It was originally available as only Mac OS (X) Update 10.4.4. The edition addressed layout as well as CPU usage matters, among other enhancements. Safari 2.0.4 became the final edition of this product to be launched entirely on Mac (OS) X systems.

From the perspective of macOS, Safari operates as a Cocoa program. It utilizes Apple's Web Kit system for rendering website pages and operating JavaScript. Furthermore, Web Kit comprises of Web Core (running on Konqueror's KHTML machine) and the Java Script Core (initially based on the KDE's JavaScript machine, known as KJS). Same as KHTML and KJS, JavaScript Core, and WebCore work as free applications and are released within the phrases of GNU Lower General Public Licensure. Some Apple enhancements to KHTML user code are assimilated again into the Konqueror program.Furthermore, Apple recently launched an extra code for open source dual-clause BSD-like licensure. Up until the Safari 6.0 version, it comprised of a built-in internet feed aggregator which supported both the Atom and RSS standards. Present features include aspects such as Private Browsing (consisting of a mode whereby no information record concerning the user's internet activity is reserved by the web browser).

Additionally, some websites have an "Ask websites to avoid tracking me" user setting, which has the capacity to archive internet content in the Web Archive format, plus ability to email whole web pages instantly from the browser menu, ability to hunt for bookmarks, as well as share tabs existing between the Mac and iOS appliances running suitable editions of software through an iCloud account (Carleton, 2013).

2.4.9. Presto and Others

The Presto system was developed as a browser machine of the Opera internet browser from the launch of Opera 7, which was made from 28th January up to the launching of Opera 15 which was done officially on 2nd July 2013, by which period Opera had already switched to utilizing the Blink engine which was initially developed for Chromium. Furthermore, Presto was equally applied to run the Opera Mobile and Mini browsers.

Besides, Presto was built as a dynamic machine. The Web pages may be re-rendered wholly or partially responding to DOM activities. Its releases witnessed a large amount of bug fixes as well as optimizations for improving the swiftness of the JavaScript machine. It's proprietary and basically available in form of Opera browsers.

- **ECMAScript Machines:** A sequence of ECMAScript machines have been applied together with Opera. A few Pre-Presto editions of Opera have been launched which utilize the Linear A machine. Opera editions which are based on Presto Core forks include the versions 7.0 up to 9.27, commonly used for the alternative Linear B engine.

Besides, the Futhark engine often gets used in some editions on the Core II fork of Presto, such as Opera 9.5 up to Opera 10. When launched, it became the quickest engine around, though in 2008 a fresh version of ECMAScript machines from Google (V8), Apple (SquirrelFish) and, Mozilla (TraceMonkey) went a step further to introduce native code creation.

Additionally, this allowed for possible heavy computations in the client-side and Futhark, which apart from being quick and efficient, wasn't capable of keeping up with the times. By 2009, Opera had already introduced the Carakan machine. It consisted of catalogue-based bytecode, native encryption generation, programmed object classification, as well as general performance improvements. The early access for Opera 10.50 pre-alpha revealed that it's as rapid as the quickest competitors; in fact it ranked among the best in most of the comparisons (Carleton, 2013).

2.4.10. Old Opera

The Opera Company has a rich history of developing inventive Web browsers. As a matter of fact, many things that we don't take seriously in our internet usage emerged from this Norwegian-based browser, such as the tabbed interface, combined search and popup blockers. Following an initial loading up process and consequently stripping itself of special features, the Opera browser has returned to inventing and differentiating itself, together with integrated ad-blocking, pop-out films, a battery saver, turbo compression structure, and now also a free integral virtual private network, commonly known as VPN, which is as quick as many premium solutions.

The firm behind Opera recently consented to be bought by a Chinese organization which intends to continue the brand's tradition of invention, strong privacy functions, and independence Installation for the Opera system is very fast compared to other existing browsers. Basically, you download a rather small stub installer that accordingly installs and downloads each full browser within no time flat (Sklar, 2011).

Likewise, the Installation options allow you to select from an impressive 50-plus languages available on the Opera browser. For the original step, a dialog requests if you need Opera to function as your default Internet browser. However, the browser app defaults to transferring usage and crash information to Opera's servers that work exceptionally. Opera operates through Windows XP system via Windows 10, as well as Mac OS (X) 10.7 Lion, and later five renowned Linux distributions. This is the final major browser that still supports XP together with its numerous security updates. This is a common 32-bit application, plus a fresh installation consisted of 136MB on the hard drive, in comparison to 406MB for the Google Chrome App and Mozilla Firefox's 92MB.

- **User-Interface:** Opera has a pleasing user-face comprising of square tabs which have somewhat rounded corners, kind of a central ground between Microsoft Edge and IE's flawlessly square tabs as well as Firefox's perfectly round ones. Generally, the background tabs retreat, making it perfectly clear whatever you're watching. The Opera browser's tab-preview function is available from a down-facing chevron found at the right side of the app's title bar.

For the current browser, simply clicking on it provides a dropdown catalogue for all your tabs, besides hovering the cursor above any of these systems showcases a preview for the website at the center of the browsing window. Some users also prefer the original Opera tab previews which emerged as thumbnails whenever you hover the mouse pointer over the real tabs found at the very top point of the database window, as well as Edge's work.

One actual differentiator that Opera interface provides is the Speed-Dial homepage found on the website tiles. Yet another quality feature is menu button which is found at the top-left corner of the browser, rather than being a typical triple-line multilevel option found on the right-side, same as those found in modern editions of all other key browsers.

Furthermore, for Opera systems the browser won't close whenever you shut the final tab. Instead Firefox provides a viable option for this, though like the rest, upon closing that final tab, then the Firefox browser would be closed down on default (Sklar, 2011).

There are two interface functions missing in Opera, though available in both Firefox and Edge, which are the reading mode as well as social sharing button. But for modern webpages filled with ads and various other unnecessary content, such as auto-play tapes and pop-over found on-page ads, then consider the reading mode system.

This same principle can be applied for simple sharing across social networks—which is among the primary elements of modern-day Web systems. The Opera browser handles bookmarks separately from the competition, also. Even though the Speed-Dial functions more like a bookmark element, the real bookmark feature displays a network of thumbnails that lists all the bookmarked sites. Users can create as many folders or subfolders as they want, while the browser shall directly import bookmarks coming from the other key browsers.

Additionally, Opera has a functional Video Pop Out feature. Its latest video pop-out element allows you to easily play videos in a different desktop window—which is ideal for viewing programs like PCMag's regular Random Access video display, while still continuing to use your computer.

Whenever a video gets played on an Opera page, there's a small double-boxed arrow that immediately shows up. The video will immediately detach and show up in a resizable Opera window on the PC desktop. Plus, the on-page video shall still continue playing, in case you wish to see the content on the page. While pop-out function didn't actually perform successfully for the live-stream Facebook video, it still holds up well with regards to convenience and reliability (Sklar, 2011).

Chapter 3 Web Evolution

CONTENTS

3.1. INTRODUCTION

In this day and age, the web has become an evolving field that has brought together a dynamic universe of hyperlinked web pages, photographs, web apps, interactive content, and streaming videos. However, despite all these technologies, many users still do not know how the web has been developed over time. With the evolving web technologies, new advanced generations have been developed by web designs creating helpful and immersive web experiences. The web being used today is the very result of hard work efforts of a diverse community that helps to define this web knowledge which include as HTML5, CSS3 and WebGL and ensuring that they are supported in all web browsers. The different color bands represent the different interactions that occur between web technologies and the browser that normally give life to many powerful web apps that are used daily. The web also is known as the World Wide Web (WWW), which is the collection of information that is only available only by the internet and is also served on top of infrastructure while the internet is the global networks of networks which is the infrastructure.

The purpose of the internet was to act as a US government weapon during the war 50 years ago. Web 1.0 was created as the static web in 1990s, while web 2.0 is the web concerned with blogging, web services, mapping, and many other services. Web 2.0 was also referred to as "pieces loosely joined together". Then later web 3.0 arrived and it appeared that web applications can understand the main content of web pages. Thic concept was also referred to as semantic web which can read, analyze the stream of data available on the websites (Lytras and Miltiadis, 2010).

Before 1999, the web experts used to refer to the internet as the Reading-Only Web. The internet was by then restricted to the reading the information only and the best examples of this web 1.0 era are millions of sites that were started up during the dot-com boom which led to the famously known dotcom bubble. With no active communication information strategy between the consumer who has the information and the producer of the particular information, this did not hinder the birth of the information age (Figure 3.1).

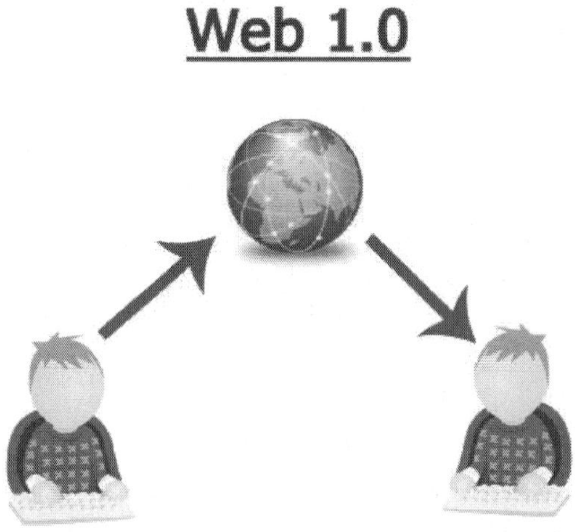

Figure 3.1. Web1.0 was initially considered as the read-only web

Source: https://thebusinessofsocial.wordpress.com/2015/03/14/web-2-0-to-web-3-0-or-when-do-i-get-my-hoverboard-2/ (accessed on 2 April 2020).

There was very little user interaction or content availability because the earlier webs only granted permission to browsers to only search what they need and read it. The first shopping cart applications that most e-commerce website owners used in some shapes or forms normally fall under the class of web 1.0. With their main goal to present products to prospective users such as the catalog or brochure, do to retailers who create a method through the website for anybody in the globe to buy their products. The creation of 2.0 webs was created due to the failure of proper interaction between the previous web and the users. With remarkable contributions from the live journal which was established in April 1999, and the blogger in August 1999, which all signified the starting of the reading and writing publish era. The new web has allowed even non-technical users to keenly communicate and give back to the web by using various types of blog platforms. This interaction between the users and the web has allowed a big change in the background of web development. The 2.0 web has a very big capability that is not yet searched. The new age has given knowledge to the users new ideas like the use of blogs, streaming of videos and social media. Some of the few developments of this web are Twitter, Facebook, Flickr, and eZinearticles (Lytras and Miltiadis, 2010).

3.2. CHARACTERISTICS OF WEB 1.0

- The web 1.0 contains information very helpful for users but there is no reason for users to return to the site later. The personal web page has always the same information which never changes. However, web 2.0 contains blogs or "My Space" accounts which can be constantly updated.
- This web site doesn't contain room for user interaction; users can only access the pages on the sites but they cannot have a positive say on these sites. It is only a look-read site with no comments to be added.
- The web 1.0 is a privately-owned software application because the users can only download but they do not know how the application runs or even alter. While the web 2.0 source code is freely available because it's an open-source, whereby the users can freely download the works, make new changes, or even advance the programs. Such an example includes the Netscape Navigator which was the sole owner of the 1.0 web era. Later came Firefox in web 2.0 which provided creators with all the necessary tools and equipment that they need to build the new advanced Firefox applications.
- In web 1.0, the comments of the users were normally stored in the Guestbook page; they were not attached to the content site.
- The web 1.0 era did not give support for the server-side scripting which is very necessary for the webserver to present a form. When the key of submission was clicked on most requests the website e-mail client would start, and where the user had to e-mail their request form to a particular address that was provided by the site.

The web 1.0 has various examples of its advantage and this is in the information resource, for example, the free online Wikipedia which is an encyclopedia source that grants permission to its users to alter any article they think might need change. However, with all users, having a say on what is right and what is not, accuracy depends on everyone's article but with all this, false information or even deceptive information can be posted. People with an evil mind can damage the article's integrity by altering or changing the facts, despite moderators who constantly keep a closer eye on these sites to eradicate vandalism there is no possibility to know if the information that was entered is 100% accurate. Another example of an advantage of web 1.0 being good is on restaurant web pages where their menu is created to let the visitors know what is offered and this is a good example of where change or alteration is not needed. The evolution from 1.0 web to 2.0 webs took over slowly over time as the web servers were being upgraded, speeds increased on the connections and the creation of new knowledge learned and skills and techniques which were upgraded. With the evolution taking place in late stages of the year 1990s, by then the web 2.0 had made drastic changes in the web site by the year 2006 but with all these changes there are still small traces of web 1.0 still being used silently in the corners of the web (Lytras and Miltiadis, 2010).

The guestbook in the web 1.0 was the best solution that granted permission to visitors to comment without dragging down the website or even the content pages and the visitors were allowed to comment, this was because the pages were consisted of long lists of visitors commenting that was taking a very long time to load during the dial-up connections. During the 1.0 era, blogging was not so common or even accessible to the common users, blogging depended on several factors like in-browser text editing, server-side scripting, databases, and other features found in web 2.0. During this era, constant website updates were necessary but they required more practical skills than what is required today.

The web 2.0 is also referred to as participatory or participative while social platforms refers to websites that put more light on user-generated content, simple use, participatory traditions, and interoperability which similar to the other products, systems, and devices for the users. These web-only deals with the designing and the use of websites and does not put restrictions on any technical changes. The evolution took place slowly and over time and no specific date can be said that web 2.0 took place. It grants the users the possible ground to interact and collaborate within themselves via social media chats as pioneers of the user created content in an effective society. This created a very big difference because the web 1.0 had restricted the users to see the information only without editing. Web 2.0 involved social platforms and even the social sites which include Facebook, blogs, wikis, videos like YouTube, Folksonomies which include classification of keywords and links. With the 2.0 creating room for debate and interaction between the web and users, it also opened a window which has led to increased spamming, hate speech, increased cyber bullying and insults. The elimination of group members who are not serious or their impact to the group is very small, creates the chance that serious members will withhold their efforts and free rides on the contribution of others, at this point the pioneers of the web site to perform the radical trust procedure. The web 2.0 has very many characteristics such as rich user, full participation of the users, lively content, metadata, web standards, and value. By use of participation things like openness, freedom, and intelligence all makeup web 2.0 as opposed to other websites which state that the visitors should contribute fully to the user-created content to have access to the website and to eliminate the free rides (Lytras and Miltiadis, 2010).

3.3. CHARACTERISTICS OF WEB 2.0

- The free sub-groupings of content have granted the users permission to be able to sub-divided and search for the content they need to be it within websites, images, videos or links this is known as Folksonomy.
- With the rich user content, there is the availability of content that allows the user to click on a particular image by zooming in or even to learn more from it.
- The information flows in two-way traffic whereby the owner of the site and the users interact well by commenting online and review. The developers of the site also develop the user-generated information that is easily visible to other users, for example, the use of Wikipedia which allows anybody to write or delete articles.
- The use of (SaaS) software as a service created the APIs that granted the usage of the web app or the software application.
- The vast mass participation has led to different ideologies from different groups like the traditional internet user base to different users.

3.3.1. Technologies behind Web 2.0

Ajax and JavaScript frameworks are web browser technologies that were used to create web 2.0. The Ajax program uses both the JavaScript and Document Object Model (DOM) which are used to pick out specific areas within a page without loading the full page. Granting the users access to mingle, information like data requests that go the server are alienated from the data streaming back to the page. This means the user waits for the data to be sent back to them before, they can perform any other work on the page, and still the user should wait for the page to load up. This increases the performance of the site as the requests sent can be quick to complete their actions, and be sent back to the client. The data that has been collected by the

Ajax is normally formatted in JavaScript Object Notation format or XML. These two are the most vital data formats, and because these two formats are well known to JavaScript, they can be used to pass on the structured data in their web applications. When Ajax receives the data, JavaScript then uses the file Objected copy too widely update the web pages based on the new information collected, thus granting permission to the user for quick and easy communication. The Google Docs is a technique that the designers have used to build up a web-based word mainframe, and by creating pages that work like desktop tools. JavaScript, Flash, and Ajax have become accepted widely as a means of creating the web 2.0 (Miltiadis and Lytras, 2009).

The web 2.0 can be categorized into three classes which are:

- **The Rich Internet Application (RIA):** This refers to the knowledge that is passed on from the desktop to the browser which has interactive features.
- The web 2.0 has well-structured web-oriented architecture (WOA) which defines how well the functions can control and incorporate in their functions to provide richer applications. This includes the news feeds, RSS feeds, and web feeds.
- We can see how the web 2.0 tends to cooperate with the user making the user a vital part of the website by adding information about their profile, upgrading their comments on the information, uploading new content, or even adding the user-generated information (Figure 3.2).

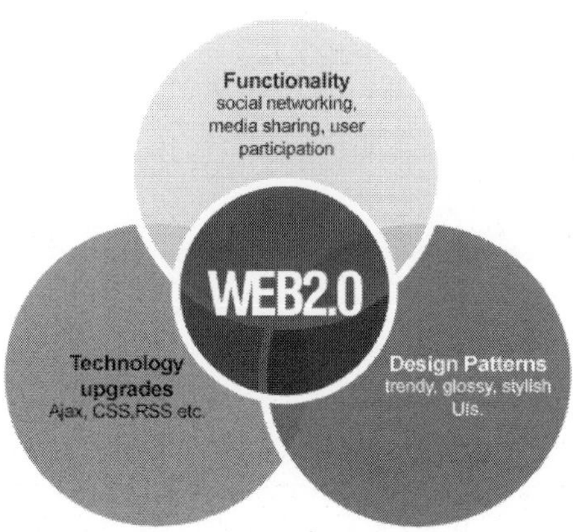

Figure 3.2. *Web 2.0 brings together the abilities of the client and the server-side software, information syndicate and network systems.*

Source: https://medium.com/@SoftwareDevelopmentCommunity/web-2-0-an-introduction-8230eb8fa6ce (accessed on 2 April 2020).

The standard oriented web browsers normally use plug-ins and software extensions to manage information and user relations. This web 2.0 equips users with information storage, creating, and distribution abilities that were not there in the web 1.0 (Miltiadis and Lytras, 2009).

Andrew McAfee referred to the following parts and techniques as the short form slates:

- That search is the sourcing out of information through its keyword search;
- Links together content from various sources using the model of the web;
- The constant updating of information leads to the sharing of the work between the authors. The perfect example is the wiki users who can prolong, edit, redo, and even undo their partner's work and the comment section has allows granted permission to its learners to share their thoughts;
- The classification of the information by the readers adding tags which are either short one or two words normally help in the search. For example, a user can tag a metal song as death metal this is the Collections of tags build by many users within a single system. This concept is referred to as folk taxonomies;
- The software extensions that create the web application platforms include the Adobe Reader, Adobe Flash, Quick time, Microsoft Silver light, Oracle Java, and the windows media; and
- Signals use such as the RSS feeds used to alert users of the information changes.

Slates are the backbone of the formation of web 2.0. They consist of the discussions of self-services information technology, the demand for information technology and many other enterprises uses under the web 2.0. Files that make up the 2.0 can be determined by the measures that are connected to such quality elements such as accessibility, completeness, and credibility with their participation with timeliness, reputation, readability, objectivity, uniqueness, and usefulness.

- **Marketing:** Organizations, companies, governments, and non-profit organizations all use web 2.0 for their interactive marketing. The marketers are widely using web 2.0 to team up with consumers to develop the products to improve customer care and to conduct promotions. Organizations have used the 2.0 as a tool to help improve their partnership with the partners in business and also the end consumers. The employees within these organizations have created wikis which have greatly helped the users to edit, delete, and also comment about the products and the services. The marketing web 2.0 has created a platform whereby the consumers can use the online community to talk about different topics they wish too. The web 2.0 has drastically increased the usage of media and greatly promoted the media hubs such as the Times of New York, PC magazines and the Business week. The user web content can be used to measure the satisfaction of the consumer (Miltiadis and Lytras, 2009).

- **Destination Marketing:** In the tourism field social media usage is the most powerful tool to attract travelers and by endorsing the tourism products and services by interacting with the clients. Brands can be created through the marketing campaigns on social platforms and also by interacting with the clients, by creating more knowledge awareness of what is available. A good example is the Walt Disney World whose main role is giving advice and giving answers to questions about family vacations at the Walt Disney World. Due to their advanced knowledge base in the Disney world, several moms were picked to represent the campaigns. This can be done on various social media platforms like Facebook and also through constant online communication with the clients. With travel 2.0, granting access to users in order to build their information and be able to talk freely globally through advanced features. The tourists can suggest what they need, see the images and estimate their expenses and also be able to book hotels and decide their travel destinations through the help of online travel agencies, with help of social platforms especially travel 2.0 websites holds an important position in the decision making of the tourist. Thus, travel 2.0 has been a big help especially for first-time tourists who want to easily know their way around, whereby they trust the information that has been provided on the social platforms as opposed to what they have provided by the travel agencies. In turn, it greatly helps the travelers to eliminate risks and be sure of what they need before purchasing anything. But the social platforms can be very dangerous because when clients complain and give negative feedbacks this can greatly damage the image and face of organizations and the companies (RichiNayak, 2008).

Nevertheless, companies can develop platforms which will help them curb and manage the negative feedbacks that are being posted on the social platforms, even if the user-generated information and the rating on this social media are out of the organization control; the managing team needs to keep a close eye on the conversations and interact with the users to increase their client loyalty and also develop good customer ties.

3.3.2. Education

The 2.0 has made education grow and become more interesting to the learners. Students can use blogs to socialize with other learners within and outside the classroom setups. The 2.0 has greatly increased the knowledge within the society to better appreciate science and in turn, improved decisions that are made within the government. Proper knowledge can greatly improve communication between the societies and the learners to have more interactive discussions.

3.3.3. Web-Based Applications and Desktops

Ajax has greatly encouraged the creation of applications for example word processor, blogging, spreadsheets, WYSIWYG wiki, and slide show presentations that duplicate most essentials of the PC applications. A great number of web-based requests imaged during the bubble of the dot-com and later on disappeared because they did not meet the required customers' numbers.

3.3.4. Distribution of Media

1. **XML and RSS:** Important procedures like FOAF and XFN, found within the social platforms prolong the performance of the pages and permit the consumers to communicate without limits. The procedures that grant permission to these pages are the really simple syndication (RSS) that is also referred to as web syndicate or the RDF, and the atom which all make up the XML procedures.
2. **Web APIs:** Web 2.0 uses engine sources, such as REST and SOAP, to communicate. Interactions that happen between the APIs consist of JSON or XML payloads. Through self-

explanatory messages and hypermedia as a power source of the request condition, the source URI is acknowledged. The best way of advertising a SOAP request program border is using WSDL, commonly known as the web service description language. This generates a wide class of web service requests.

3.3.5. Criticism

According to critics, web 2.0 does not stand for the revised version of the World Wide network but its continuation of the previous web platform. Ajax could not substitute the earlier HTTP but instead it creates other ideas to expand it. Earlier, web 2.0 implemented many features that were already in use. The web source ensured that every workspace had a dedicated IP address that was always connected to the network. This made file sharing or printing pages very easy like. The term 2.0 is very unclear and very confusing because even according to most professionals it cannot be well-defined. According to Scott Laningham and Tim Berners-Lee, web 2.0 is referred to as jargon because nobody can explain what it means. Other people criticized the 2.0 and called it the second bubble which meant that too many organizations were trying to create similar products with a lack of a proper model for the business (RichiNayak, 2008).

The political market criticizes the 2.0 as an exploitation of labor because these web sites use terms of the agreement to ask for licenses to particular user-created information and later on use this information to build new profiles of the clients and later sell them to the marketers. This is observed from the close supervision of these sites about the user movements within web 2.0. Besides, it can be used by the governments who want to keep a close eye on rebel citizens; with the imaging of the Ajax sites information rendered on the users has intended that the clients who used the previous hardware's are provided web sites which fully composed of HTM, whereby the creation takes place on the computer servers. Some say that web 2.0 technologies are attached to a specific political mindset. The web 2.0 can be a big problem because the web is doing extra work for consumers to achieve their standards of entertainment. A few examples include Twitter, which grants users access to online features which they can use to build their tweet. Hence users are putting in extra effort to produce quality media information. The web 2.0 was not a big problem for social media platforms like Google and Facebook because the users were curious to discover and exploit the net, this web wants people to be involved more and build more information. This is because more user involvement builds up new information and profile information that is used for third users such as national security and advertising agencies. Control of privacy that is created into a model of any business that uses the 2.0, it should not be attached to the hopeful thought that this 2.0 is the next big step in the revolution of online media (RichiNayak, 2008).

The web 2.0 permits users to interact and communicate with each other through social media platforms as pioneers in the user-created information in an essential community. The difference between them is that first generation of 1.0 web is that people were restricted to viewing information in a passive way.

3.4. APPLICATION DOMAINS OF WEB 2.0

3.4.1. Government

The 2.0 government defines the government programs that target join together technologies and interactive features within the internet to build an open way for the computer platforms. Here transparency is improved within the government structures, inventive companies, and the citizens. The 2.0 brings together the basics that govern the 2.0 with e-government by radically increases the participation of the nationals by use of open source venues that permit the growth of new apps, widgets, and also websites. By offering open statistics or data, services within the web and also open venues as a ground for proper infrastructure are all government main roles.

3.4.2. Business

The 2.0 business had a big growth before the readers and the advertising fields. With the rise in the fortunes of and technology within new companies, the 2.0 business was not able to bring profit. In an attempt to bond with the big masses of readers who depended on the news from blogs, 2.0 businesses started up a chain that consisted of staff-written blogs.

3.4.3. E-Learning

The CSCL is also known as the processor-supported joint learning this is methods created with guidelines that are used to support and motivate the learners in working jointly on the tasks and in turn permits communal learning. This computer-supported collaboration is related to the term 2.0 e-learning. With the improvement of 2.0 webs, it has become possible for numerous people within the web making it easier and increasing users.

The most essential reason for it been used is that it's ground creativity and encouraging educational actions. This particular learning is very dissimilar from when the instructor was the only key to knowledge, 1.0 e-learning even known as neologism refers to the instruction given direct which are used to the computer-based knowledge and also the training methods. These apps have been a big aid in helping learners and also the teachers freely socialize even when studying. They help learners to revise their work well and also enjoying doing it, in turn, the learners enjoy studying and become busier and also gain more important knowledge. By the involvement of games, students create a progression state, enabling the students to be more motivated and reliable while also improving in their studies. The (MUVEs) or multi-user virtual environment which is online is the definition of 2.0 classroom, which brings together learning institutions within a wide geographical scope. The computer-support collaborative learning or the CSCL permits students who are indifferent institutions to interact and share their knowledge which greatly improves learning levels and encourages the integration of culture also referred to as e-Twinning.

3.4.4. Health

The term 2.0 health started as a subgroup within the health care industries with features that mimicked the web 2.0. This consists of social platforms, user-created information, cloud-based, and technologies in mobile. This web 2.0 has given patients control over health care and bad medical practices. However, with it have come various disadvantages, such as no patient privacy and wrong information being circulated. Health 2.0 was created with the main intention of altering the health care industry and e-health was created in the later years of 1990s. Nevertheless, in the late 2000s, there was increased usage in social networks and the internet, which sparked increased interest among clinicians, patients, librarians in the medical field in adopting these important tools for health care management and purposes. The health care system has created its own health 2.0 with the idea of improving the standards of health care globally. However, health 2.0 has several opposing terms which might not have a precise meaning which is linked health care, modern health, medicine 2.0, and mHealth; all this play a major part in the system of health care, by the use of reform in the technology set up and hence improving the relationship between the medical staff and patients.

- A personal search is concerned with user knowledge;
- Groups that can understand the knowledge of the caregivers and

patients and can able to elaborate it to society;

- Provision of good working tools for information delivery and dealings; and
- A better combination of information and data.
- Several criticisms have been noted about the usage of 2.0 in the health care industries as stated below:
- It was only applicable in scenarios that had very unique signs and symptoms which are normally used as research terminologies. Thus, its results couldn't be fully trusted.
- Besides, there is fear that patients seek online medical help because first. They depend on online methods to give them a solution to their symptoms.
- User-created information can be misleading for the patients, false information about the medicines in the market or even the vaccines being introduced to curse different sicknesses.

3.4.5. Science

The science 2.0 is the new technique in this field that specifically adopts data sharing and communication becomes possible with this web. It's motivated by web 2.0 technologies which are a replica of research which open and science. The benefits of science 2.0 include transparency and sharing, regarding research ideas and solutions. Science 2.0 first gained ground with some websites flourishing yet still; there is resistance within the communities of scientists about different terms and the definite meaning of the terms. Significant talks are taking place between the scientists concerning the adoption of model science 2.0 if it will work or not and it has led to these scientists slowly implementing these tools in their respective fields. 2.0 terms in science compare traditional methods of science 1.0 with more advanced technologies approaches. Also, it can be used to solve problems with a variety of everyday issues.

3.4.6. Sci-Mate

This is an open channel of communication for scientists who use the 2.0 web software to tackle problems in the academic field and the transfer of information. Providing a free pass to a variety of web 2.0 software features that makes researchers and builders combine their knowledge, tools, and society. Featured articles on offer answers to the scientists on how to pass their knowledge into articles that are open to being accessed.

3.5. WEB 3.0

Web 3.0 is the third age group that uses the machine-based knowledge of data to create bases of webs which are semantic and governed by data. The main purpose is to build more knowledge bases, connections, and free accessible networks. Web 3.0 is also known as the semantic web. Machines can still study the net pages just as humans do. The main purpose of this web is to reinforce the web which is current so that information can be developed that exists on the WWW, by learning it and solving problems has helped the human race to acquire new knowledge, and through it, there is a widespread of knowledge among the society and even data sharing is open as opposed to documents which were just stored. 3.0 web or commonly known as semantic is dyeing and this is because the language used was very difficult to understand and this has enabled other smarter webs to beat, the technology was very difficult and very unclear and was made for the learners (Gopalan and Adikesavan, 2014).

The web 3.0 browser is a particular form of software that is used to search the semantic web, this is an expansion of the WWW that normally functions by joining together information and their origin as ordinary web links do, and they are also referred to as hyperdata browsers.

When purchasing products and services the browser first searches the web and brings a detailed list of what other consumers have bought. It also provides a list of different selections of products and later proposes the right product to purchase. In short, web 3.0 is a learning site which has improved and providing knowledge. Web 1.0 was mainly determined by the information that came from the business or the organization for its clients. Web 2.0 made things a little difficult because it permitted users to share and upload their information on the site directly. Web 3.0 permits online requests and sites to receive content that is available on the website and provides the latest content or data to the users.

Webs 3.0 helps businesses to grow by gaining a competitive advantage through semantic system of joining information from several places found within the internet. It greatly helps identify needs.

- Below are number of the properties that make up the web 3.0:
- One important element is semantic network. This refers to the

network of information which can summarize all the information on the web and create connections and links that join the computer webs and the society together and when it will become successful machines will be communicating with others hence to create the age of intelligent agents. The 3.0 consists of two fundamentals which are semantic and artificial intelligence (AI). Semantic assists to teach the computer what information means and involves AI that is used to exploit that data or information. The main idea was to create a web-like structure of information and knowledge across the diverse internet in turn aid the proper understanding of words and their meanings to share, create, and communicate well through the research and summarization. Due to the metadata, 3.0 webs will significantly help in connecting information; hence, the knowledge level of the users greatly evolves.

- Computer science is also known as machine intelligence is the knowledge that is exhibited by these machines as opposed to the natural knowledge that the humans and animals displayed. AI has made the machine evolve and become more knowledgeable to meet the user's daily demands. The AI will permit sites to select and present the most appropriate data achievable. People are the most common of the biggest aids in improving web 2.0, but we as humans cannot be trusted as we can give feedbacks that are positive to boost a negative thing and that are when AI comes in because it has the power to distinguish right and bad and providing quality data.
- 3D graphics-3.0 technology has a very big impact on the net growing from web 2D into a more realistic three-dimensional imitated worlds. The 3D creation has been applied widely in webs and services in 3.0 webs which include games online, real estate agencies and also e-commerce. As foreign, as it can be people across the globe are getting to socialize through games online such as the second world or life. Whereby the users are more concerned about their online players themselves. Examples, where 3D is being used, are in graphics in museums, computer games, and movies.
- The thought of being present or being everywhere and anywhere at a given time was seen in web 2.0. A good example is the websites of the social platform such as Instagram, whereby the users can take pictures on their cameras and later on they can upload the

pictures and circulate them so they can be visible everywhere. The big growth in mobile appliances and free access to the internet will help web 3.0 be accessible everywhere at any given time. The 3.0 is also referred to as the web which is everything and is everywhere because all things are joint, together to the internet.

3.5.1. Implementation Challenges of Web 3.0

- The information provided can at times be very vague and fuzzy logic is used to rule it out.
- There is too much uncertain information provided. A good example is when a patient seeks medical attention online and are provided with symptoms that are similar to different sicknesses that do not match up to what they are suffering from.
- Data which is not consistent can cause irrational challenges and unpredictable data within the web 3.0.
- AI will deal with sorting out the data, but if the data was entered to be all wrong that is when cryptography procedures are applied to curb and provide a solution.

3.5.2. Advantages of Web 3.0

- Their helpful communication between the web servers and the users.
- Knowledge sharing by connecting the online information creating a web joined together for information.
- Marketing of goods and services becomes very easy and effective with the 3.0 web.
- Well organized net search.
- Good communication structures are created.
- It greatly increases human contact by increasing interactions between different cultural groups.

3.5.3. Disadvantages of Web 3.0

- Equipments and devices which are not up to standard will not be able to manage 3.0 webs.
- web will be assumed to be outdated.
- The new users will not be able to understand the new websites; it

will take them time to understand.

- Citizens will use most of their time on the net browsing and other things.
- The use of 3.0 webs has made it possible for privacy and private content to be linked.
- There will be no mystery.

Tim Berners-Lee was the man who created the 3.0 web or the semantic net, and at first, it operated on the language of HTML. The net is divided into two classes the original 1.0 web and the 2.0 web which was an improved version of 1.0 web and the adding up of social platforms and internet fields. However, there has been disagreement on the meaning of 3.0 webs; its main advantage is that the 3.0 web will make the internet much quicker and even very easier in searching for information. From when it was introduced in the market, it has been undergoing constant changes in order to satisfy the users' needs (Gopalan and Adikesavan, 2014).

3.6. WEB 4.0

This 4.0 web is referred to as an intelligent, well connected and an open source web, with the arrival of these web pages on sites will be able to download faster and producing perfect outcomes and results. It will run similar to the brain of a human. Web 4.0 is usually described as OS web; this is because the whole system that makes the web is a single functioning structure that allows information to easily move from one given point to any other receiving point. Web symbiotic is also another name of web 4.0. The main objective of the web symbiotic is to create a mutual relationship between the humans and equipment. The 4.0 will enable a smooth relationship with the users and it will create a world that is always running and linked together, individuals will be able to interact freely and exchange crucial knowledge (Lytras and Miltiadis, 2010).

The 4.0 is assumed that it will create an era in which individuals in a society will have a drastic change in their behaviors and also an ego that will enable them to interact more with new knowledge for example machines which are intelligent. The 4.0 can also be referred to as the web which is always active. The previous web version used search bars which are still very important in providing vital information which can be used to solve the client's needs. However, the 4.0 will be very different from the 3.0, when it is fully factional; despite it eradicating several procedures in web 3.0, it will be precise on point and very undetectable. The search bars will not be eradicated fully but they will be incorporated into essential tool assistants. These essential tools will be able recognize the verbal language as well as written to them and be able respond appropriately. This network will even recommend things on its own. All this advanced technology is with us but most of us don't know these features because they are very new. For example, when the virtual helpers have mastered the user's tastes and behaviors, they can use the information to book hotel reservations and wait for final confirmation. Presently, cable, and alarm companies have created the capacity to join together businesses that are not similar for a mutual relationship. Users now can afford access to very economical home security using affordable web cameras and pre-existing broadband.

A symbiotic relationship will make web 4.0 an agent for personal users. Using facial recognition technology, it will be able to acknowledge individuals whenever they use internet or other services. The user can change their appearance and character through the avatar simply by asking the assistant a question. In the daily functions smart devices will be connected to the web and will be able to run duties without human supervision. For example, a refrigerator that uses the RFID (Radio Frequency Identification Tags) can detect it doesn't have milk and gets in touch with store to order milk. Later on, it will send a text message to the owners' phone to go get milk at the store. The RFID are used in vehicles that use the tax highways as tracking systems. They are also seen in supply processes and motor vehicle assembly and also in agriculture fields. Webs 4.0 will permit grocery store attendance to tell what they can manage; hence, the web will help drastically cut down the wastage of delicate foodstuffs like fruits and kales. With the 4.0 being introduced in the daily activities even travel routes will be updated and easier to understand and also be accurate.

3.6.1. Medicine

The knowledge of creating a biomedical chip is still underway. These biomedical implants when fully developed will help eradicate many sicknesses, and web 4.0 plays a major role. Such examples include the people who have problems with their eyesight's and after successful operation their eyesight is restored, this is achieved by the chips that inserted in their eyes. That permits these chips to talk to the brain and be able to return the eye functions which were affected. However, the most disabled individuals can be able to speak again mainly because can control most things on the keyboards by implant which help them to manage the cursor on the screen of the computer.

3.6.2. Virtual Reality

Virtual reality (VR) is widely used in everyday life. when Google has been used to find lost keys or a lost phone is an example where VR is being used. With the wide spread of 4.0 webs, travel agencies are able to improve their services by combining stories, coordination, navigation, and Google maps. However, the most important and widely used is the addition of social platforms in traveling apps.

One of the most critical developments of 4.0 webs will develop during the relocation of online functions into the physical globe. Such as, trying to find our homes when lost especially on Google. Trying to find car keys or the remote control. The Challenges of the new web will be facing, are those concerning industry standards such as wireless connections, telecommunication lines doing the actual connection and Challenges and disadvantages of 4.0 webs. With privacy issues in the websites, 4.0.

With privacy issues in the websites, 4.0 webs will also be facing the same as no proper rules and regulations have been installed yet to curb this problem. The other challenges the 4.0 web will encounter are those involved in industry levels such as telecommunication wires and wireless connections, which involves all links connected by the devices which do not use the same language to interact.In summary, web 4.0 will create a strong link between the devices and the users in order to build new information and data in a mutual relationship. High hopes will greatly influence many aspects of the everyday life. Intelligent information and VR will become more wide spread. With the radio frequency, identification (RFID) tags fitted in household appliances will greatly improve the relationship between devices and the users and still improve their interrelations between the devices.

The imaging of the 4.0 will greatly alter the hope of both the medical fields and businesses. The RFID tags will alter the shopper's skills, because it will have the consumer's best interest and they will have maximum say on what they want. The intelligent buildings is the process of using sensors and IP systems to constantly revise the data about the occupants who are available at the hotel, this relationship in the future might lead to no hotel staffs working. In the medical scope, this relationship will permit patients with know-how of how to get treated online without attending a hospital set up.4.0 web is meant to transform the day to day lives of the society.

Consumers will acquire unique connected social and individual lives. This connected, intelligent, and open sourced will be hope for a better net in the future. Several scopes of field use SODA for strategic option development and analysis procedures used to solve difficult problems. It is better to apply this procedure in rapidly growing areas or the under explored parts of information which is very important to help summarize mechanisms and the connections that join them. When the strategic option development and analyzing procedures were used five aspects were recognized and this are web symbiotic; things of web; social computing in web; invasive web and ubiquitous. Each individual aspect has something in common such as persistence and omnipresent computing their elements are the same and in the situation of work they are considered as synonyms; other aspects that share elements things of web and social web computing they are required to use the big data algorithms and the surfacing of M2M communications that originated from the use of net of artificial knowledge.

Chapter 4

Web Servers

CONTENTS

4.1. INTRODUCTION

The Web, famously known as the World Wide Web (WWW) is an interconnection of different computing devices which support sending and receiving of documents with advanced appearance via the global network of networks. Some computing devices might act as the storage locations for the most wanted resources to be requested via the internet while others might act as the devices requesting for these resources.

Most documents in the global network are created by special scripting. Some of the scripting languages used in creation of these documents are "Hyper Text Markup Language", JavaScript language, Cascading Style Sheet language which is mainly used for enhancing the general appearance of the whole document by adding special features to it which cannot be added by the other languages, among other types of scripting languages. These scripting languages allow adding of multimedia information such as graphics, videos, audios or a combination of all the multimedia formats of multimedia information.

The different documents are connected to each other depending on the topic they discuss. If they are the topic being discussed is related, they are connected together with special links. Links are a special set of words which are added to a document specifying the location of a different document which discusses related information with the current document. The links are renamed to specify the information which they represent. Such link names include the "next" name tag which informs the user that, once they click on that link, they will access the next document which is a continuation of the current document's information. Other name might include the "previous" name tag, for accessing previous document of the current one, or the title of the document to be accessed.

Generally, these documents are accessed by typing their domain name in a web browser tab. Domain name are special names given to a document allowing a user to be able to remember the documents name. This is because; the computers in which the documents are stored in use special set of numeric characters for identifying the document name and its specific location once it has been requested. A Domain Name System is used to translate the user-friendly domain name to a computer friendly Internet Protocol address for the computer to reply to the request made.

The documents availed in the Web are referred to as web pages. A Web page is basically a hypertext media, meaning it is interconnected together using different links, which has its appearance being advanced by use of special features provided by the different scripting languages such as the Hypertext Markup Language (HTML) and the Cascading Style Sheet among others. This Web pages are further grouped together to form a website. A Website consists of a homepage, which is linked to all the other pages making up that specific website. The Homepage is specifically the main page of a website in which visitors to that website find hyperlinks to all other pages. It does also contain a brief summary of what the whole website is all about and some contact information to allow a visitor or a client to be in touch with the firm the website is representing its information.

4.2. HISTORY OF THE WEB

The web originated as a result of the internet. The internet was invented by the American Army as a way to coordinate their communication techniques during war period. The internet was advanced with time to improve the security of the information being shared through it. This enhanced the security of the information to an extend that, if a certain military base containing all the computing devices was attacked, the information which was stored in them would not be lost due to several backups. And in situation were hackers tried to gain illegal entry to the system, it would not be possible because the data was highly secured by use of several encrypting techniques (Silva, 2012).

With the advancement of the Internet and with its commendable security features, the world web was invented so as to avail all sorts of information to its different users in different places. The Web did continue to grow in terms of the number of pages which were added to the internet. As of the year two thousand and fourteen, the web had accumulated over thirty billion web pages handling different topics in different areas associated with our society and it is still growing.

4.3. GENERAL OVERVIEW OF THE WEB

There are different ways in which the various website presented on the web can be viewed. Some can be viewed as personal website for they are created by individuals who have the interest of sharing information on areas they love most. Some individual may present information on a topic which deals with their passion areas, their greatest fears, and their opinions about different happenings in the world among others. Other website can be organizational website, maybe advertising the products offered by a certain organization to the larger market available on the internet. Other websites are educational website which presents educational support materials for learners to access them via the internet.

Most websites need payment of subscription fee and creation of accounts for one to access their information. Many educational websites fit in this category for they do ask for a subscription fee before one is allowed to view the information they are offering to them (Silva, 2012).

Websites may be interconnected with each other by use of hyperlinks. This interconnection of the websites does bring in confusion on the category which a certain website can be viewed in. This is because with this interconnection, both personal website and organizational websites are interlinked making it hard for categorization process to take place for the website are two different things. Though the main advantage of interlinking different categories of website is for reference, purposes (specify that a certain idea was borrowed from this website and for further understanding, one can visit that website).

4.4. TYPES OF INTERNET WEBSITES

There are several types of websites availed on the web via the internet based on different website client needs which need to be addressed. They include:

Static websites are websites which content does not change. It is always presented to the different users in the same format. The reason is that static websites are created by HTML, which is the commonly used scripting language. Static websites do not support interaction between the clients and the owners of the website because their content is always the same without any changes or improvements. Static websites are mostly used for clients who need to access information of topics which have remained constant in terms of their information such as topics based on the happenings of some historical event which has not changed and does not have a future of ever changing even for a little bit (Silva, 2012).

The dynamic websites have their content changing constantly with every view of the website. They are coded using a special coding language which allows for information to be updates effectively at any time of the day. The famous JavaScript scripting language is the language which does mostly specializes on creation of this kind of website. This website is basically created by use of HTML and Cascading Style Sheet language used for enhancement of its general appearance but JavaScript still remains to be the most important language. Dynamic websites operate by using the initial format created by use of HTML and cascading style sheet to display the use of the recent updated information by using JavaScript language which kind of overwrites the initial content and replaces it with the new up to date information. This type of websites allows interaction between the clients and the website owners hence also referred to as Interactive websites.

An affiliate website does major in selling the products of a third party. Such products might include the contents of a may be a certain research conducted by a third party. The selling maybe through a website portal created by a seller. The seller does receive a commission for selling the products to a third party via a website (Silva, 2012).

Archive site is a website used for the safe storage of useful past information threatened with extension. Such information might include old news contents which might act as a basis for the research of historical happenings and if not well preserved, it is faced with the danger of being lost for good and the history fails to be recorded. An example of archive website includes Internet Archive which has preserved billions of old the web pages, which were among the first websites to ever be created after the amazing invention of the WWW, for several decades.

Attack websites are among the growing types of website for with this new technological era which we are in, the rate of cybercrimes is tremendously increasing. This type of websites is used to launch cyber-attacks to the electronic device of a user, either a laptop or a mobile phone, if the device does not have strong up to date antivirus software. Users who have experience with cyber-attacks are more likely to get through the attack for most of the will have the knowledge of evaluating a certain website Uniform Resource Locator (URL) and be able to discover that the website they are about to access might contain some malicious files. This Websites are created mostly by hackers who want to gain unauthorized access to the information in the vulnerable device under attack. This leads to loss of valuable information or alteration of information on a client's device (Silva, 2012).

The weblogs are websites which are used to post more of a daily report or daily diary information based on the area the blogger (the one creating the website) is really interested in. Blogs may be created by bloggers who have been paid by a certain organization to research on maybe a trending issue and write a blog article expressing their opinions about that specific issue. Most information available on blog sites can be based on the political trends in a country, sports, gaming trends, fashion or maybe an epidemic which might be affecting a large population in a certain country.

Brand building websites are basically used to promote the brand of a certain organization's products. For example, accompany which has majored in the development of maybe different robotics design, may create a website to promote their robots brand since most probably they are not the only company developing robots. For them to have a fair competition with their competitors, they have to promote their brand in the market (Brian, 2006).

In this new era which we are in, people tend to be more interested in celebrity information. Therefore, celebrities are going out of their boundaries to create website which inform their fans of their life history and update them of their daily activities. Fans might also go beyond their limit and create celebrity websites to inform their fellow fans of the life happenings in their celebrity's life.

A comparison-shopping website has been created to help customers be able to evaluate different products and services offered via online through e-commerce platforms. This website combines different products from different e-commerce platforms and display them to the online customers for them to compare the prices, quality, and quantity of services being offered to them. This allows them to select the best quality products or services allowing them to experience maximum satisfaction.

As many projects are being developed in the world to make human life better, the funding to such projects might be a problem. This has led to the development of crowd funding website which is used to mobilize the society to chip in some of their earnings towards the development and completion of such projects for the betterment of human life (Jones, 2006).

Community sites are websites used to allow different people from different communities to communicate with each other maybe through chats via the websites. This communication shrinks the world population uniting different people as one community.

Content sites are used to inform the public on different issues with each passing day. They are updated on a daily basis for the world is keeps on changing with each passing day and new information is being discovered or made with each passing day.

Corporate website is majorly designed for different corporate organizations so as to provide valuable information to the public informing them of the structure and functioning of that organization. This kind of information is of great value to job seekers for they are able to gather some background information before deciding to seek for a job in a certain company. It does help them during interviews with these corporate organizations for they at least do have some background information on the different task and procedures conducted in that organization.

The advancement of the technology is kind of making different people to be very antisocial hence making them opt for online chats. This issue has led to the development of several dating websites were people are able to meet their dates and maybe try out their luck in the famous mystery of falling in love. Others might use the dating websites to seek friendship. Some dating websites do charge for the services they offer but as competition increases, several of them are opting for more users hence offering their services free of charge.

Electronic commerce websites are websites being used to offer goods and services for online sales. They allow online transactions for customers are allowed to order for goods and services online. The delivery is made within the shortest time possible for the transaction has already been made (Silva, 2012).

The internet is corrupting the minds of different people. This is because people have opted to use the internet to make dirty money. Fake news websites are being developed to present clients with fake information and promotion of different goods and services for the developers to profit from such activities and make easy money.

Cloud computing which is the storage of information in the cloud space has led to the development of Gallery websites. This website is mainly used to store art gallery or photo gallery which might be used for commercial or non-commercial purposes.

Government websites are being created to inform the citizens of a certain country about the operation conducted in the government administration. Such information might also be useful in the tourism sector; for tourist will be able to have some prior information about the country, they are about to visit and how that country does conduct its activities.

The gaming industry is immensely growing. Several gaming websites have been created to allow gamers in different locations to play one game online and earn some virtual rewards. Games or lotteries are also being played via these websites (Silva, 2012).Comedy is becoming a great industry in the world. This has led to the development of several humor sites which satirize and amuse their clients through use of different humor materials.

Mirror websites are more of a replica of an original website. They are mainly created to allow access of the same information by several users all at the same time without any delays. They might also be valued for their ability of allowing large downloads to be downloaded.

News sites are used to update the public on different happenings within their region immediately as they occur.

Phishing websites are websites mostly created by hackers for them to access information such as the passwords or back account details of their target. They are a clone of the original website manipulating the targets trustworthy to giving out their details without them having any clue of what is happening (Silva, 2012).

Political sites are used to share different political information either in certain country or worldwide.

Question and Answer websites are websites which allow users or their clients to gain more knowledge by asking questions on their area of interest and the websites do provide possible solutions to the question at hand.

Religious sites share information on different religions activities. They inform the public about believes, and their general way of life and the reasons behind the existence of their religion.

Review sites are websites in which different users do present their insight about different information availed on the internet, good, and services offered via the internet among other reviews. They allow a stranger maybe to a certain website offering different goods and services to be able to gauge if the products are worth the price or they are just a scam.

School websites basically present information of different educational institutions. The information might be about their administrative structure, the courses offered in that institution, the fee payment, and their different modes of teachings. Such information is of great help especially in situations of school searching for one is able to gauge which schools best fits their needs or requirements.

Warez sites are websites developed to host different materials such as music, movies among other entertainment materials.

The search engine website is used to index material on the internet allowing clients such for information and present them with the results based on the search terms they used. This allows quick navigation of a certain website saving on the time used to access required information.

The website types discussed above are just but a few of websites types. This is because there are a variety of different types of websites and more are still being invented as the human needs keep on growing too, with each passing day, meaning more and more website types are yet to be invented.

4.5. MEDIA FORMATS TRANSMITTED VIA INTERNET

Most of the media formats which are transmitted or accessed via the web include images, which are formatted in a format that will fit their display on any web browser by changing their extension type. Videos, which are also formatted into a suitable format, are transmitted via the web. Text documents which might have images, videos, and animations incorporated in them too are part of web media formats. With the advancement of the web, more, and more media formats are being compiled.

4.6. THE SERVER

A server is a computer device offering the services of hosting different resources required by other devices known as clients. The hosting services are aided by use of different programs which have to be installed on the host or server computer. These programs allow the server computer to be able to handle different types of resources hosted in them, ensuring proper functioning of the computer. There are different models of the server connection that are defined based on the number of servers and the programs installed in each server computer. For instance, in the client-server model, it is made up of a server that has other programs connected to it. The server controls all other devices and is like the overseer of all the operations that are occurring (Bowen, 2007).

As the name implies, the server does provide services which guide the operations that occur within a certain model. The services include carrying out computationally functions for the client as well as sending data and sharing resources among the clients. A server is set up to handle multiple clients. A client can also be connected to different servers. While connected to the server, the client can still run and carry out other tasks such as sharing of email services. There are a variety of servers available for any certain client computer based on the type of resources it needs to gain access to. They include the file servers, print servers, game servers, database servers, mail servers, application servers, and web servers (Bowen, 2007).

4.6.1. Types of Servers

- **Windows Communication Foundation Based Server:** This type of server acts as a platform or framework to be used for the development of various service-oriented applications. It facilitates the sending of data from one service point to another without any transmission complications. The information which is usually sent in the form of asynchronous messages which do not follow any timing procedures of protocols. The WCF based server employs the use of other servers such as the IIS web server and vice versa. For instance, the WCF based serve can be hosted by other servers such as the IIS.

The information on the server can be composed of a several characters which might sometimes add up to a word that is sent in as a collection of binary data. It can also be in form of a complex combination of different sets of words. In the WCF server, the end point can be in different forms. For instance, the end point could be a client waiting for feedback after having requested for information. If the client does the feedback for the request made for various types of information, then the end point would be a service endpoint.

Dashboard application and the Silver light applications are some of the applications which were present before the generation of the WCF server therefore acting as the guide to the development of the end points making the whole process to be an easy process. Therefore, this type of server does offer a more efficient approach of generating web servers and web service clients.

Windows Communication Foundation Server is made up of a variety of servers which include the service orientation. The WCF server allows users to create server based oriented applications. This brings about the service-oriented structure. This structure places more emphasis on the web services of being able to send messages in fulfillment of a request as well as receive request from client computers. The use of this server is efficient as it allows clients created on different platforms to connect to the server of choice but this will only occur if the requirements for the connection to a certain server have been well laid out and perfectly met (Bowen, 2007).

The server also has interoperability features that allow it to incorporate the modern standards to allow web servers to work together without any errors. They also have the capability of sending multiple messages in different pattern. For the WCF based server, the most common pattern is the reply-request pattern. This pattern involves an endpoint requesting information from another end point and the end point requested for information gets to send a response based on the request. There are other patterns such as the duplex exchange pattern, which operates by having both the requesting end and the sending end point sending and receiving replies all at the same time simultaneously.

It also has the service metadata feature which is a publishing service that makes use of tools such as the WSDL, WS-policy, and the XML scheme which are all categorized as formats. The metadata is used in the generation, configuration, and authorization of clients for connection with the server before they can access the WCF servers. It also has data requirement features which must be met before access is allowed as well as code friendly ways of availing the constraints to be employed. The WCF server has a classification model that classifies data by grouping it hence making it easy to handle data. It automatically creates the metadata thereby allowing clients to suitably work with the provided data types designed without any complications (Bowen, 2007).

It also has security features such as encrypted messages that ensure the privacy and protection of the information for only the sending and receiving end is able to understand the message being transmitted. This avoids security issues such as tapping, which is having unauthorized access to data by redirecting the communication, and also cases to do with eavesdropping are avoided, which is listening to information channels to get information, among other security breaches. The protective measures involve the users authenticating themselves before accessing the message so that they are given access to the messages. There are standards also used in ensuring the safety of the information. They include the WS-Secure conversations as well as the secure socket layer (SSL). These are but some of the features that ensure the smooth running of the WCF based servers.

- **Cloud Servers:** These are among the latest trends in the computing world. The cloud servers are also known as the virtual server. Virtual meaning that is not physically tangible. This server is internet based. This means that the user needs to have internet connectivity so that they have access to this server. The cloud server can also be referred to as a logical server, meaning that it only operates by executing some logical commands as programmed during its invention and creation. The cloud servers are not different from other servers. They carry out the same roles as other servers in terms of functionality. The difference is that the cloud servers are accessed through the cloud service providers which are only available once one is connected to the internet.

A cloud server is generated as a cloud-based service model. There different types of cloud servers. The two main types include the physical cloud server and the logical cloud server. For the physical cloud server is made up of two or more logical servers each of which contains its own operating system, applications, and the user interface for easy interaction with its uses. In most of the physical cloud servers, they have similar components as the common physical servers (Bowen, 2007).

The logical servers are referred to as logical as they give of information through server virtualization. This means they gauge the commands fed in to them from their users with the commands which have already been programmed in them and give responses as required of them by their manufactures.

The major difference between the physical servers and the cloud servers is that the physical server is not distributed and shared amongst multiple users for it can only be accessed by either one user or just a limited number of users unlike the cloud servers which can be accessed by millions of people all over the world all at the same time.

For the cloud servers, they have specific software installed in them to cater for them allowing them to function and run independently as a unit (Godbole, 2013).

Cloud servers can also be categorized as either private cloud server or hybrid cloud server. The private cloud servers operate by being segregated to service only specific request made by only specific clients and not just any other client.

The hybrid cloud servers respond to requests made by multiple clients all over the world without having to check if they meet any specific qualifications which might make them to be segregated or different from other client computers or client devices.

Some of the features of the cloud servers include the easy maintenance. This is because cloud servers have automatic updates that allow the server to give out better services to its clients. They are also easy to maintain and the updates are made in such a way that every device is compatible with the upgrade. It also has a large network access thereby allowing users to upload or receive data from just anywhere in the world. It also has an automatic system that carries out analysis so as effectively control their functioning and monitor the operation of the server. When it comes to security, the cloud serves make use of the cloud security. The cloud security if well modified in that they are able to keep records of data in case the server gets damaged. It is also reliable as information stored in these servers cannot be accessed by hackers due to the high rate of techniques used for encryption of the information stored in them. The encryption techniques are rated high and as superb as possible for they keep on changing with each passing day such that hackers do not have a chance of cracking or getting an idea of the encryption technique (Godbole, 2013).

- **The Web Servers:** As the name indicates, the core function of a web server is to host different web pages availed on the internet. They insure the delivery of the specific web page requested by a client computer by either stating its domain name as stored in the domain naming system (DNS). They basically handle the web requests made to them within the shortest time possible by avoiding any transmission errors from the server computer to the client computer. They might be physical computers who basically store different types of information in their system. Some of these physical computers might contain soft wares installed in them which help in the handling of the large bulk of information stored in them. Generally, they contain multiple websites with other many webpages in them.

During the delivering of responses to the request made by client computers, web servers make use of different protocols, (which are rules that govern the transmission of the web pages or the whole collection of web pages, the website, from the client web server computer to the client computer). The protocols ensure that there are no errors or complications whatsoever during the transmission process from one end point to another (Godbole, 2013).

The most commonly used protocols for transmission of web pages is the Hypertext Transfer Protocol (HTTP). It is mostly used for most web pages for most of them are created using of a scripting language the HTML. The protocol, HTTP, got its name for it allows or it governs the transmission of documents which have been interlinked together using links allowing a user to navigate from one document to another, documents handling the same topic, from within. HTML documents mostly contain images, scripts of words among others. As discussed earlier, the HTML documents are decorated or have their appearance being advanced by use of the Cascading Style Sheet. The images in HTML documents might also be designed in a way that they are able to act as both images and as a link, an interconnection to another image or a document either elaborating more on the use of that specific image or any other topic related to that image's information.

The communication between a client computer and a client computer is initiated by a web browser. As mentioned earlier, a web browser is mainly used for surfing or accessing information via the internet from web servers. Once a user keys in the search terms in the search engine, the domain name keyed in is translated into an Internet Protocol by the Domain Naming System (DNS), part of it containing the source Internet Protocol number, which acts as the identification number for the device requesting for the information. The same domain name does help in identifying the end device containing the information being requested for. As mentioned earlier, the translation process is for the proper functioning of the computer, for a computer functions well by use of the machine binary language, which is in either zeros or ones. Once the location has been identified, the response information is prepared for retransmission process from the server computer to the client computer, and then transmitted. This process is designed to take the shortest time possible for most users requesting for information from the client computer are required to take the shortest time to be replied (Godbole, 2013).

The requested information can be received in different forms. Some websites do make use of forms before authenticating the user to access their information. The user must first fill in the forms the requested information. Most websites developers use this technique to get to know customers better. Once the information is accessed, there might also be forms to fill. Most of the forms to be filled at the end of a web page or website content is used to allow users to share their opinions with the website developers about the satisfaction they have had in accessing that information. This process does also help website developers to know ways, in which they can improve their website to satisfy their customers, gain their trust or have more customers come in. The websites might also present customer testimonial before a user gains access to their requested information. This is to ensure that the user does have more confident in the information they are accessing for it has been accessed, assessed, and approved by other users to be worth it.

The documents requested for can also be uploaded to the web servers and downloaded by the client computer. This does save on the storage space available in the web servers. Once the user requests for a certain information from the web servers via the web browser, they are responded with links which will guide them in downloading an either an executable file or a PDF file format to be read offline whenever they require it (Silva, 2012).

A web server is referred to as the backbone of the internet. The internet cannot be in existence without the presence of the web servers. A web server is the server that carries out the process of hosting website applications. It is a kind of a link. For instance, it controls the incoming and outgoing messages within the server. It links the user with the information that they want to obtain. The web server decides on what application process is to occur. For instance, for incoming messages, there is an application used and a traffic that is to be followed.

The web server will receive the in bounding traffic depending on the ports that have been used. It afterwards has to decide on how the received requests will be processed. There are various ways in which the web server can handle requests. The ways are referred to as processing models. It allows the user to handle the requests either in a single thread or it may have to develop a new thread for the individual threads. The single thread includes the Node. JD. It is composed of worker threads that allow it to carry out a variety of tasks but on most cases, they specialize on carrying out selected kinds of work. The thread-per-request process model works by selecting a thread from a collection of threads to be used do a specific request.

There are request-response patterns in the web servers. These request patterns are used in the response process. These patterns are present to ensure that once a client keys in a request, it is able to get feedback. For clients who are using the internet, the web server will tend to use the HTTP during the communication process.

Hypertext transmission protocol does allow updating of the database (contains a collection of related information) in the web servers without altering the display format of the entire website or web page. The use of server-side scripting does allow this process to work effectively. This process involves use of the JavaScript scripting language to change the information in the active server pages (pages which keep on changing) of a website without altering the format and the location. The location is not altered because of the use of the Hypertext Processor scripting language which ensures that the database is kept intact in its location with the only alteration being made on the contents the database does contain. This constant updating of information on the web servers does help in preserving the visitors of a certain website for they are rest assured that they will be updated on any changes that occur in their area of interest (Bowen, 2007).

Websites in the web servers need to be managed properly and maintained error free. This is because, the competition between websites offering the same kind of information is high, and if one website does fail or have any errors, customers will not hesitate to jump to another website offering the same information. The management process is affected by having a standby team to fix the website errors within the shortest time possible. This ensures that the customers barely notice there was any occurrence of an error in the functioning of the website. The team needs to examine the website frequently to ensure that any sign of possible errors occurring is curbed before the disaster sets in.

Web servers can also be made part of any computing electronic device such as printers, routers, or web cameras. They may also be part of a complex system so as to monitor its operation and avoid any errors during the functioning of the entire system. This means that there is no need for installation of system software to monitor the operation of a web server. Embedding web servers on most of electronic devices has made the only requirement to access information in them from a client computer, be the availability of a web browser is nowadays being brought automatically installed in a computing device operating system.

In terms of hosting web servers, the operating system, the web server can either be hosted in the most inner component of the operating system which is the kernel or the outermost component of the operating system, which is the user mode part or the shell (Bowen, 2007).

If hosted in the user mode, it means it be part of application software. The web server being part of application software means that it will have minimal chances of fast operation. This is because requests made by the application soft wares to the kernel are not given that much attention. Most of the requests are preserved in buffer storage locations to await their execution to be approved based on the priority order given by the kernel part of the operating system. This leads to slow response to client request due to the slow operation of the web servers. It also leads to wastage of buffer storage for there will be many requests made by customers which will need immediate responses, hence filling up of the storage space available for storing information which needs to be processed (Bowen, 2007).

Once the web servers are hosted in the kernel part of the operating system, the execution of customer requests will be fast and effective. This is because, the kernel part of the operating system is the one which is in most control of the activities of the operating system, and thus it gives the first priority to the functions of the task assigned to it before considering the tasks assigned to the user mode component of the operating system. Hence, it is advisable for web servers to be hosted most of the times in the kernel part of the operating system.

4.7. WEB SERVERS LOAD LIMIT

Due to the increasing numbers of clients who are able to access information form web servers, most web servers are experiencing lots of loads which limit their functioning. The main characteristic of a web server failure is that it takes a longer duration to respond to customer request. With the rise in this load issue, most web server designed has come up with a technique to try and curb this disaster which has been causing dissatisfaction to customers.

A web server limit is designed based the Hypertext Transmission Protocol type which has been put into place. The web server settings are also being modified to allow support of only a few requests at a time and avoid overload of client requests. The hardware used in most web server locations is being upgraded to ensure that it functions at its maximum level. The soft wares are too being upgraded to avoid any delays to responding to client requests based on their functioning speeds (Bowen, 2007).

Generally, this upgrade is of great importance, for with each passing day, more, and more client computers are being set and allowed to request for information. The upgrading of web servers in all perspectives needs to be upgraded too with each passing day so as to meet the standards of handling client requests without any delays.

- **Client-Server Architecture:** The client server architecture is basically made up of two parts the client and the server. The client is the computing device requesting for information from the via the web browsers while the server is the computing device responding to requests made by the client computer.

The client server architecture consists of all the computing nodes connected in a network and a central device which either controls or governs their functioning. It is essentially entails the remotely accessed processors used by the users requesting and obtaining service from a main server which is known as the host computer.

The clients and servers are usually not located on the same location. The clients may be in their workplaces while the servers in a different location. This simply mean that the device used by the clients and the servers are not the same. The servers are usually located amongst relatively powerful machines. This client-architecture model is among other computing models used but this model is more effective. This is because the client and the server get to be located at two different places and the allocated time for access of information for each is different same as the set frequency.

It is mostly used in big institutions such as universities and larger firms. In such institutions, there is a lot of data processing involved. For instance, a client may be running an application program involving entry of student information while the server has a program running that will manage the data in the database. In the database, the data will be permanently stored. As demonstrated in the image, several clients can access the server. The benefit is that clients can access the information in the server at the same time and the client can get to carry out other activities while connected to the server. For instance, the client's computer can be streaming songs while still connected to the server (Bass, Clements, and Kazman, 2012).

The client device or computer creates a platform to allow a computer to request for services which can only be provided by the server. The server gives back a response which the client computer will display at its web browser. For the severs to give off any information, they first wait for a request from the clients so that in turn it gets to give a response based on the request made. The systems, hardware, and software, used to provide the service are usually not known by the client. This is because of the transparent interface that is standardized provided by the server.

There is a deviation between the client-server model and the mainframe model. The client server model uses artificial intelligence (AI) while the mainframe model has the central device perform all the tasks and govern the functioning of all devices connected to it. Hence, it is also referred to as "dumb terminals" because it does all the tasks without ever complaining (Bass, Clements, and Kazman, 2012).

4.8. TYPES OF WEB SERVERS

4.8.1. Internet Information System Web Servers

It is a product of the Microsoft Company in the NET platform and is used in the various windows operating systems (OS). Some users tend to combine the IIS server with other systems and set it as their preference but in most cases, it does likely lead to improper working of the other devices in the system. The IIS server is one of the best servers amongst other systems present in the computing world. There other systems such as the Macintosh operating system developed by the Apple company among others from different companies. However, the IIS server is the most commonly used as it is more stable. There are also some upgrades that are made on it frequently so to ensure that the services offered are much better than the previous versions.

- **Features of the Internet Information System Web Servers:** The IIS Web server contains several features to ensure smooth running. The variety of features come in handy as the IIS server has to carry out a variety of tasks. Depending on the type of task to be performed, the features are generated to suit that specific task. For instance, while hosting the ASP.NET web applications, the IIS is fitted with authentic options such as the ASP.NET, Windows author and the basic. These options are also useful in hosting static websites. Apart from hosting, the authentic options are useful in helping the server conduct its roles which include it being used as File Transfer Protocol server as well as offering host WCF services.

The windows operating system owner is required to create an account so that their account details will be used if there is any windows active directory environment which needs to be addressed with immediate effect. With such an option the user is able to automatically sign into a given website application using their domain account. The IIS also has security features to ensure the safety of the information. The security features consist of the authorization rules which are made up of a set of rules specifying the requirements of one who gets to access certain information. There is also the request for keying in information before logging in. The File Transfer Protocol security options which are specific in nature, request filtering which is used in white listing or black listing traffics used as well as a TLS certificate (Bowen, 2007).

The IIS web server also has an application pool among its features which is an important element of the as it is used to help the web server host applications. The IIS also makes use of some features that it cannot automatically access such as the remote management. Therefore, it is managed using other tools such and the PowerShell and the CLI (Bowen, 2007).

Apache web server was developed and maintained by the Apache Software foundation group. It mainly functions well with the UNIX family OS. This family includes OS such as the Kali Linux, Ubuntu, and Debian among others. It first authenticates the functioning of different client computers before giving them access to the information in the apache server databases. Virtual hosting or installation of the apache servers allows them to be able to store as many websites as possible without any complications. It is mostly used in computers which support Graphical User Interfaces for it kind of prefers use of graphical representation of information for it to function properly.Apache servers provide us with a variety of multiprocessing modules to allow multiprocessing of multiple user requests on different modules. This ensures that each user request is services or responded within the shortest time possible without any errors. The modules are created by use of different time-frames, more of the synchronous multiplexing technique, to ensure that each request is response is fixed to a specific transmission path all through avoiding conflict of access to server services (Bowen, 2007).

The apache servers come in different versions. For effective functioning of the servers, one needs to gain access to the latest version of apache servers. If you already have access to an apache server, it is advisable to update it every now and then for it to function well and properly and also so as to satisfy the clients requesting for information every now and then.

This kind of web server is one among the best for it does not have any complex requirements for it to service a client's requests.

4.8.2. NginX Web Servers

The NginX web server is a type of web server which can be used to service web requests made via the web browser on the internet by kind of holding data having the high possibilities of being selected temporarily in a location which is more of a Hypertext Transmission Protocol cache memory. This type of web server was developed by Igor Sysoev. It is an open and free software type of a web server meaning it can be downloaded and installed on any computer without having to purchase its license and its developments codes can also be modified so as to fit the user's requirements. The alteration process is kind of guided by a standard set of requirements which must be met to avoid creation of totally different software which does not serve the original main purpose of the NginX web servers (Jones, 2006).

This type of a server makes use of the asynchronous technique of responding to clients' requests. By this, we mean that it responds to requests based on their rate of request and not based on a set time frame for response. This enables it to provide more chances for the predictability of its performance in times of high loads of client request.

NginX does outperform the performance of the Apache servers for it does not make use of the synchronous technique of responding to customer requests but rather it makes use of the asynchronous technique of responding to customer requests which is more efficient and faster to use (Jones, 2006).

4.8.3. Google Web Server (GWS)

Google web server commonly referred to as the GWS is a web server created by Google for hosting of different web pages. It is a proprietary software meaning that its codes are hidden from the public hence it cannot be altered to fit a user's requirements. If a user needs to use it, they are forced to have to bear with all the negative features of it that they do not like. It also means that one has to buy the license key code for them to gain access to its usage and for one to be able to host their web pages or website content in it. It is frequently updated to keep up with the ever-changing technology trends.

Chapter 5

Software Architectures

CONTENTS

5.1. INTRODUCTION

Software is a set or collection of data put together that control and instruct the computer how operate. The computer software controls the processing of data, control the flow of data and the functioning of the operating system. There are three major types of software consisting of the system software which is divided into operating system and utilities. Programming software is used in coming up with software programs and also the application software used in developing software applications. The computer software therefore needs to be synced together with the computer hardware to make the software able to accomplish its task. There are different types of software available and they are selected according to the user requirements. For the software to be in existence, they need to be developed. This brings about the software technologies (Figure 5.1).

Figure 5.1. *Showing software.*

Source: https://www.bitdefender.com/Downloads/ (accessed on 2 April 2020).

Architecture is a term that refers to construction and building. This term can be used in the building industry. In computing, architecture is used to refer to designing in the sense of computer design systems. The knowledge in architecture is used in identifying the type of hardware and software systems to be used in a computer. For instance, based on the knowledge on the operating system used on is able to identify the most suitable software that can be used in controlling the computer operations. Therefore, software architecture refers to the design of the computer software systems (Bass, Clements, and Kazman, 2012).

Software architecture refers to the basic and important structures of a software system and the principles used in the creation of such computer structures. The knowledge on software architecture is used in decision making in making of computer systems. A good software architecture must contain all the principals that a software architecture requires such as amorism. There are different types of software architectures which include the:

5.2. CLIENT-SERVER ARCHITECTURE

The client server architecture consists of the computers in a network and a central device.

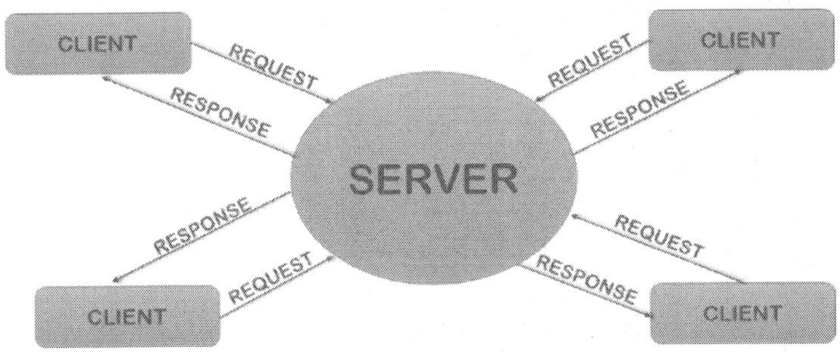

Figure 5.2. *A client-server architecture.*

Source: https://msatechnosoft.in/blog/tech-blogs/types-of-client-server-architecture (accessed on 3 April 2020).

5.2.1. A Server

A server is a computer-generated program that facilitates the functionality for other programs and devices that are referred to as clients. (Barroca and Hall, 2000).

The name "server" reveals its purpose. The server provides services which are functionalities that occur within the model. There are a variety of servers available for the user. They include the file servers, print servers, game servers, database servers, mail servers, application servers and web servers.

The following are some of the major examples of servers:

1. **IIS Web Servers:** IIS refers to the internet information systems (IS). The IIS is among other systems present in the computing world. There other systems such as the Macs developed by a different company. However, the IIS is the most commonly used system as it is more stable. There are also some upgrades that are made on it so that the services offered are much better than the previous versions (Figure 5.3).

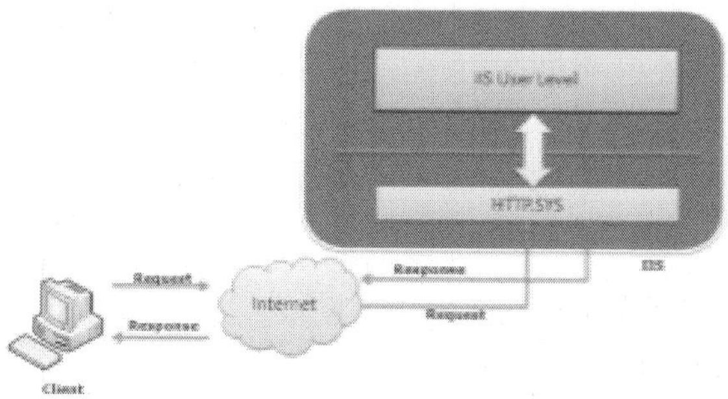

Figure 5.3. *A IIS web server.*

Source: https://yrrrakeshpandian.wordpress.com/2014/10/18/what-is-iis-7-0/ (accessed on 3 April 2020).

For instance, the HTTPS uses traffic 443 while the HTTP uses traffic 80. The HTTP is the default traffic that is used. This is because in most cases as the user enters the request, they usually do not specify on the traffic that is to be used therefore once they key in a request the traffic 80 is the one used.

The IIS Web server contains several features to ensure smooth running. The variety of features come in handy as the IIS has to carry out a variety of tasks. Depending on the type of task to be performed, the features are generated to suit the task.

The windows author is used if there is a windows active directory environment. The IIS web server also has an application pool among its features and it is an important element of the IIS server as it is used in helping the web server host applications.

2. **WCF based Service:** It is also known as the Windows Communication Foundation. It is a platform or framework used in developing Service-oriented applications. It facilitates the sending of data from one service point to another. The Dara is usually sent in the form of

asynchronous messages. It can also be hosted in an application.

The messages in the server can be composed of a character or word that is sent in form of a XML or a collection of binary data. It can also be in form of a complex. Both the WCF server and the end point vary greatly. For instance, the end point could be a client in a server. When the client in a service requests for information then the end point would be a service endpoint (Hofmeister, Nord, and Soni, 2000) (Figure 5.4).

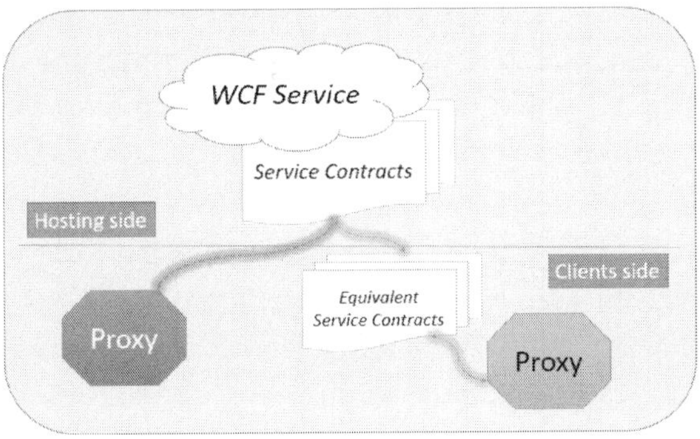

Figure 5.4. *A WCF server.*

Source: https://chsakell.com/2015/10/15/wcf-proxies-from-beginner-to-expert/ (accessed on 3 April 2020).

Dashboard application and Silver light applications are some of the applications present before the generation of the WCF server therefore making the development of the end points to be an easy process. It therefore offers a more efficient approach of generating web servers and web service clients.

WCF server is made up of a variety of servers which include the service orientation. The WCF server allows users to create service based/oriented applications. This brings about the service-oriented structure. This structure places more emphasis on the web services being able to send as well as receive data. The use of this server is efficient as it allows clients created on different platforms to connect to the service of choice but this will only occur if the contracts laid out are met (Hofmeister, Nord, and Soni, 2000).

The server also has interoperability features that allow it to incorporate the modern standards to allow web service interoperability. Hey also have multiple message pattern features. This allows numerous messages to be transferred using a given pattern. For the WCF based server, the most common pattern is the reply-request pattern. This pattern involves an endpoint requesting information from another end point and it gets to send a response based on the request. There are other patterns such as the duplex exchange pattern which is more complex.

It also has the service metadata feature which is a publishing service that makes use of tools such as the WSDL, WS-policy, and the XML schema which are formats. The metadata is used in the generation and configuration of clients before they can access the WCF servers. It also has data contracts features as well as code friendly ways of availing the contracts to be employed. The WCF server has a classification model that classifies data grouping the data making it easy to handle data. It automatically creates the metadata thereby allowing clients to suitably work with the provided data types designed (Hofmeister, Nord, and Soni, 2000).

It also has security features, such as encrypted messages, that ensure the privacy and protection of the information. The protective measures involve the users authenticating themselves so that they are given access to the messages. There are standards also used in ensuring the safety of the information. They include the WS-Secure conversations as well as the SSL. These are some of the features that ensure the smooth running of the WCF based servers.

3. **Cloud Servers:** These are among the latest trends in the computing world. The cloud servers are also known as the virtual server. The cloud server can also be referred to as a logical server. It is hosted and availed with the use of a cloud computing platform. The difference is that the cloud servers are accessed through the cloud service providers (Godbole, 2013).

The two main types include:

- the physical cloud server
- the logical cloud server

The physical cloud server is made up of two or more logical servers each of which contains its own operating system, applications, and the user interface. In most of the physical cloud servers, they have similar components as the common physical servers. The logical servers are referred to as logical as they give of information through server virtualization.

The major difference between the physical servers and the cloud servers is that the physical server is not distribute and shared among the users unlike the cloud servers (Godbole, 2013) (Figure 5.5).

Figure 5.5. *A cloud server.*

Source: http://buydedicatedserversinindia.blogspot.com/2018/02/information-about-cloud-servers.html?view=snapshot (accessed on 3 April 2020).

For the cloud servers, they have specific software catered for them to allow them to function and run independently as a unit. There are different types of the cloud servers which consists of the private cloud server and hybrid cloud server.

Some of the features of the cloud servers include the easy maintenance. The cloud servers have automatic updates that allow the server to give off better services. It also has a large network access thereby allowing users to upload or receive data anywhere in the world. It also has an automatic system that carries out analysis and monitors the server. When it comes to security, the cloud serves make use of the cloud security. The cloud security ensures that administrators can keep records of data in case the server gets damaged. It is also reliable as information stored in these servers cannot be accessed by hackers (Godbole, 2013).

5.3. CLIENT

Client refers to the computer systems (software and hardware) that are given access to server-side services. The client and the servers are usually on different computer systems. There are different types of clients consisting of the thick clients, thin clients, and hybrid clients. Thick clients are independent as they are able to carry out the processes without essentially relying on the server. The thin client is one that displays data that has been processed through the use of an application server. The hybrid client is a combination of the thick and thin clients. The hybrid client relies on the server for different uses such as storage of data (Vogel et al., 2011).

Some examples of clients include:

1. **Web Browser:** The web browser is an application software used by users to allow them access information in the World Wide Web (WWW). The user asks for information and the web browser has to obtain the information from the web server and presents the retrieved content in the user's computer. There is a difference between web browsers and search engines (SE). The search engines need the web browsers in order for them to connect to website servers. Examples include Chrome, Firefox, Internet Explorer (IE), and Opera among others.

The browsers have features including bookmarks so that they can easily access the used site and private mode features that allows users to browse information confidentially. They also have extensions, sync services as well as user interface features.

2. **WPF Application:** The Windows Presentation Foundation is a user interface platform used in creating desktop client applications that run on Windows operating systems. This application makes use of frontend languages as well as backend languages which are XAML and C#, respectively.

The WPF applications have the interoperability features, alternative input, imaging features, template features, and the data binding features.

3. **HTML5 Application:** It is a web application generated with using the version of web content standards. This application is designed for devices such as the handheld devices. This application allows users to carry out a variety of tasks at a minimum number of software.

The features include geo-location which is able to acquire the current location of device. It also has the camera access, canvas, and web storage among others.

4. **Mobile Application:** It is a software application modified for the purpose of running a mobile device. There are different types of the mobile applications consisting of web-based apps, hybrid apps and the native apps. The hybrid apps are a combination of the web-based and native apps. Some examples of the mobile apps include Bitmoji, trackers, and scanners among others.

5. **Silver Light Application:** This application is mostly used as a development tool to create mobile applications. It also creates engaging user experience on the web. The most common is

Microsoft Silver Light application in Windows operating systems. The application has a variety of features, such as security features that ensure of the data used in this application.

5.3.1. Client Server Models Examples

1. **Web Server (Apache, IIS) Web Browser:** Apache is used by most of the web servers in the world. The server software is fast, secure, and easily customizable so that it can be installed on a variety of platforms. Apache works effectively with no disruption on Windows and Linux web servers. Apache was developed by Apache Software Foundation. Below we discuss Apache in more depth, touching on topics, such as Apache users, web servers, features, and disadvantages and advantages of Apache.

Apache webservers serve more than 43% of the world's population. Apache is used by major companies all over the world ranging from IBM, eBay, Adobe, Paypal, LinkedIn, and Facebook amongst others (Bass, Clements, and Kazman, 2012).

One of the most interesting features is that Apache is open-source software which source code can be seen and used at no expense. Since Apache is open-source, it has been used by many developers to configure it further. Apache started being used in 1995 and ever since it has assisted web developers to develop internet. The web servers are a major part of websites but they do not a personal connection with the browser of the web. Apache is a software foundation founded in the US as a non-profit corporation which main function is to assist and provide the needed support to Apache software projects. Apache is a decentralized community of many people who are involved in working on Apache (Sklar, 2011).

Apache's function is to accept requests from the clients or browser so that web servers can gove back the desired response to those requests. The Apache server can perform many functions since it is equipped with features that range from loading dynamic modules, handling static files, access directory configuration support, IPv6, and gzip compression amongst others.

The following are some of the advantages of Apache server. It is open source and therefore it is accessible by any individual at no cost at all. Its code can be changed at any time to meet users' needs. It can add more features and therefore it is flexible. It can be relied on to perform required functions. Its performance is very high and its installation is very easy. Overall, the software is very flexible and is regularly maintained by the community.

The following are some of the disadvantages of the Apache server:

- It is not that secure since it easily configures invitations to various threats and therefore, it can lead to major problems.
- Because it is easily customizable, it contains plenty of new bugs and unexpected errors.
- The strict updating policy has to be followed at specific intervals, which poses several disadvantages.
- IT disables unwanted services, which poses several disadvantages.
- It creates a lot of traffic and therefore, it becomes slow.

Apache is currently very popular today and is being used by many developers. Despite all this market share, it does not stand as a single web server in the market today.

2. **FTP server (FTPD)-FTP client (FileZilla):** The FTP server, that is also known as the FileZilla, is a software program that is free to use to transfer files from a local computer to a remote computer. FileZilla comes in two versions: client version and server version. To understand FileZilla better we need to look into its features.

Filezilla has many features to perform its functions. It acts as a site manager to manage sites and store a list of FTP servers. It also enabled individuals.to compare and contrast between information in directories. Filezilla also assists individuals to manage files. Lstly, it shows the status of file transfers.

Filezilla is a cross-platform software and is compatible with Windows, macOS, and Linux clients. IT is supported by FTP, SFTP, and the FTPS protocols (Bass, Clements, and Kazman, 2012) (Figure 5.6).

Figure 5.6. *FileZilla logo.*

Source: https://infofly.es/ftp-filezilla-client/ (accessed on 3 April 2020).

The advantages of FileZilla include:

- It enables people to share a lot of files and directories at time;
- The transfer of the file will continue in case the connection was lost, therefore it does not start the process all over again;
- It also enables users to add files to the existing download queue ;
- The users can plan transfers;
- It does not limit the users in terms of number of transfers they can make and therefore one can transfer as much as they want;
- The users can use a command line interface;
- Users can sync with each other anytime;
- Its transfers are performed much faster than others, such as HTTP;
- Lastly, it has a lot of support.

Disadvantages of FileZilla users include the following:

- It is not secure as passwords are sent clearly;
- Achieving connections is quite difficult;
- Information can easily fall to the wrong hands and therefore it is not trusted as being very confidential;
- Scripting involves a lot of hard work;
- It is not the most preferred when compared to HTTPS and others; and
- If it is used by people who lack experience, loss of work may be a major outcome.

3. **Email Server (QMAIL)-Email Client Outlook:** An email server is a software installed in computers and other technological devices to send emails to other users. It acts as the virtual post office. The purpose of the email server is to receive incoming mails from the sender and sends emails out to another user in form of reply. The mails that are received are stored in the email for future reference. In the technological devices is mainly known as Email and therefore it is commonly referred to as an email and when the software is also referred to as an email (Godbole, 2013). The email server is commonly used by a large population of people and therefore it is a popular application. For one to use the email server they are required to first download the application or they can also use the internet to gain access to it. They then create an account with their username and their email

and once they are done their email is set. It has replaced the post mail because many people prefer to use their computers to read their mails than having to visit the post office so that they can the mails. It is also cheaper since the post office one has to pay for the mails but when using the mobile phones, computers, and other technological devices, they are assured that they do not need to pay for it. It is very fast in sending the mails than the post office and the sender is assured that the email will be sent and this kind of assurance they may fail to acquire when they use the post mails since the emails may get lost along the way. (Godbole, 2013).

4. **SQL Server-SQL Server Management Studio:** SQL server express is a database management system which aim is to store and access data in many different databases. It is a free Microsoft-developed software. The SQL server contains a lot of features that are used for business intelligence or reporting. There is an enterprise edition of the SQL Server and this is equipped with features that are very costly for small companies to afford. Aside from this edition, other editions come with the SQL server that is provided by Microsoft and they include: aerver enterprise, business intelligence, standard, web express and many others.

The advantages of SQL server include:

- It is completely free. This is advantageous because it enables individuals to save costs.
- SQL contains also free features. With other application you normally have to pay for premium features but SQL offers everything for free.
- It is secure. SQL can be backed up and secured with a password. After all, data cannot be lost to other individuals and therefore the data is secure.

Disadvantages of SQL server include the following:

- SQL database engine has a maximum memory of only 1GB and therefore it limits progress.
- It has a maximum size of 10GB memory.
- It also limits the buffer cache.

5. **Bittorrent Tracker-Torrent Client (uTorrent):** BitTorrent is a computer software application whose main aim is to start, transform, download management and upload data and

information using the BitTorrent. BitTorrent is an application that enables individuals to download files from the internet and it is very crucial software that is needed to manage the ongoing downloads. It is software the enable the support as it is given support by most OS (Figure 5.7).

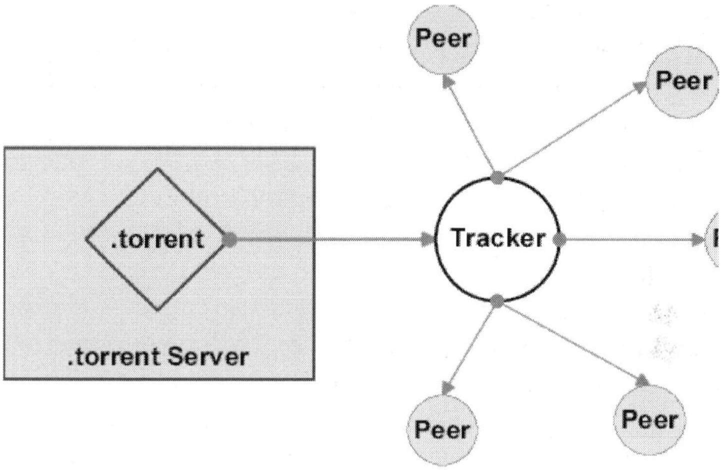

Figure 5.7. *Bit torrent tracker.*

Source:-https://www.researchgate.net/figure/BitTorrent-architecture-consists-of-centralized-Tracker-and-torrent-file_fig2_3454643 (accessed on 3 April 2020).

The design of BitTorrent enables sharing and passing of information through tBitTorrent sharing protocol. Its design also enables downloading of information, such as movies, using BitTorrent applications. BitTorrent enables seeding of data and providing a connection between peers. Therefore its design is complex (Lytras and Miltiadis, 2010).

BitTorrent client is also an important software application since it enables local users to be able to find a torrent that they want to download. This enables individuals to avoid wasting a lot of time looking for torrents and prevents the disappointment of not having to find a torrent. Various data can be downloaded from the BitTorrent that ranges from PDFs, movies, music, EBooks, and many others.

An advantage of BitTorrent is that is free and therefore when individuals want to download a torrent they do not have to encounter any cost. All that is needed is a stable internet connection and then the torrent is downloaded and therefore it is easily affordable. In case the internet connection is lost and it comes back, the torrent will continue with its download (Lytras and Miltiadis, 2010).

6. **DNS Server (Bind)-DNS Client Resolver:** DNS server is a name server whose main aim is to manage the names that are given to various internet domains and keep a track of them. In short, the DNS server is the application that has the work and obligation to give the domain name to web hosts. The full meaning of DNS is the domain name system. The name itself states the aims of the DNS server which is to give names to the internet domains. The goal and work of a DNS server are to deliver and give out websites to the users of the internet through the internet itself. The domain name system was invented as hardware that controls the domain name system software and it is connected to the internet or network at all times. The domain name system also keeps a database of the names of different domains in a safekeeping record. Aside from the domain names it also stores the internet names, network names, internet hosts and many other names. The main aim of the domain name system is to transform the domain name to the respective internet protocol address. When one is searching for a particular domain, the records that are held by the domain name systems are used to search and when the domain name is found, the domain name record is taken back. In the case where the Domain name is not under the domain name system, it is searched for in the other domain name servers until one with the name record is discovered (Vogel et al., 2011).

The domain name system is designed primarily with the function of delivering websites to web users at the end over the internet or the network. As noted above the Domain name system is initially designed s hardware that controls the domain software and it is always connected to the network or the internet at all times.

The domain name system server has the names of many different domains networks and even the internet and it has the function an obligation of transforming the name of the domain into the internet protocol address. The internet, therefore, should be always connected to the domain server or the domain server should be at all times connected to the internet server because there is need to transfer the websites to the users and also there is need to keep a record of the domain names and all these are functions of the domain name server (Vogel et al., 2011) (Figure 5.8).

Figure 5.8. *DNS server hardware.*

Source: https://www.learnabhi.com/what-is-dns-server-how-dns-works/ (accessed on 3 April 2020).

Domain name servers are free and therefore no cost is encountered when the users are using the domain name server to store and manage the name of the domains. IT is also advantageous since the domain name servers can keep records of the domain name and therefore they manage these names and these possess as an advantage. Domain name servers are therefore an important part of any internet and network (Vogel et al., 2011).

7. **DHCP Server (Wireless Router Firmware)-DHCP Client (Mobile Phone/Android DHCP Client):** A wireless router is a hardware device that gives the infrastructure for a home or an organization. It is involved in a process where the three network components are put together in a single box. The wireless routers are given the obligation to connect the wireless devices so that they can have access to the internet where they can upload, download or share content. A Wi-Fi router is connected in a house or organization where it offers or acts like a hotspot to any wireless devices that may be connected to it.

The Wi-Fi router also plays a role in providing IP addresses to computers. IP addresses are important because they enable computers to have access to internet network. Different computers should be given different internet protocol (IP) addresses to prevent any complications that may arise with the connections.

The wireless routers enable internet and network connections to reach many individuals in the room. Whereas the wired router may fail to reach some places in the house or office, the Wi-Fi router is likely to reach most places of the room. The process of using the Wi-Fi routers is very easy and fast and therefore many people prefer using it. Additionally, Wi-Fi routers are affordable and easy to access.

8. **SMB Server (Windows)-SMB Client (Windows):** Windows is software produced by Microsoft. It consists of more than one OS that can operate specific functions. Windows exists in many versions with each being more improved than the previous one. Each version is equipped with a graphical user interface that enables individuals to view files and folders in windows. In most personal computers (PCs), Windows has been commonly used for over 20 years. Microsoft Windows has a design that helps individuals and professionals to perform duties using their PCs at home or in the office. Hence, Windows suits both types of users.

5.3.2. Evolution of Windows

Microsoft Windows has evolved over the years from editions that could be used at home which included the windows 3.0, 3.1, 95 and 98. These editions were developed before 2000. In 2000 the Millennium Edition was developed, which was later followed by Windows XP in 2001. Later, we saw Windows 7, and Windows 9 being rolled out. Other versions designed for professional and business purposes included Windows NT 3.1. Windows can run on x86 hardware, for example in Intel, which enabled it to be installed in various hardware, such as Dell or Sony computers. Windows is still used and installed in some homemade computers and works very well. Newer versions of Windows OS were rolled out with touch screen features, which started the era of smart phones. Windows 7 was also introduced in tablets and smartphones, such as Samsung or Nokia.The advantage of using Windows is that it is easy to use. This means that many people prefer using windows when manufacturing the systems because they will be able to use them easily and efficiently. Windows is also advantageous because it helps gaming industry professional and hobbyists. Gaming fans have advantages if they own Windows because they can use the operating system for gaming anytime. Windows 7 is the most preferred OS for gaming as it has many gaming features.One disadvantage that Windows has is that it has high resource requirement. This may end up making Windows expensive. Windows also may lack security and therefore it may be easily hacked and users can lose their valuable information. This is definitely a disadvantage because it makes the information and data organization very vulnerable as it can be stolen at any time.

5.4. TIER/MULTITIER ARCHITECTURE

The multitier architecture is almost similar to the client-based architecture. The main difference is that the framework is divided into several pieces by having separate databases separate, which ensures that applications are handled separately. Some of the multitier architectures may have both the external and internal applications using the web-based applications. This architecture has application servers which are used in the communication of these devices. For instance, the database server communicates to the applications servers. There are different types of applications used in the multitier architecture. They include the two tier and the three tier applications among others. In most cases this architecture is installed in the client's workstation (Figure 5.9).

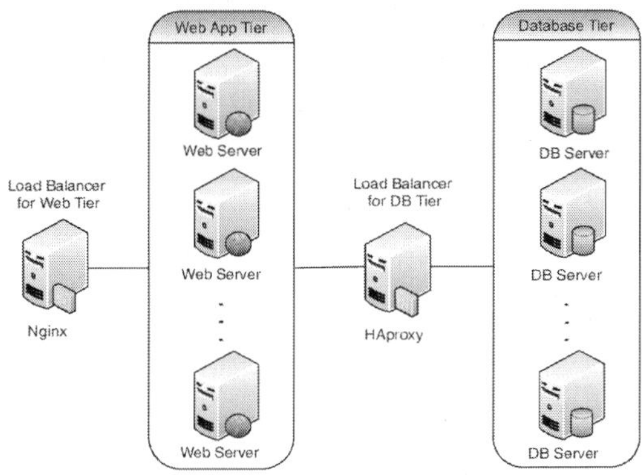

Figure 5.9. *A multitier architecture.*

Source: https://www.researchgate.net/figure/Benchmark-multi-tier-web-application-deployment-diagram-showing-web-tier-and-database_fig1_328341880 (accessed on 3 April 2020).

In a multitier application architecture, the logical operations are separated and allocated into a specific operational layer. The number of applications depends on the number of required applications. Often the three-tier application is the one used in the enterprises. The multitier application is also referred to as the n-tier application/architecture. Using this application, it is much easier for users to create reusable and flexible applications. It enables the modification of a specific layer in the application. The different multitier architecture applications are composed of different tiers. For instance, the three-tier architecture consists of the domain logic tier, data storage tier and the presentation tier (Bass, Clements, and Kazman, 2012).

5.4.1. Advantages of Multitier Architecture

There are several advantages of using the multitier architecture, which include scalability. The multitier architecture can be used on either a small or a large scale thereby making it convenient for an enterprise. For instance, if there is larger number of users or work stations, the architecture is modified to accommodate this quantity. The scalability is due to the fact that it has the capability of having a multiple tier development.

It also allows better load balancing. This is attributed to the fact that each application is assigned to a layer.

Therefore, the tasks are evenly distributed. For instance, the logic application is divided between different servers. There is also the reusability aspect in that since the applications are divided into several layers it makes it simpler to incorporate re-usable elements. For instance, a component in a given layer may be accessed by other components in different layers simultaneously (Bass, Clements, and Kazman, 2012).

It is also reliable. It is incorporated into different servers making it a simple process to increase the reliability of system. This is done by creating several levels of redundancy in the architecture. This architecture allows data integrity. The data integrity means that the data within the server are not changed or granted to unauthorized individuals. This also means that only data that is crucial/valid will be updated in the database reducing chances of biased data entering the data base. Therefore, this architecture allows such making the user able to access credible data.

5.4.2. Disadvantages of Multitier Architecture

There are some downfalls of the multitier architecture. For instance, by using this architecture there will be a heavily loaded network. This is due to the fact that the processes are divided into different layers.

This means that more exchanges with reference to communication will take place thereby congesting the network.

This will lead to the slow response from the server as well as the request being delayed and may end up not reaching the server. As this architecture is more complex, it makes it difficult to program it as well as test it. Usually in the architectures, the more the complexity the more difficult it is to program it. Another disadvantage is the fact that this type of architecture is very expensive.

5.4.3. Applications

The multitier architecture can accommodate a number of users ranging from 100–1000. This contributes to it being used in most enterprises. It is also used in businesses and organizations.

5.4.4. The Three Tier Architecture

This architecture is made up of three tiers that is the presentation tier, data tier and the logic tier. The presentation tier which is usually at the highest level in the application. It is the user interface within which tasks are translated thereby the user is able to understand. The logical tier makes logical evaluations and decisions. It also processes commands and coordinates application. It allows the movement of data between layers. The data tier is involved in the storing and retrieving of information. It is connected to the database thereby allowing to the logical tier and to the user. The three tiers is a client-server architecture patterns are created and sustained as individual modules in different platforms (Bass, Clements, and Kazman, 2012) (Figure 5.10).

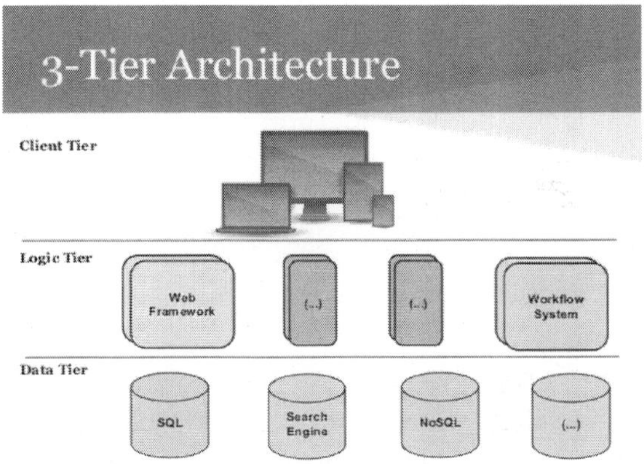

Figure 5.10. *A three tier architecture.*

Source: https://www.quora.com/What-is-the-role-of-a-web-service-in-a-three-tier-architecture (accessed on 3 April 2020).

The three-tier architecture is created in such a way that it allows upgrading and replacement of individual technologies. For instance, if modification was to be done to the operating system that is present in the presentation layer, the user interface code will be changed.

In terms of web development, the three-tier architecture is known as the website. It is built using three tiers. It is built using a middle dynamic application server, a back-end database, and a front-end web server. The three-tier architecture involves the use of protocols such as the SNMP. NET, COBRA. Java RMI and the UDP. The composition of the multitier architecture may change (Barroca and Hall, 2000).

The three-tier architecture is the most commonly used multitier architecture as it has several benefits. For instance, when it comes to development speed it is the best. The modularizing aspect gives individuals an opportunity to create and modify a product as a faster speed compared to generating a single code. The three tier is also beneficial in that it allows efficiency in development. This is done by placing more emphasis on the core competencies. This has involved individuals being assigned to develop layers that they have specialized in. For example, some individuals specialize in developing server front or back-end while others data-back end.

It is also beneficial as it allows scalability. Due to the fact that the layers are created individually, they can also be modified individually in terms of the scale. Meaning that one can scale the web servers without accessing the application servers. Modification can also be done on the application servers to accommodate large application requests. When doing this, the web servers are not required. It therefore allows the user to allocate the load to individual layers independently. This increase the performance with a reduced use in resources. The individualization in the modularization of the tier gives room for deployment chances allowing one to decide whether their web server should be hosted in a private or public cloud. It gives the user various options when it comes to the hosting of applications and web servers (Barroca and Hall, 2000).

The three-tier architecture also offers high reliability and availability. As the layers are separate, different parts of an application can be hosted in different servers. This ensures that no server crashes and also the performance is not affected as well. By allowing the applications to be allocated to different layers, it ensures that when a server crashes, the performance is not affected in anyway.

The layers in three-tier architecture are developed differently. For instance, the three-layer is commonly developed using one tier like the work station. There are different layers in the multitier architecture. The four major layers include the application layer, data access layer, business layer and the presentation layer (Barroca and Hall, 2000).

5.4.5. Presentation Layer

It is also known as the front end. This layer is used in the presentation of data. As the name front-end suggests, this layer is at the top most level when it comes to the three tier architecture layers. It presents data in such a manner that it is well-defined, accurate, and of a given standardized format. The presentation layer made do the work of translating the data within the application layer and the network format. The presentation layer is modified to allow it to present data in various formats with the use of the different available sources. It therefore has a role of ensuring that the data is integrated into a standard format that will facilitate effective and efficient communication.

The presentation layer is a user interface. In nature, it tends to be graphical and is accessed through a web-based application or a web browser. This layer is in charge of presenting information or content that is required and relevant at the user end. There are various technologies used in building the presentation layer. They include the HTML used in providing the standard structure of sites. The CSS which is used in handling the formatting, layout, and presentation of data while JavaScript manages the behavior of different elements in the website. Other web development frameworks are also used in building the presentation layer. They are able to communicate to other layers through the use of API calls (Barroca and Hall, 2000).

5.4.6. Presentation Layer Responsible for Visualizing Information

The presentation layer is involved in the user interface meaning that is layer that user interacts with the web server. This involves it being associated with the visualization of information. This is in terms of graphical display of information. In other words, the presentation layer is responsible for the visualization of information. This is made possible through the special features in the applications used in this layer. There is a sequence of processes that occur to being about the visualization of information.

The computer sends a request to the server. The server then sends a response. The presentation layer makes use of the application layer to translate the information into a format that is acceptable. The information is formatted according to the sequence in which the data was to be presented. Mostly to present it in its original format. It is equipped with formatting features as well as a logarithm to assist in the visualization of the information.

It also makes use of applications that will assist in the presentation of the data. It has graphical features that is useful in the graphical visualization of information. This increases the quality of the visualized data.

5.4.7. Presentation Layer Providing the User Interface

The presentation layer is the top most layers in the three-tier architecture. Being the top most layer means that it is the layer which the users get to interact with. As the user will be required to interact with the device, a user interface is required. The user interface allows the translation of the computer language or codes into a form which can easily be understood by human beings. The presentation layer provides the user interface for the application. It has features that make it easier for users to interact with a computer of server (Hofmeister, Nord, and Soni, 2000).

For instance, website code is not easily understandable by humans. Therefore, the presentation layer carries out decoding of the codes and afterwards it encoded it to a format that will enable a user to easily understand the codes. The presentation layer also referred to as the presentation tier by providing the user interface allows the displays information on things that relate to services such as purchasing and browsing for merchandize.

In order to provide the user interface, the presentation layer also needs to have good communication with other tiers such as the client tier allowing it to present the information requested.

In conclusion, the presentation layer is the layer that users interact with and is easily accessible to them. They include the operating system's GUI and web pages among others (Hofmeister, Nord, and Soni, 2000).

5.4.8. Application Layer

It is also known as the business tier or middle tier. It is the layer that follows the presentation layer. This layer is involved in monitoring and influencing the performance of an application. It consists of different elements that avail the business logic required in an application. This layer provides the functionality relevant to a given business domain for example the e-commerce sites. Usually the key functionality is located in the application layer. For instance, it is used by the presentation layer to aid in the visualization of information as it has some tools that will enable such (Vogel et al., 2011).

The application layer programs can be located in the client or in the servers. It plays a variety of roles that include the following: identifying communication partners. The application layer has to identify available communication partners that will assist in the transmission of data from one layer to another. It also determines the available resources for instance it identifies the network resources that are sufficiently available for use when there is a request for information.

It is created to carry out this task within a short period of time ensuring that little time is taken in the requesting and response of information. The application layer also synchronizes communication meaning that the communication layer handles the communication process within the application ensuring that there is communication within the applications/tiers.

There are various technologies used in the application layer, the Java EE, technologies. They include the Java persistence API entities, JAX-WS service endpoints, JAX-RS restful web services and the Enterprise JavaBeans components (Gosselin, 2010).

The application layer has different services that aid in its working. The services of the application layer include the network virtual terminal. This service allows users to be able to log into a remote host. Therefore, the application will generate a software emulation of a terminal in the remote host. Once this is done, the computer communicates to the software terminal which will relay the information to the host therefore allowing the user to log on.

The other service is the file transfer, management, and access. This service allows users to access, retrieve, and manage files in a computer even though it may be remote. The application layer is therefore able to manage different file sequencing. Addressing is also a service of the application layer. Addressing is required so as to facilitate communication between the user and the server. For instance, when a user makes a request, the request has its own address and also knows the address of the server. Once the server responds, it has the address of the destination and it relays the information to that given destination. Therefore, the different addresses include the server address, client address and the destination address.

The application layer is also responsible for naming the network devices as well as formatting messages. There is also the mailing service which is involved in the sending and receiving of mails. The application layer is usually in charge of forwarding of the emails as well as their storage. The application layer enables the user to make use of services in the network and therefore useful in the creation of network-based applications.

In conclusion, it is established that the application layer is responsible for the functionality of an application through the use of tools that it contains. It also provides the system logic for the application (Gosselin, 2010).

5.4.9. Data Layer

Data layer may also be referred to as storage tier. The data layer involves data mechanisms such as the databases and the file shares. It also consists of the data access layer which makes use of the data mechanism and therefore allowing the exposing f data. The data layer is composed of a database as well as a program that is used in facilitating the read and write access to the database. The data tier can be hosted in other parts of the servers such as the cloud. There are systems used by the data tier in allowing the read and write access. They include Microsoft SQL server, Postgre SQL, Mongo DB and MySQL. The data tier is therefore a self-contained unit composed SQL server. This also means that the data layer can also be referred to as the database layer.

The data layer is located after the application layer. It keeps record of data that has been accessed by the user. The data layer is an example of a Java script array. It performs different functions including storing key attributes if a web page. It is at time used in the tracking process as it gives off logs on data that has frequently been accessed by the user. It also allows the sending of information from a website to a given container tag. The container tag is part of the tag management system which is used in the managing of data (Gopalan and Adikesavan, 2014).

The data layer plays a major role of ensuring that data of the system is well managed. It therefore employs the use of various tools including the databases to assist in the managing of data. This layer also controls the access to data thereby allowing users to access given quantities of information while some get to access all the data.

5.5. SERVICE-ORIENTED ARCHITECTURE

Service orientation is a type of design that aimed at designing computers and inventing computers in the form of services. Service oriented means that the computer is more based on oriented on service. The service-oriented architecture is aimed to ensure the functions are carried out in separation from the software. The service-oriented architecture has been used widely since the year two thousand and five because it provides a lot of benefits and is a promising architecture of many promises.

5.5.1. Design Pattern Based on Discrete Pieces of Software

A design pattern is a solution that is designed or made to come up as a solution to a problem that has occurred in the design of the software or that may occur later in the design of the software. A design pattern is not a complete design and it can be changed into a code. Its main aim is to provide a solution and act as a solution to many problems that may arise in the design of the software that may arise. Therefore, the design pattern that is based on discrete pieces of software is made to provide solutions to the problems that may arise in the design of the software (Hofmeister, Nord, and Soni, 2000).

The use of the software design systems include;

- It speeds up the process of developing a software because it utilizes the design pattern in developing a software
- It prevents and solves problems very fast, which reduces time in the development cycle

Service-providing architecture is a type of designed patterns based on discrete pieces of software providing application functionality as service to other applications because they are designed to provide and ensure that the functions are provided as software in separation to the software. A service-oriented architecture is designed in consideration of several principles that are set that include the following:

Using the service orientation results in units of software that are set into the capabilities of the operation. Each service-oriented operation is designed to solve a particular problem that is of concern. As noted above, service orientation has been used widely for the last years from the year 2005 because it has a lot of promising benefits. Therefore, service-oriented architecture is preferred and has many benefits, such as making the process of developing the architecture faster. Therefore, it is a type of designed patterns based on discrete pieces of software providing application functionality.

5.5.2. What Is Service?

Service is a piece of work performed by any service provider. The service-oriented architecture provides the same client with some desired result by some input parameters.

Service-oriented architectures mean a set or group of principles or rules that are used by the developers of the software and engineers of the software who engineer the software to make and come up with the software in the form of interoperable services. These services are designed with a lot of specificities that aims to ensure that the components can be reused for many other works than the one that it was made to perform. Due to this fact, the interfaces are practically defined that gives an allowance of using across different applications and therefore they can be used and have access to many different platforms. The main aim of the service-oriented architecture is to make a business more agile and by this it means, to make the business more vigorous to increase the sales and the profits and this is achieved by enabling the businesses to settle down more quickly and have the flexibility to fit into changes that may arise at any one time. It also enables cost efficiency which is the cost that is used is much lower than before and therefore a lot of savings are made than before since it enables cost efficiency to the changes in the market and adaptability to the market changes. The service-oriented architecture fits in and works appropriately in components that are defined appropriately which individuals who manufacture computers design in such a way that they are accessible as services over a network. The advantage of this is that it allows the service-oriented architecture to operate on many different platforms that are far apart which the different networks have access to. The act of sharing of data using the different application where one sends data from one application to another application is as a result of the service-oriented architecture business applications (Hofmeister, Nord, and Soni, 2000).

The service-oriented architecture business applications were made in such a way that they perform their duties hand in hand with the help of APIs that bring about a positive result that ranges from the togetherness of the applications and the sharing of a function, therefore, easing work. The systems that are found in a singular organization and those found in different and separate organizations can accomplish their goal of getting the togetherness in the business process when they follow the set business process model. The service-oriented architecture is a database that has a lot of data and information that is not constant but continuously changes with time and interacts effectively. The advantage of this is that it enables the passing of information and data between businesses and organizations via the services provided by the web. The measures that are taken to test are done within the system-oriented architecture and there is assistance that is given to the workflow (Figure 5.11).

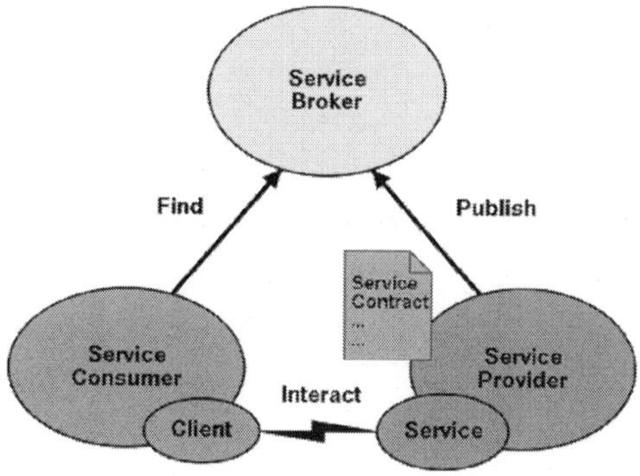

Figure 5.11. *Service oriented architecture.*

Source:-https://link.springer.com/chapter/10.1007/978-981-13-2330-0_15 (accessed on 3 April 2020).

Some policies and processes that include set rules and methods that are important to the service-oriented architecture that is involved in the service-oriented architecture treasury. Service-oriented architecture can allow the passing of information that is the communication from one platform to another platform and linguistics by using a system which is referred to as the loose coupling system. The presence and knowledge of the service-oriented architecture have been there and people have known about it for so many years back then but it has risen gradually and is being recognized even more in the past few years like past ten years where it is now being used majorly in developing technologies that are involved in software.

Loose coupling is the process where a user of a certain service can manage without the use of that service that is required. The advantage of this and an important fact is that the user which can also stand for a service can pass information even though there might be a lack of any connection between the user and the service itself. The communication and passing of information are enabled by implementing a certain set interface that can permit transmitting data and information (Hofmeister, Nord, and Soni, 2000).

The ability to pass information and data without any hindrance from the service is seen clearly when using coding languages to pass information since there is no use of service and the service does not offer any hindrance. There are very many different languages that are used by software platforms which are not necessarily invented and they do not have any fluent interaction that fails to have issues of passing information between them. The advantage of applying the use of service-oriented architecture is that the user is not forced to know about the service but they rely on a structured interface that enables the passing process between the service and the user. A service-oriented architecture is different from micro services architecture (MSA) and therefore it is of very great importance that individuals get to know the differences that exist between the service-oriented architecture (SOA) and the MSA.

5.5.3. The Advantages of Service-Oriented Architecture

Service-oriented architecture comes with a wide range of benefits and advantages that are used to provide benefits to the business organizations especially based on web services. These advantages and benefits are discussed in the section below and they include; creating reusable codes, promoting interaction, allowing scalability and reducing costs.

1. **Creating Reusable Codes:** First of all, service-oriented architecture can create reusable codes, and by the reusable codes, it means that the codes can be used more than once. The ability to create reusable codes is the basic fact that has seen most companies move from other architectures and opt for service-oriented architecture. The reusing of codes means that the codes can be reused not only for the same application but also for other applications that may exist and may need the code. The advantage of reusing the code that exists within the service is that the companies will face an easier time in the process of coming up with a process and therefore it will be way faster than expected and therefore spending less time than it would if the codes were not reused. Aside from benefiting and saving on time, reusing codes also makes the development of applications way cheaper than before because individuals who are designing the applications will not incur any more costs that are needed for the code and therefore they can save more. The service-oriented architecture enables changing of languages that are used to pass information and therefore the engineers and designers of the applications are less worried about the environment that the services will function

in. this allows them to have more time to place their focus and aim on the society interface that is applied at that time.

2. **Promotion of Interaction:** It means enabling the interactions. A common con that is visible when one uses Service-oriented architecture is that the amount of interoperability is easily attained if the service-oriented architecture is implemented appropriately. When using the service-oriented architecture there is no hindrance in the passing of information from one platform to another and this hindrance is mostly brought about by language but is not applicable in this architecture and therefore it is advantageous. Immediately a standard protocol for passing information is set in place. Hence, platform systems of having different languages do not apply any more. Therefore, transmission of data and information from one client to another is still enabled. Another advantage attached to this is those service-oriented applications can hack into firewalls and therefore organizations can share services that are important in work.

3. **Allowing Scalability:** During the coming up of web services, a common problem that is normally faced is that there is the capability of there being a way to increase the service scale to ensure that the user's needs are met and this method must be discovered. The individuals developing the services must, therefore, find a way to discover the way to improve the work output so that it may meet the standards and needs of the clients and therefore it may pose as a disadvantage because it is not an easy process. This problem is however not applicable and present in the service-oriented architecture since there is a communication standard which is set and is in place and therefore they can easily meet the standards and the qualifications of the users or the clients and therefore it is advantageous.

4. **Reducing Costs:** Any business aims at ensuring that the costs and the amount of money used are as little as possible to ensure the profits that are gained are more than the losses. Even though most organizations want to reduce the costs and spend an as little amount of money as possible they also have to ensure that their standards are still high and the quality is as desired. The use of service-operating architecture has seen a positive advantage in reducing costs since very little money is invested when comparing with others and the quality does not change therefore it is more preferred.

Chapter 6

Emerging Web Technologies

CONTENTS

6.1. INTRODUCTION

Emerging web technologies is a term to cover technologies that are still developing or are under review. These technologies represent essential innovation and are typically characterized by fast development, major impact, and ambiguity. The major impact of emerging web technologies will be clear in the future and hence, the development direction is often vague. Examples of innovative ideas include Pixar and Apple companies created by Steve Jobs. There are different types of technology that are under the Emerging Technology and these include nanotechnology, information, cognitive, robotics, educational, psycho technology, and artificial intelligence (AI). The developments of new knowledge in the field occurring as a product of technology uniting together from different systems developing into a common goal. The uniting of earlier dispersed technologies for example telephony tools, information, and video jointly all equally divide resources and mingle together hence building new competence. Upcoming technologies are technical creations that stand for progress within a particular area for competitive benefits, different fields that are likely to be flowing towards strong interlinked and same goals. The standards of the impact rank and economic capability of several upcoming and coverage knowledge differ. Over the years, modern methods and advanced technologies have been created and exposed. These technologies are mostly created through hypothetical research and the rest from profitable investigation and growth. Technology developments are incremental techniques and disorderly technology. This includes the previous slow roll-out of digital video disc or famously known as DVD as an expansion of intended to follow up on the earlier technology of solid disc. Disruptive knowledge is whereby emerging techniques take over the earlier technology and creates it redundant, this includes the automobiles, and various vehicles have taken over from the horse-drawn vehicle.

6.2. EMERGING WEB TECHNOLOGY DEBATES

Scientist Bill Joy had recognized several technologies that he thought were very important to mankind's race. He gave a very strong reasoning that the knowledge of technology can be used by different people as media for doing wrong and right. This would use it as good ambassadors for doing just to the mankind race or even make up their minds that everybody is not required and drive for accumulation extermination of those people who were not important. People who see the best in the changing technology normally anticipate that with the uprising of a new technology their will drastic improvement in the state of mankind. Throughout mankind, evolution genes evolve very gradually as opposed to technology which has been evolving very fast. History considers man to be even while the technology to be uneven. Some advocates of technology cautioned the human race that some technologies can be a ground of potential dangers and even lead to the extermination of the human race completely but all this were critics towards the technology. Others stated that as the technology continued to grow and with the creation of robots and other technology will significantly turn to lack of employment because these machines and software will give the humans competition and also surpass them in doing their duties. With the drastic growth of robots and knowledge, advancing skilled jobs can be endangered. Computer technologies that include engine learning will eventually permit the computers to do many jobs that consign to the knowledge that entails major education. This will, in turn, lead to a lack of employment. It will lead to user's becoming more depressed due to lack of money to use to buy their products and services that are built by the companies (Li, 2009).

6.3. TECHNOLOGIES THAT ARE EMERGING

The augmented reality is an interactive knowledge of the world environment where the matter that exists in the actual world is improved by the creation of the computer created information at times through many types of technology which include illustration, acoustic, and olfactory. The real aim of Augment reality is to build a mechanism whereby the user is not able to differentiate the real world and the essential expansion. In this modern age, it is mainly used for leisure, military education, engineering device, robotics, industry, and many others. Today it is used in medical education, and it's widely used in MRI equipment to doing very sensitive surgery. Augmented reality systems can be used to deliver actual information to the management area to support analysis, operation procedures and management ideas, and with a device known as AccuVein which can scan various networks of the veins of the patient, surgeons can make plans ahead before even operating. Several technologies have been applied together with visual projection, monitors, handheld applications, and exhibit applications that are normally used on the person's body. The HMD or commonly known as the mounted head exhibit is a piece of equipment worn on the person's temple like a helmet or a harness. With augmented reality, marketers will no longer have restrictions from the physical globe to be able to market their products (Li,

2009). Augmented reality is positioned to becoming a significant element of advertising and user experiences.

1. **Augmented Reality:** It is normally used for entertainments for engaging the customers more, to even gaming applications to building to browsing with augmented reality that give more information for what is seen on the cameras, with this field being enhanced at a first speed leading to development of many companies; as different thoughts are created we have hope in the future of augmented reality which will play a big role in the society.
2. **Responsive Web Design:** It is an advanced reaction that states that the plan and growth should react to the user's manners and surroundings based on the size of the screen, stage, and course. It creates a good image of the web sites making them appear good. The responsive web design commonly uses the HTML and the CSS; the web plan is not a JavaScript and program. These pages can be seen on diverse applications which include tablets, smartphones, and desktops. Despite the application being used, the content should always look applying and very simple to use. These pages should not elevate some information so that it can fit the screen but it should become accustomed to fit all the information. Besides, when this information is resized, conceals, minimized, and expanded or transferring the information to make it appear to look good on the screen, they normally use HTML and CSS. Adaptive web designs normally load much quicker than responsive web design. Adaptive web design is not made of one layout but a number of diverse layouts for numerous screen sizes. The web site recognizes' the type of application being implemented and delivers the set outline of the application. Since the adaptive design only moves important materials to each application and this is normally seen the user is using the adaptive site on a very high valuable show here the images will load faster based on the content being used. Responsive web design and web adaptive design are very much connected and assumed to be the same. By reacting first and completely to any transformation that what responsive web means while adaptive is the easy customization for a new idea and circumstance. In responsive design sites repeatedly and gracefully alter based on various elements which include viewpoint width, as adaptive websites

are created to a group of today elements with both combining the create an excellent formula for useful sites. Mobile sites are very light but they cannot depend on the new code base and browser sniffing on all of them can be a very big barrier to both the user and the creators (Assimakopoulos, Oshri, and Pandza, 2015).

3. **Ambient Intelligence:** Or the AMI is the electronic surroundings that are responsive and receptive to the attendance of people. Ambient intelligence was a protrusion on the future telecommunications, computers, and used electronics. These applications would help humans accomplish their daily activities in a more instinctive way by using content and knowledge that is captured by neural networks. With these applications reducing, becoming more linked and more integrated into our society, the knowledge structure being them would vanish into the environment until when the use of border remains perceivable by the clients. Ambient intelligence model is created upon persistent computing, ever-present computing, profiling, information understanding and individual-centric computer interface design which is consists of systems and knowledge which are:

- Most network applications are incorporated into the surroundings;
- These applications are about to acknowledge the user and the state of the information;
- They are modified to meet the user's needs;
- They are very adaptive according to the user needs; and
- They can foresee the requirements without awareness negotiation.

A good example of the ambient intellectual surrounding is home but it can also take place in work areas, open areas that are determined by applications such as street lighting and hospital setups.

The Hypertext markup language (HTML) is a major language for creating websites. The content of HTML websites is fixed, which means it cannot be altered according to user's actions. HTML is very easy to learn and does not need special pre-requisites (Binder and Dustdar, 2009).

Cascading sheets style (CSS) refers to a style page to give a summary of the content that is printed in HTML. CSS, JavaScript, and HTML represent the main foundation of the WWW. The cascading style sheet is created to assist the differentiation of the appearance and the information which are the outline, colors, and words. This differentiation can greatly enhance the information which is accessed, by granting more elasticity and power in the requirement of the appearance individuality alloying numerous web pages to contribute equally to formatting the related cascading style sheets in different cascading sheet styles folder and meanwhile decrease and difficult and duplication in the structural information. Differentiation of the style and the information also is made possible to the score page in separate styles for the separate representation procedures which include the screen on, by say, print in or even the Braille concrete procedures. It also has regulations' to changing the style of the information which is presented on the mobile phone application. The term cascading is derived from a particular main concerned system to decide which particular approach the law applies to if many laws are compared to specific content. This cascading main concern system is predictable. It has a very straight forward sentence structure and implements several digits of the English main words to identify the details of the names of a different approach to elements. This sheet page is made up of a register of regulations. Every regulation is made up of several selectors and a statement mass (Binder and Dustdar, 2009).

6.3.1. Ajax

Ajax this is a collection of net progress procedures that use several net applications on the user's side cater to web technologies. Ajax can recover information within the server without bothering the display and the manner of the obtained site. Ajax permits the web sites and the prolonging of the web technologies to alter the information without the necessity to load the whole site page. Today technology normally uses XML or JSON. This is not a single application but instead, it is a collection of applications. CSS and HTML are both connected to mark up and approach the content. The site will then be customized by use JavaScript to widely display and the client content interaction. Ajax is not an emerging technology or even a special language being used but they are existing applications that are being applied in the latest methods. The web pages were structured on comprehensive HTML sites, every user act states that a whole new sheet is gotten from the server. The procedure was unproductive as stated by the client's knowledge all the page site information vanished and eventually the new sheet was seen. Every occasion the net loaded the site all the information had to be sent again but only a fraction had changed. In return, this created extra work loaded to the servers and the bandwidth a restriction feature on its show (Binder and Dustdar, 2009).

1. **Technologies of Ajax:** Ajax refers to a large class of web applications which communicate with the main server without disturbing the present condition of the site. Below is the summary of how they are used;
   - Both CSS and HTML are used for appearance;
   - DOM is used for the vibrant show and contact with information;
   - Both JSON and XML are used for content exchange. XSLT is used for its exploitation;
   - XMLHttp request items for the interaction purpose; and
   - While JavaScript is used to bring together this application in one place.

With time several growths in the application have been implemented in the Ajax technology. The management of the information does not need XSLT or even the XML for information operation. The JavaScript object Notation is usually used as an option plan for the information exchange but this does not mean that other plans cannot be used the use of the plain page and the HTML is being used. A range of commonly used JavaScript libraries which are the JQuery consist of abstractions to help in performing Ajax requirements.

2. **Drawbacks of Ajax:** Every client whose computer does not hold up to the XMLHttp Request and JavaScript nor has its features not functioning will not function well to the sites that rely on the Ajax. Going back to JavaScript is the appropriate way to ensure that the function operates well to enable the client to use it. Some technologies are created in a way the content cannot be interpreted on the monitor and these include JAWS. Moving back and forth of different web pages is not recommended but if tracking the site required the use of fine-grained can be used the use of the pre-HTML5 method was normally used for unseen frames to activate changes in the monitor's records. Vibrant site page updates normally make it hard for the bookmark to return to the specific state of the technology. Answers to the trouble are there and most of them use the URL identifier. The Ajax concentrated sites seem to work as technology instead of information, bookmark acting states which hardly make logic. However, the answer is given by the HTML5 for the previous trouble also is relevant (Li, 2009).

The character of Ajax technology may disturb the client relations due to dynamic sites being updated especially if the network link cannot be trusted or it's slow. Most of the main internet crawlers except Google they do not a JavaScript system so that the search bars can be able to run the web technologies should be able to give an option for finding the information required that would be recovered by Ajax.

The Ajax is still in use today as the main way that JavaScript in a site page requests an in-page to the monitor. Ajax makes it possible to download a particular web site and not necessarily the whole document.

6.3.2. API

Application programming interface (API) is a communication procedure involving various sections of the computer plan to make things easier for the application and upkeep of the software. API consists of a creation of the net system, working procedures, record system, monitor hardware or even the software records. API deals with different structures (routines), information structure, object program, variables, or even distant calls. ASPI, POSIX or even Windows API are all various types of application programming interfaces. Lately, the term has frequently been used to illustrate a precise type of link that happens between the user and the monitor (Li, 2009).

1. **Purpose of the API:** API is normally used in building technology much easier by giving the original achievement and only revealing substances or the procedures that the builder requires. The graphical border of an email user normally gives the user the switch that does all the procedures of attracting and highlighting all the new incoming emails. The application programming interface for the record can key in or even key out giving the developer a feature that duplicates a record from one place to another and not necessary for the developer to comprehend the whole system file procedures that run at the back of the scenes.
2. **Remote API:** The application programming interfaces remote permits the builders to control distant income via the procedures, particular values for talking that permit the various applications to coordinate together despite the verbal communication or stage. However, the application programming interface is very vital in sustaining the object idea in objective learning training, a technique called that is done in the vicinity on a substitute object involving the matching technique on the distant object by use of the remote procedure and finds the outcome that should be used in the vicinity as they revisit value.

3. **API Webs:** The application programming interface is a term used to define which particular connection has taken place between a project and a request that normally uses its resources which also are the service rank agreement or the SLA to identify the useful supplier and the inter-presentation of the repair.

In circumstances were the creation of the web is taking place, the application programming interface is mostly described as the group of terms like the HTTP or the hypertext transfer protocol that asks for the texts together with the meaning of the arrangement of replying the texts normally in the XML (Extensible markup language) or the JSON (JavaScript entity Notation) plan.

The application programming interface plan has a very major impact on its procedure. The standard procedure of hiding then content defines the job of the encoding interface allowing the modular encoding by hiding the performance information of the modules so that clients do not recognize the design inside.

6.3.3. Biometric Authentication Biometric

Biometrics is a scientific term used for body size and calculations. It describes the features linked to human personality. This realistic authentication is applied in the mainframe science is a way of recognizing and admission control and is also used to recognize particular persons in an area that are under close watch by the government. Biometric authentication identifiers are mostly divided into physiological versus behavioral individuality. The physiological individuality is connected to the outline of the body. This is like but not restricted to fingerprint, appearance recognition, hand geometry, and scent, while behavioral features are connected to the sample of the actions of the individual. Driver's license or passport and information-based recognition systems, for example, personal identification numbers are some admission control. However, biometric authentication is very different and very distinctive to every person (Li, 2009).

1. **Adaptive Biometric:** This system plan to constantly revise the templates or even copy to the intra-class difference of the prepared information. The advantage of adaptive biometric is solving the dilemma of the restricted preparation of the information and tracking of time variations of the contribution of information via editing. Lately, the adaptive biometrics has established an important part from the investigative society. The investigation

is anticipated to increase the drive because the solution is promulgated. With this system, no one is supposed to gather big figures of samples of biometric throughout the employment procedures. It's no longer essential to employ again or restrict the process from zero to enable it to adapt to the changing society.

2. **Recent Advances with the Biometric:** Biometrics has developed signals on the brain study known as electroencephalogram and heart study known as an electrocardiogram. With this study, it showed that the human has some dissimilar heart and brain patterns that vary in each individual. Others include the finger layer acknowledgment by the use of blueprint acknowledgment procedures that use pictures of the vascular design of the human. Despite the advancement of this application, it is tiresome and still not accurate. Biometrics of intent is the new era of biometrics. This technology will summarize physiological elements like eye progress, body high temperatures, and the breathing movements and calculate unsafe manners or hostile intentions before it turns into action. Vendors are widely adopting the miniaturized biometric authentication systems or the BAS; in turn, they reduce cost and save more (Li, 2009).
3. **Operator Signature:** An operator signature are biometric forms which record the manner of the person by use of a tool or difficult procedure and this is known as verification pattern, the major use of biometric signature is to differentiate amongst the remote clients of telerobotic operation procedures that use open internets or communicating.
4. **Biometrics in Animals:** Instead of using tattoos and tags to recognize animals, the biometric application has proven even to be the best in recognizing each animal, and with its stripes of zebras, prints on muzzle, appearance acknowledgment and the spots on koala all have been tested using the biometrics procedures.
5. **Video Biometrics:** Video biometrics has become an obvious way of recognizing content. There are specific elements in the videos that analyze how strong specific areas of the frame are as opposed to others which also helps in acknowledgment.
6. **Dignity in Humans:** Biometrics has also become very active in the growth of state power. By making the human topic into a set of biometric parameters, also dehumanizing the person, break

physical integrity and eventually upset the human self-respect. Some have insisted on the globalized world which is faced by huge groups of people with missing identities. The developing countries have undependable credentials and the poor people in society do not have trustworthy credentials. And without good documents, there is no sureness of rights or even civil freedom.

7. **Likelihood of Full Disclosure of the Government:** The national population is sad about how the biometric information is being applied but the full revelation will not be imminent. The United State government states that it is good to defend and to even mask the true degree o national abilities in particular areas which are concerned with the behavior of security linked activates.

6.3.4. HTML5 Canvas

The HTML5 canvas is a component that is normally used to sketch graphics through the use of JavaScript. Canvas has different techniques for sketching paths, boxes, circles, messages, and also adding pictures. The canvas is made up of a sketching area that is described in the HTML system with height and width features. The JavaScript system may have the right to the area via a set of sketching features that are alike to other common APIs 2D. Hence creating a wide created graphics. It is used in the construction graphics, animations, games, and picture composition (Binder and Dustdar, 2009).

6.3.5. Microsoft Azure

Microsoft Azure which was previously windows Azure is a cloud computing application built by Microsoft which is used for construction, testing, organization application, and services by the use of Microsoft-managed information centers. It gives the SaaS (software as a check), PaaS (platform as a check) and the IaaS commonly known as infrastructure as a service) and joins together many programming features, equipment, and frameworks which consists of Microsoft-particular and third-party software and procedures.

– **Services:** Microsoft has a list of over 600 Azure services.

- Computer services the essential machines permit the user to initiate an all-purpose Microsoft application and Linux virtual types of equipment. The net job technologies can be sent to an APP service surrounding to execute the backdrop processes that can be invoked on the agenda, on command or even operating endlessly. The table, Blob, and queue application that are used to converse between web jobs and web Apps and to offer condition.

- Mobile services are the mobile commitment that gathers actual-time that normally emphasizes the behavior of the user. It gives a notification push to the mobile device. The Hockey App can be implemented to create, allocate, and beta-test mobile technologies.

6.3.6. RSS Feeds RSS

The RSS is the short form of Really Simple Syndication. These are records that are simple to interpret by a computer known as the XML records that update the content without any human intervention. The content is received by a computer known as the RSS feed reader that changes the records to the newest updates from sites in a simple to read the plan. A normal XML record plan makes sure it's consistent with various types of equipment and programs. These news feeds are very important to the readers who want on-time updates from their best sites or by combining information from the various sites. By subscribing to this RSS feeds eliminate the necessity for the reader to manually verify the net for new information. Their monitors keep a close eye on the web and alert the readers of any new feeds. The monitor can also be set to instantly load the new information for the reader. The feed information is offered to the readers by software known as the aggregator news. The aggregator can be created into a web page or even downloaded on a computer desktop or downloaded on the mobile gadgets. The reader constantly checks the reader's feeds for fresh information and they can instantly load it when that feature is working (Binder and Dustdar, 2009).

1. **RSS on Emails:** Some applications send the Simple Syndication to the mailbox to transfer the client's individual choice and schedules.
2. **Current Usage:** Various important websites, such as Facebook and Twitter, rolled out really simple syndication feeds but they have decreased or eliminated support for those features. However, its broadly used readers such as Shiira, FeedDemon, and Google Reader have been stopped having shown decreasing fame in the RSS. Really Simple Syndication sustain was removed in OS X Mountain Lion's versions of letters and expedition, even though the features were to some extent restored in 8 Safari. Mozilla

eliminated the Really Simple Syndication support from Mozilla Firefox 64.0 version, uniting Chrome Google Chrome and Microsoft Edge which do not comprise RSS hold up, hence the departure of the Internet Explorer (IE) as the last main browser to include the Really Simple Syndication support by defaulting.

6.3.7. Ruby on Rails

Ruby on Rails or Rails is a server-area where the net request structure designed in Ruby based on the MIT license. This is a model-controller-view (MVC) structure providing evasion of an information base, a net service, and net sites.

The rails surface in the year 2000 and had a great impact on the net application creation via new features which include the faultless folder table developments, migrations that allow quick technology growth. The rail's controls on other networks remain obvious nowadays.

1. **Framework Structure:** The rails are divided into several parcels which are the active records, achievement pack. The web 2.0, rails also consists of the action net service parcels that are currently replaced by active sources. Typically, the parcels builders would make plugins to prolong the present parcels.
2. **Deployment:** The rails are usually installed by RubyGems a management package that is incorporated with present versions of ruby. Most open Unix-like systems also maintain fitting of ruby on rails and its dependencies via their local package organization scheme. Rails are usually deployed with a catalog server such as MySQL or even the PostgreSQL and a network server such as Apache running the Phusion Passenger component.
3. **Philosophy and Design:** The principle over the pattern means that the creator needs only to state an exceptional aspect of the request. The rails conventions are only direct to reduced code and reduced recurrence. By reducing recurrence means that the content is positioned on its own and its unmistakable position. For instance, the use of the Active files unit of the Ruby on Rails the builder is not required to identify the file feature especially the names of the students in the classroom. However, the rails can be able to restore the content from the file based on the name of the class.

6.4. ADVANTAGE OF EMERGING WEB TECHNOLOGY

The advantage of emerging web technology is that it has greatly made big progress in the lives of many within society. With the technology progress it has helped people to efficiently complete their tasks, also keeping them safe and in good health and even keeping the environment safe.

6.5. IMPACT OF EMERGING WEB TECHNOLOGY ON THE FUTURE

With the evolution of the web technology robots are taking up the workforce jobs and with it, they will create a loss of employment for the humans, hence they will not be able to sustain themselves and will become further reliant on the robots.

Chapter 7 Uses for Real-Time Web Technologies

CONTENTS

7.1. INTRODUCTION

The web is also referred to as the World Wide Web (WWW). It is a collection of internet system servers that give support to specially formatted documents written in the markup language format called Hyper Text Markup Language. This language supports links to documents, audio, and video files. Technology refers to the equipment and machines that have been generated through the application of scientific knowledge. There are various types of technology which include the mechanical technology among others.

Therefore, the term web technologies refer to the ways in which computers among other devices are able to communicate with each other via the markup language and multimedia packages. There are different types of web technologies, which include the cascading style sheets, XML, Hypertext transfer protocol (HTTP), and common gateway interference. The real-time web refers to networking webs that use technologies and practices to facilitate reception of information within a short period of time.

The real-time web technologies have been widely used. Some of the uses of real-time technology include:

7.2. AGILE SOFTWARE DEVELOPMENT

Agile refers to the ability to respond to change. Agile software development refers to a collection of frameworks and practices based on principles stated in the manifesto of the agile software development. The frameworks include scrum, feature-driven development and extreme programing. The practices include test-driven development, stand-ups, pair-programming, sprints, and planning sessions. The agile software development is the most commonly used method in software development. In most agile software development cycles, quick and iterative development cycle is needed to ensure efficiency. In real-time development, all the characteristics of the software have to be met by the iterative in the development cycle (Carleton, 2013).

Agile development software makes it to easier to create software given the time constraints or deadlines. The agile software development allows creating multiple software elements without disturbing each other's timing requirements. It employs the use of timing analyzers that check the real-time characteristics of the software program. It also employs the use of normal tool chain during the development process. The agile software development involves the incorporation of the cores and values of it manifesto to assist the software developer create a good software that is within a given context.

The agile software development is majorly dependent on the collaboration that the developers have. This development requires contribution from the members of the team. This enables to get proper solutions to the challenges encountered in most software. The agile software development majorly focuses on discovering new ways and proper methods of developing software and sharing the knowledge enabling other individuals to be able to create the software. The agile software development majorly depends on feedback. Feedback is essential as it enables them to identify problems encountered in software that have been developed and they can now develop software that will overcome these challenges. This is why the collaboration between the developers is important as they will be able to share different ideas (Carleton, 2013).

With the advances in technologies, there are new programming languages that have been developed to enable the creation of quality software. The programming languages are among the markup languages used in software creation. They avail a variety of tools that can be used by software developers to enable them to come up with good software. The agile development software as illustrated above follows a given process in development of the software. The first stage involves planning. Here the developers gather information on the software that is to be developed. They identify the properties the software should contain. They also look into the agile software development manifesto for guidance during the development process. They gather all the tools that they will require. After preparation, the next step involves designing.

They create various design of the software. They then choose among the designs which are the best design. After designing, it is the developing process. Here the web technologies are used in visualizing the chosen software designs. All the ideologies of the software are incorporated into the software being developed. The next stage involves testing the software. This involves the software being given to testers who will test the running of the software identifying any bugs if present in the software. If there are bugs present, the software is returned to the developers so that they can rectify the bugs and return the software to the testers (Carleton, 2013).

Once the software has been certified, it is deployed and afterwards it is reviewed to ensure that is suitable for use. The final step involves it being launched. The software is put in the market for users to install in their devices. The agile software development method assists in equipping software developers with tools and knowledge enabling them to face any unpredictable situation while in the process of developing software.

The following are some of the advantages of the agile software development:

- It allows stakeholder engagement meaning that it allows collaboration between the project team and the client;
- It ensures high levels of transparency;
- It enables the developers to have predicable delivery;
- It ensures predictable costs and schedules after the sprint; and
- It improves the quality of the software produced to become more user-centered

7.3. CONTENT MANAGEMENT SYSTEM (CMS)

This is a software application that is used in creating and modifying digital content. It is mostly used in web content management as well as enterprise content management. The web content management is used to allow the collaborative authoring of websites while the enterprise content management allows integration of document management therefore paving way for collaboration in the workplace. It also allows digital assessment as well record retention functionalities. The web content management and the enterprise can be dividing in to two. That is the content delivery and management applications (CDA and CMA).

Some examples of the content management system include the Joomla, Magneto, Square space, Wix, Drupal, and the TYP03. The content management application allows the user to handle the design, modification, innovation, and the withdrawal of content. This is beneficial as the user does not have to have knowledge in HTML in order to carry out this process. The CMA is therefore a graphical user interface. The CDA facilitate the backend services that are required in the support management as well as the delivery of content. This is after the content has been generated in the content management application (Webuters, 2018).

There are various platforms/software that provide the CMS which include the SharePoint which allows the easy storage, management, and sharing of digital information. The Joomla which provide feature such as the blogs and allow the support of language internationalization. Word press used as a hosting service and can be utilized as a web server.

There are three types of the content management systems that consists of the open source CSM, software CSM and the proprietary CSM.

Some of the common features of the CMS include:

Reduced server requirement that have brought about the ease of accessing information from the servers. They also have adjustable/customizable templates thereby allowing users to use templates of their choice and preference. This is provided by the publishing functionality features. They also have integrated file managers that facilitate the easy management of files and proper recording of data in a well modified system. It also has an admin panel which allows user to select the language they are compatible with to be used in the system. The system has features that allow easy installation of wizard-based applications.

It also has revision features that facilitate the updating of content more so those that have been published. This feature keeps records of all the publications that have been updated either by the author or the user. There is the formatting feature which allows the modification of the document into the format required by the user. They also have the in-built SEO features that allows the creation of user friendly URLS as well as Multi-platform capabilities.

Some of the benefits of CMS include having control over the website content, being able to refresh the content, offering good website security, and allowing content updates.

7.4. INTERNET MARKETING

Internet marketing also referred to as digital marketing. It utilizes internet and digital technologies to market their products and services. This is one of the latest trends in technology. There also some digital platforms that have been generated to be used in the marketing of the products. This trend is on the rage among business enterprises as it enables them to get access to a larger audience therefore creating a much greater awareness on the products they have.

The use of internet marketing has replaced the traditional means which included employees going from door-to-door to market their product. This was time consuming and also allot of funds went into it. For some businesses, not much profit was made from the process. There are different internets marketing strategies that have been employed by businesses. Most of them entail a combination of the different digital marketing. For instance, in most cases search engines (SE) and social media optimization have been combined to improve the online marketing (Godbole, 2013).

Other form of internet marketing used include social media marketing, e-commerce marketing, content marketing, content automation, campaign marketing, e-book, display advertising, influencer marketing and gamification. Social media marketing is more common. It involves the individuals marketing their products across the different social media platforms such as Facebook and Instagram. It also involves companies setting up blogs. The blogs give them a platform to write more on their products. It also creates an avenue for them to get feedback from the consumers. The post pictures of their products and also give their contact information so that the consumers can co tact them at any time.

Internet marketing also makes great use of websites in their marketing strategies. Almost all companies in the current world have websites. The websites are created based on the commodities or services they offer. The website also contains contact information so that consumers can get more clarification. A major asset of internet marketing is communication (Godbole, 2013).

Communication between the sellers and the customer. This communication will enable the business men to give any updates of the products they have and also on any changes added to their products.

7.4.1. Features of Online Marketing

They include the SEO tools. These tools are useful in knowing the status of on-page keywords. The tools should also assist in assessing the SEO strategies identifying which strategy is effective. In websites, the SEO tools help on identifying pages that are not of good quality and would therefore need to be upgraded. Another feature is the web designing tools which are useful in creating websites of good quality so that user experience is good (Vemula, 2017).

Some of GE benefit of internet marketing is that it gives business owners a larger platform to market their products. Also, individuals are able to get employment as web designers and content creators.

7.5. OBJECT ORIENTED PROGRAMMING

Object oriented programming is a programming model used in the organization of software designs that use data. They make use of programming languages. Different from other programming models, this object-oriented programming compatible with its name focuses more on the object that are to be modified in the software different from others that focus on changing the logics of the software. It is therefore unique from other programming models. This programming approach is mostly used in programs that are complex and are relatively larger. It us durable for programs that require to be frequently updated and need high level maintenance (Jones, 2006).

It therefore works by first having the program developer to identify the objects in the program that will be manipulates. This process is also referred to as data Modeling. Afterwards the object can give more information about the data that it contains. There are four main pillars of object-oriented programming. They include encapsulation, which involves restricting data from accessing public methods, thereby hindering it implementation. Therefore, the data is kept private and restricted access.

There is also the abstraction involves the using of other ideas in that are not related to programming to aid incoming up with good programs and also it brings about a new perspective in the creation of the program. There is also polymorphism which is divided into static and dynamic polymorphism. Static polymorphism employs the concept of overloading while dynamic polymorphism employs overriding concepts. Inheritance revolves around relationship between two things. For instance, a code used in JavaScript may have a different meaning if used in a different programming language (Jones, 2006).

Examples of object-oriented programming include Python, Ruby, Scala, Small talk, Eiffel, Emerald, Self, and Jade. The programming languages include Simulator, Java, Python, Ruby, C++, Smalltalk, objective C and Visual Basic. Net. The object-oriented programming is mostly used in creating mobile apps. For instance, it is commonly used in IOS mobile apps.

Features of the objective-oriented programming include inheritance features allowing the creation of relationships codes in different programming languages. They also have the polymorphism features consisting of both static and dynamic. It contains data hiding features that hide data from public sources. There are encapsulating, overloading, and reusability features. They are all used together to allow the creation of good quality programs.

Benefits of the object-oriented programming include easy trouble shooting. This is made possible through modularity. Therefore, the program developers can easily identify problems and bugs in the programs created. This employs use of encapsulating features. It also allows the reusing of codes therefore programmers do not have to generate new codes over and over again. This is made possible through the use of inheritance features.

It also allows flexibility facilitated through the polymorphism features. It creates an avenue for one to develop problem solving skills among other benefits (Jones, 2006).

Object-oriented programming is made often in the surrounding of objects. The object-oriented programming model changes data to the form of objects and it shows the content of the objects and how they behave by declaring classes (Vemula, 2017).

7.5.1. Features of Object-Oriented Programming

- Encapsulation which enables the structure of object-oriented programming has an easier management system because there are well-defined boundaries that are present behind the implementation of boundaries.
- Polymorphism which is implementing the abstract entities in several methods.
- Inheritance meaning the organization of fragments for implementation hierarchically.
- Object-oriented programming is advantageous because it enables easy and simple programming. Other advantages that are associated with it can be used more than once, it can also be factored again and it is extensive and it can be maintained and it is very efficient and therefore it can be relied on.
- Object-oriented programming is and it has been a preferred model for programming for the last very many years close to more than ten years. The use of object-oriented programming is that it allows programmers to create a software in small amounts rather than developing them in big chunks and therefore this is a more manageable and effective means and it is more relied upon.
- Object-oriented programming is beneficial since when dealing with the objects, they do not have any limit whatsoever. Also, information can be kept aside from the method which ensures that a problem or crackdown does not occur those which were found previously. Object-oriented programming is, therefore, a method that is being applied by many programmers and they are also used to avoid any bugs.

7.6 PROJECT MANAGEMENT

Project management is putting the resources that belong to an organization or business to ensure that a project that was being carried out is completed. Project management can be the management of a particular project or it can also involve a project that has been carried out for some time.

Project management has been used mostly in fields like engineering and it has been introduced in other fields like medicine and healthcare and with time it found its way into information technology. It involves managing a project and coming up with a complete and functioning end product that will work effectively (Vemula, 2017).

Project management is the same and works in the same way in all the fields and it does not have any differences in different fields. It mainly aims at ensuring that any project that was started or that is started comes to completion and that it is completed most effectively and that it is functioning effectively. It also ensures that the system or project has high quality and it can reach and maintain this standard.

7.6.1. Important Things to Take Note of on Project Management

Project management involves a process where one must first be organized by planning and efficiently executing the project and also the project is kept an eye on to ensure that it does not fail. These steps should be followed to ensure the project is completed and it is functioning.

There are different methods that a project can be managed and these techniques are applied in different ways which may be in either the olden ways that were used or the agile and modern ways.

Project management takes place in different steps that need to be understood and followed. First of all, the project is planned. Planning is an important process since the project is organized in such a way that it will flow to ensure that it succeeds. After the planning stage, there is the initiation process where the project is introduced for the first time and then it is followed by execution where the project is carried out in the way it was planned. The project is then monitored to ensure that it operates in the way it is supposed in. Lastly, there is the closing of the project if the project is a success. Every project operates on a budget that should be followed effectively (Vemula, 2017).

7.7 SKUNK WORKS

Skunk works is also referred to as sunk work project. It is a smart project that involves a small number of individuals who are not part of the company's research and development team. The origin behind skunk works name is a hidden secretive research and development team that was situated in Lockheed Aircraft Corporation and they were the ones who were responsible for coming up with a jet that was used for fighting during the world war two. It was asked by the US army to make military jets for America to use against the Nazi in the world war two and therefore they needed to be kept secretive or they could be destroyed.

How skunk works transitioned to business include; A certain person named Johnson prepared and designed a management strategy that he used in coming up with the hidden project that had fourteen rules. From what Johnson developed, other individuals came up with better versions that were more improved than what Johnson had designed. A certain individual called Martin tern was among those individuals and from this it enabled the more generic and real version of skunk works. Skunk work projects came up with more innovative products that were used to improve their line and helped them in becoming better.An advantage of skunk works innovation is that it enables people to have a break and a time off from their main work and routine and therefore individuals have an opportunity to have some time off from their normal work procedures. however, with the coming up of the new school it has brought up a new meaning of companies where it stated that companies should not be based on innovation and with these, it has proven a disadvantage to the skunk works since they are now only based on innovation and this caused disruption (Carleton, 2013).

7.8 SOCIAL MEDIA

Social media is an internet website or applications that allow people to share content and information. It also promotes communication and many social platforms were invented which include WhatsApp, Instagram, twitter Facebook and many others that are being designed and invented daily by software designers. The ability to share content and photos has brought about a new phase in the life of people where people spend most of their day engaging in social media and communication and passing of information from one individual to another has become faster and more effective as it is way simpler than before. To understand the social media, we will have to first have to understand all the types of social media.

Instagram is an online social media platform that has the intention of sharing uploading pictures and posting pictures in your stories. Instagram has brought many people together since an individual can view how an individual in another country can post their pictures and another individual in another country can view their posts. People can also communicate through the Instagram platform and send information to people in other places and they can get feedback from their friends and family (Webuters, 2018).

7.8.1. Types of Social Media

WhatsApp is a social media platform that enables communication of individuals in different countries since it involves the passing of information from one person to another. WhatsApp is a more preferred platform since it involves the sharing of information in a cheaper way than the other social media platforms and therefore it is more preferred as it is more affordable than the others. WhatsApp is also more confidential and people cannot be easily hacked and the information cannot easily leak and therefore people who want to send a confidential message will opt using WhatsApp than the others.

Facebook was among the initial phases of social media platforms. Facebook was invented long ago where one was required to create an account with a password and then when they have their account, they were required to post pictures, and they gained "likes" and many friend requests. The coming up of Facebook was among the reasons that the other social media platforms developed with time as they gained their inspiration from Facebook. With the passing of years, Facebook has been improved and it has led to the coming up of better versions for communication and social life entertainment. Some of the improved versions of Facebook include Facebook Lite (Webuters, 2018).

Other social media platforms that have been invented include the all social that connects people all over the world. There is also the twitter that enables people to criticize negative comments that people may post or discuss politics, discuss individuals in power and this has made the world a global community or village where you communicate with a person in another country like you are communicating with a person who is next to you. It has also promoted entertainment where people are entertained with what other people post and with these; they can find something to spend their time doing (Webuters, 2018).

7.8.2. Advantages of Social Media

Various advantages come with social media that has enabled the success of real-time web technologies. Some of the advantages that are associated with social media include:

Social media enables communication. Communication is the sending of information from one individual to another. With the coming of social media platforms, it enabled communication of people who are far away from such that one can send a piece of information to an individual who is as far away as another country or continent and they get feedback immediately. By using social media platforms, it is way faster and cheaper than having to travel to the other countries to pass the information.

Social media is also a source of entertainment. Many people spend their free time in social media as a way to entertain themselves where they can share or upload their pictures, view other peoples' pictures, watch videos that are posted by other people and like as they follow other accounts. By engaging in social media, it enables individuals not to get idle and indulge in activities that are harmful to example engaging in drugs and substance abuse. It also boosts the creativity level of an individual that makes them be able to think and come up with new ideas.

Social media enables and promotes entrepreneurship such that individuals who are selling goods and products can advertise their goods through the social media platforms in that they can create groups that the main intention is to upload their goods and let people know about them. The advantage of social media in business is that it enables many people to get information about goods that the entrepreneurs are selling as compared to advertising using traditional ways. It also enables entrepreneurs to acquire new market for their goods such that people who had no information about the goods can now get informed about the availability of the goods and where they can acquire these goods from.

7.8.3. Disadvantages of Social Media

Since nothing that has an advantage lacks a disadvantage, social media also has its advantages. Among the disadvantages of social media include:

- It is addictive and therefore individuals who use social media for a long time may get addicted to it. Users can waste a lot of time on social media that they forget to perform their duties as it is required.

The other disadvantage of social media is that it promotes sexual immorality. Great deal of immoral content, such as pornographic materials and pictures, is being uploaded on the internet and this has led to a lot of immorality in the society today. In some social media like WhatsApp, everything one sends is kept confidential and therefore individuals end up misusing this by sending nude pictures of them or other unnecessary content and therefore the moral values of the society are degraded. Every individual who is using social media, therefore, should avoid receiving or sending this type of content.

Another disadvantage is that it promotes laziness such that a lot of individuals spend a lot of time on the internet and social media such that they forget to perform their duties as it is required. Laziness can lead to many individuals losing their jobs. Therefore, some companies and organizations have come up with rules that prohibit all employees from using their phones when they are working.

7.9 REAL-TIME WEB ANALYTICS

Real-time web analytics is a type of real-time web technology where an individual is allowed to manage web sites users in an instant such that the website managers can monitor user behavior and interaction. Real-time web analysis stands for all the things that are involved in a website. This means that the managers can manage the people who are visiting the website for the first time, they can also check and monitor the likes and positive comments that the page gets, it also enables that the content being uploaded is uploaded immediately and that the dashboard has the reporting is done. Real-time web analytic enables the individuals to check on how the people who are using their website are reacting. It also enables them to carry out research on how they are to improve themselves to give better services to their users. For example, if they use the real-time web analyst to check on the reaction of their users and they discover that the users react negatively to a particular content, they can eliminate that part to ensure that the consumers are satisfied with the content and to attract new users too (Carleton, 2013).

Real-time web analytics has evolved over the past years from simple generations to more complex forms. The initial generation involved log files to glean data. It was not very effective because it could not take a large amount of data and information and it also took a very long time to process some information and therefore it was not reliable enough. Better and more improved web analytics have been created that include very reliable Google analytics.

7.10 PUBLISHING

Publishing is among the real-time web technologies which include online publishing. Online publishing aims at ensuring that the individuals and users of the online published information remain entertained and glued to that page so that they are interested with the content that they acquire from that page and that they get enough information that is accurate and properly detailed. Real-time data and information can ensure and lead to some interesting info graphics that are aimed at connecting viewers and keeping viewers entertained and engaged enough. Publishing is, therefore, an important part in the real-time web technologies.

Chapter 8

Cloud Web Technologies

CONTENTS

8.1. INTRODUCTION

Cloud computing refers to the ability to access computer system resources on demand, inclusive of computing power and data storage, without the user having to actively manage it directly. It mainly refers to a center of data that users are able to readily access over the internet. Of predominance today are large clouds which mainly have well distributed functions over many different locations from servers that are found centrally. If there is a relatively close connection to the user, it is possible to incorporate an edge server.

It is possible for clouds to be used by many different organizations. This is referred to as the public cloud. Similarly, it is possible for the cloud to be limited to one specific organization; this is referred to as an enterprise cloud. This form of computing normally depends on the ability to share resources so as to be able to achieve economies of scale and coherence (Figure 8.1).

Figure 8.1. Some of the advantages of cloud computing is the ability to decouple the management at the application and operating system level, an increase in reliability, flexible scaling, and reduced costs

Source: http://souqi.ps/2019/04/23/leading-cloud-data-choices-the-key-criteria-of-selecting-the-electronic-data-area-for-your-enterprise/ (accessed on 3 April 2020).

The people who advocate for hybrid and public clouds state that this form of computing provides companies with the opportunity to lower the information technology infrastructure costs up front. They also state that it makes it possible for companies to make sure that their applications are faster in terms of their performance, in addition to having less maintenance and a level of increased manageability. It also allows IT teams to adjust the resources in a faster manner and provide a high capability of computing performance.

The providers of cloud services normally utilize a model for pay-as-you-go. This is advantageous in situations with unexpected expenses or with no prior knowledge on cloud pricing models.

Growth in cloud computing has mostly been due to the availability of storage devices, low-cost computers, and high-capacity networks, service-oriented architecture, and hardware virtualization. The most widely used operating system by 2019 was Linux.

8.2. CONCEPTS THAT ARE SIMILAR TO CLOUD COMPUTING

Cloud computing was developed with the aim of allowing users to gain an advantage from the different technologies that are commonly used, without the user having to acquire a deep knowledge for each of these different technologies. It also aims at reducing the costs that are involved in the integration of these technologies, and also allows the users to pay full attention to the tasks they are aiming to accomplish, rather than having to deal with some of the obstacles that come with Information and Technology.

Virtualization software is the main enabling technology that is used in cloud computing. This software helps in separating the computing device that is physically available into a single or many more devices that are virtual, whereby; each one of them can be utilized and managed for the performance of tasks in computing. It is possible to allocate and use idle computing resources in a much more efficient manner, with operating system-level virtualization which mainly work through the creation of scalable systems that are of many independent computing devices. Virtualization normally helps in providing the dexterity that is needed for speeding up Information Technology operations, and for reducing expenses by being able to increase the level of infrastructure use (Godbole, 2013).

The process that is available for use by the user for providing resources on-demand can be automated by autonomic computing. By reducing the level of involvement by the user, the process is sped up by automation, the cost of labor is reduced, and the possibility of human errors is also lowered. For the provision of metrics for the used services, cloud computing normally utilizes concepts from utility computing. This form of computing deals with quality of service and reliability of other computing models.

Some of the concepts that are similar in characteristics with cloud computing are:

1. **Computer Bureau:** These are bureau service providers of computer services. They were created in the early 60s, after time-sharing, OS were developed. They made it possible for the division and selling of services provided by some mainframe computers as commodities that are fungible. They were able to grow at a steady rate due to the development of the first modems, and telecommunications. This is because they had the ability to immediately allow immediate access to the facilities of the computer from the premises of the customers themselves (Figure 8.2).

Figure 8.2. *Above is a picture of the first ever computer bureau or commercial computer. It was considered a mathematical genius that was eight feet tall. It was able to classify citizens in a sixth of a second according to their income, employment, birthplace, age group, residence, education, and sex marital status.*

Source:-https://time.com/4271506/census-bureau-computer-history/?amp=true (accessed on 3 April 2020).

2. **Client-Server Model:** This is an application structure that is well distributed. It partitions workloads between resource or service providers (servers) and requesters of the service (clients). Most of the time, servers and clients use a computer network to communicate on separate hardware. Sometimes, however, both the server and client may be residing in a common system. Server programs, either one or more, are run by server hosts, which work

by sharing any of their resources, however, they make a request for service or content from the server. Communication sessions are therefore initiated by clients with servers, which normally wait for requests that are being brought forward. Some of the computer applications that utilize this model include the World Wide Web (WWW), network printing, and e-mail.

3. **Fog Computing:** This is an architectural form of computing that normally utilizes edge devices for carrying out many different types of local communication, storage, and computation that are routed over the backbone of the internet. In addition, this type of computing is able to use the network level to handle data, on client side, end user through smart devices, for example mobile devices, rather than having to send data to a location that is remote for processing.
4. **Grid Computing:** This form of computing normally utilizes different computer resources that are widely distributed, so as to achieve a common goal. One can think of this as a distributed system with workloads that are not interactive, all involving many files. These computers are normally more dispersed geographically and heterogeneously in comparison to cluster computers. Despite the fact that it is possible to dedicate a single grid to a specific application, grids are mostly used for many other reasons. They are also considered a form of computing that is well distributed, all which are composed of computers that are network loosely coupled, where all of them act together to ensure the performance of large tasks. Grid or distributed computing, in certain applications, can be considered a unique form of parallel computing that depends on computers that are equipped with network interfaces, power supplies, storage, onboard CPUs, etc. Therefore, having the ability to be connected to computer networks, which may either, be public or private, through a network interface that is conventional, for example, an Ethernet connection. In contrast, the supercomputer has a notion that is traditional, meaning the available processors are connected through a computer bus that has a locally high speed.
5. **Utility Computing:** This is also referred to as computer utility. It is a model that oversees the availability of infrastructure management and directs computing resources to the user on demand. It also charges users for special services instead of providing a flat rate.

Just like grid computing and other types of computing that are on demand, the utility model aims at maximizing the level of efficiency during the utilization of resources, and/or for lowering the costs that are associated. Packaging of system resources as metered services, for example services, storage, and computation, is referred to as utility. For acquiring computer resources, this model provides the benefit of either a low or no initial costs. This is achieved by renting the resources instead.

6. **Mainframe Computers:** These computers are mainly used by huge companies for applications that are considered critical, such as processing transactions, census, and enterprise resource planning, and processing of bulk data. These computers are much larger, and their processing power is much more than that of other computers, such as personal computers (PCs), workstations, servers, and minicomputers. Originally, the term was used to refer to mainframes that were used for housing the main memory and CPU of traditional computers. Later on, it was mainly used to differentiate commercial machines that were considered high end, from those units that were less powerful. Most of the computer systems that were used for large scale purposes were created in the 60s; however, they have continually developed over time. Most of the mainframe computers that are used today are mostly used as servers (Puntambekar, 2009) (Figure 8.3).

Figure 8.3. Mainframe computers are similar to cloud technologies due to the fact that they are also used by large companies with a lot of data to process. Similarly, cloud storage is able to store a large amount of information

Source: https://byte-notes.com/uses-of-a-mainframe-computer/ (accessed on 3 April 2020).

8.3. CHARACTERISTICS OF CLOUD COMPUTING

There are several characteristics of cloud computing:

1. **Agility:** It is possible to improve the level of agility of organizations that use cloud computing, due to the fact that it helps in increasing the level of flexibility that users have by either expanding, adding, or re-provisioning the resources for technological infrastructure.
2. **Reduced Costs:** Cloud providers claim that the use of cloud computing can help in lowering the expenses used in the incorporation of these technologies. Capital expenditures are converted by public cloud delivery models such as purchasing servers, to expenditures that are operational. This helps in reducing the entry barriers due to the fact that infrastructure is accessible because of third parties making it available, and it is not necessary to buy it for one time or for intensive computing tasks that are infrequent.

- The independence of the location and device allow for users to have a higher level of accessibility to the systems via the web browser, regardless of where they are or the device being used, such as a mobile phone. Users are able to connect to cloud computing networks from wherever they are, because the infrastructure is offsite.
- It is easy to maintain cloud computing applications-this is because they do not have to be installed on the computer of the user, and they are available for access at any time and place, even when traveling or working in a different location.
- The fact that they are multi-tenant means that they allow for sharing of costs and resources over many different users. This leads to: centralized infrastructure in low cost locations. An example is an increase in demand for electricity such that users are not required to pay or supply equipment to achieve high load-levels.
- Information and technology experts monitor the performance, all of them from the providers of the service, in addition to having the construction of architectures that are loosely coupled via the system interface.
- It is also possible to increase the level of productivity when many users are able to simultaneously work on the same data, instead of having to wait for the data to be saved and emailed. It helps in promoting time saving because it is not necessary to re-enter the

data after matching fields and users also does not need to ensure installation of upgrades to the software on their devices.

- Improved reliability-using multiple sites that are redundant helps in improving the level of reliability, thus making cloud computing that is well designed, suitable for ensuring continuity and recovery in disasters in businesses.
- They help in providing elasticity and scalability with the help of resources that have been dynamically provisioned, whereby peak loads do not have to be engineered by users. This makes it possible for users to ensure that it is possible to either scale up or down when there is an increase in the usage need or when there is no use for the resources respectively. Approaches that are continuously emerging when it comes to the management of elasticity include using techniques for machine learning (ML) for proposing elasticity models that are efficient.
- Centralization of data and increasing resources they are focused on security can help in improving security, however, there may be some issues when it comes to losing control of data that is sensitive, and lacking security for the kernels that are stored. In comparison to other traditional systems, security in this cloud computing is considered often as good, and sometimes even better, due to the fact that providers of this service are able to make sure that resources are devoted into dealing with security issues that the users may not be able to deal with, due to finances or lack of technical skills. There may still be an increase in the complexity of security, especially when there is distribution of Information over an area that is much wider, of over many more devices, in addition to unrelated users sharing multi-tenant systems. It may also be impossible or difficult for the user to access security audit logs. The users' motivation to maintain a level of control over the infrastructure and also avoid the loss of control when it comes to security of the information helps in promoting private cloud installations (Figure 8.4).

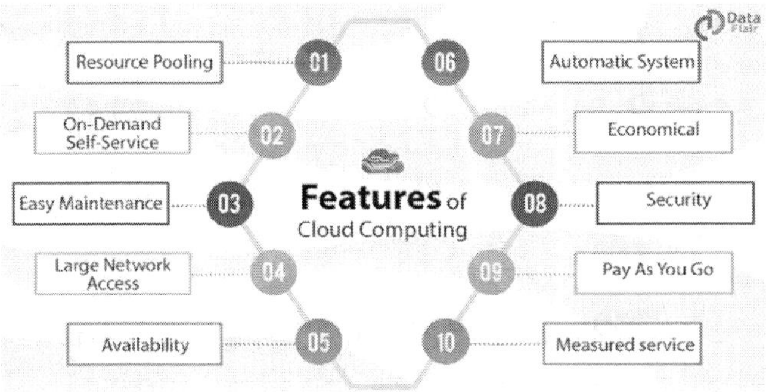

Figure 8.4. Above are some of the main features of cloud computing, which is becoming much more popular. The reason for popularity is that many organizations that seek for areas to store large amounts of information.

Source: https://data-flair.training/blogs/features-of-cloud-computing/amp/ (accessed on 3 April 2020).

There are five main characteristics identified by National Institute of Standards and Technology. These are:

- **Broad Network Access:** The networks regulates the availability of computing capabilities that can be accessed from workstations, laptops, tablets, and mobile phones.
- **Self-Service that is on Demand:** Computing capabilities can unilaterally be provided by consumers in an automatic manner, inclusive of network storage and server time, as required without having to physically interact with each of the providers of the service.
- **Resource Pooling:** The computing resources of the provider are pooled so as to have the ability to cater for many consumers with the use of the multi-tenant model, with resources that are virtually and physically different and assigned and reassigned dynamically in accordance with the demand of the consumers.
- **Rapid Elasticity:** It is possible to elastically provision and release capabilities, sometimes even automatically, so as to rapidly scale inward and outward commensurate in accordance with the demand. Most times, the consumer view the available capabilities for provisioning to mostly appear in an unlimited manner, and at any time and quantity, they can be appropriated.

- **Measured Service:** Cloud systems work through their ability to optimize and control the use of resources by having to leverage their capability to meter at a certain level of abstraction that is specific to the service being provided, such as active user accounts, bandwidth, processing, and storage. It is possible to monitor, control, and report the use of resources, thus being able to provide a level of transparency for both the consumer and the provider of the service that is being used.

8.4. ADVANTAGES AND DISADVANTAGES OF CLOUD COMPUTING

Some of the advantages of cloud computing include:

- **They are Inxpensive:** This is one of the greatest advantages that this technology can provide. It allows for the user to save a substantial amount of money due to the fact that it does not require the user to invest in physical hardware. It also does not require for the user to high trained professionals to ensure that the hardware is maintained.
- **High Speed:** Users are able to use minimal clicks to deploy services in a faster manner. This means that is possible to acquire the resources that the system requires in a shorter time period.
- **Back-Up and Restore Data:** In the cloud, once data is stored, it is very simple to receive back-ups and also recoveries, which is a process that normally takes a lot of time on premise.
- **Automatic Software Integration:** This could normally integrate software in an automatic manner. This means that the user is not required to make more effort in customizing and integrating the applications in accordance to their preferences.
- **Reliability:** The cloud technologies normally update the users on any alterations that occur immediately.
- **Mobility:** It is possible to access all the services that the cloud provides either in the office or even in remote locations. All the user requires is a connection to the internet.
- **Unlimited Storage Capacity:** The storage capacity offered by the cloud is almost limitless. With nominal monthly fees, it is possible to achieve expansion of the storage capacity provided by the cloud.

- **Collaboration:** This technology allows for communication between users from different ends of the world, thus promoting collaboration in a manner that is highly secure and convenient.
- **Quick Deployment:** with this technology, the user is able to achieve fast deployment. Once the user chooses to switch to utilizing the cloud, they are able to access the services in a very short time period. However, this time can vary depending on the type of technology being used (Figure 8.5).

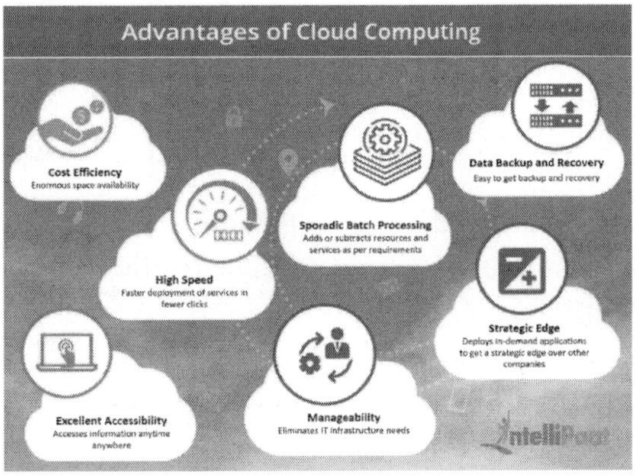

Figure 8.5. *Above is a pictorial illustration of some of the main advantages that user can benefit from when they purchase cloud computing.*

Source: https://intellipaat.com/blog/tutorial/amazon-web-services-aws-tutorial/advantages-and-disadvantages-of-cloud-computing/ (accessed on 3 April 2020).

Some of the other benefits that the cloud provides include:

- Pay-per-use.
- API access available.
- Effective and fast virtualization.
- Multi-tenancy.
- Web-based control and interfaces.
- Low-cost software.
- On demand self-service.
- Advanced online security.
- Device and location independence.

- Resilient computing.
- Always available and able to adjust to the increasing demand.

Some of the disadvantages of cloud computing are:

- **They Have Varying Performance:** Using the cloud means that the running application is using the server at the same time as many other applications being used by other business and users. The shared resource could have performance issues if there is a DDOS attack on a tenant or even greedy behavior.
- **Technical Issues:** It is possible to have some technical issues and even an outage when using cloud technology. Even with high standards of maintenance, these problems may cause issues to even the best service providers.
- **The Cloud Poses Security Threats:** As a customer, before paying for cloud services, it is important to know that using the cloud means sharing all of your information to the service provider, and therefore a third party. This makes it possible for hackers to gain access to this information, and it could get into the wrong hands.
- **Downtime:** While working with cloud computing, it is important to consider downtime. It may occur due to factors on the side of the provider such as service maintenance, low internet connectivity, power loss, etc.
- **Internet Connectivity:** In cloud computing, it is important to have good internet connectivity. Without an internet connection, it is not possible to access the cloud. There is no other way the user is able to access information or data from the cloud.
- **Low Bandwidth:** The bandwidth usage for the user is normally limited by many providers of cloud services. In a situation where the client supersedes the provided allowance, the extra cost can be very high.
- **Lack of Support:** Customers do not get to enjoy proper support from cloud computing companies because it is hardly ever provided. They tend to only provide online help and FAQs, and this can be time consuming and tedious, especially for users who are not well knowledgeable on technology.

Despite all the advantages and disadvantages, it is evident that cloud computing is a part of network-based computing that is developing very fast. Enterprises, developers, simple users, different organizations, etc. all get to enjoy the benefits that come with cloud computing.

8.5. SERVICE MODELS

There are three main forms of cloud computing: Software as a service, Platform as a service, and Infrastructure as a service. Each one of them works to provide various levels of control and flexibility over the services being bought. They each also vary when it comes to their relationship with the Information Technology infrastructure that already exists. Due to the many different variations between the types of cloud computing, it is necessary to understand how each one of them works and determine the ones that are best for the user's needs (Godbole, 2013).

8.5.1. Software as a Service (SaaS)

This is a software distribution model that works by making applications available to users through the internet, where a third-party host them, then provides them. This specific model provides many benefits; however, it also has some disadvantages. Some of the main benefits include operational management, compatibility, and accessibility. In addition, this model offers upfront costs that are much lower than downloading and installing traditional software, and this makes them more available to many different users.

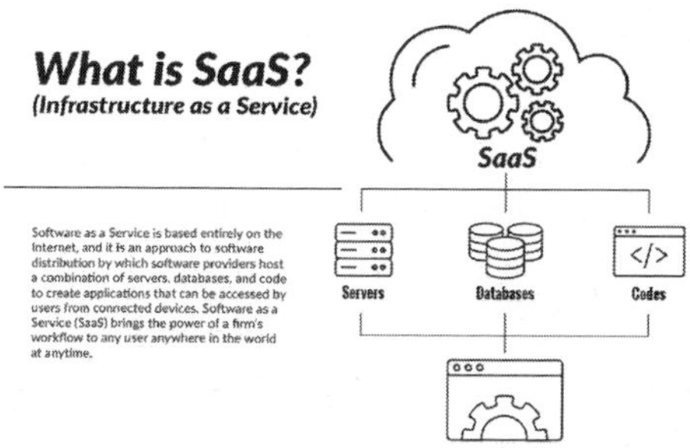

Figure 8.6. Software as a service provides users with codes, databases, and servers to create applications accessed through internet

Source: https://www.atlantic.net/what-is-saas/ (accessed on 3 April 2020).

The main disadvantage of this model is that it cannot work without internet access. This however has become less of an issue, because high speed phone networks like 5G and good broadband deals are becoming more and more available. In addition, some of the applications that use this model are inclusive of an offline mode that allows the user to use the services for basic functions. Looking keenly at the pros and cons of this model can help in better understanding how the model works (Figure 8.6).

The following are some of the main advantages of SaaS:

1. **Accessibility:** One of the greatest advantage is the ability to run on an internet browser, meaning that it is OS-agnostic. You can run the application on Linux, Mac, or Windows machines or on iOS and Android devices. As a result, SaaS is very versatile in a variety of aspects. First, the customer does not have to worry about whether their operating system will be compatible with SaaS applications. SaaS can be mobile-friendly and are utilized in many different circumstances and situations.
2. **Patches and Updates: The** provider makes software updates from the source without causing any negative effects on user's side. This is very different from the traditional software, where a level of endpoint security and compatibility testing is required before the application of patches and updates. This means that the model works while avoiding the disadvantages of testing that normally lead to the slowing down of the cycle of development It does this while still being able to ensure that the updates on security are immediately applied, in comparison to the traditional software that remains susceptible to attacks up to the point that the staff finishes the testing.
3. **Hardware:** The fact that a customer does not have to make an initial investment to use the SaaS application, is one of the greatest selling points of this model. The traditional software requires compatible software configuration with PCs and desktops. However, with SaaS a user is able to access the tools for running the software through cloud applications. In addition, this model can be easily scaled. This means that if a need arises for adding or eliminating users, the business can make an adjustment to the billing plan. This is in contrast with buying more hardware when the need arises to add more users, or even having to shelve the electronic devices that were initially expensive to purchase, when there is a need to reduce the number of users.
4. **Market Reach:** This means that the service provider is able

to supply the model to many users and businesses, rather than having to supply the service to a select and limited target. This helps in making the model much more accessible to many different businesses and users, and also making it much cheaper. The users benefit from this through the high level of accessibility to services that were previously not as available, which helps to expand and improve business services, general opportunities, and productivity.

5. **Storage and Saving:** When using traditional software, the user has to purchase disaster recovery plans and online cloud storage to prevent data loss. On the other hand, SaaS routinely saves data on the cloud. This is also very advantageous because the users are able to change devices from one to another without losing any data, all through the simple act of logging into an account on the device being utilized.
6. **Analytics and Data:** Due to the fact that a centralized platform is used for running everything in the SaaS model, it is much easier to ensure that data is captured and provided for use in analytics. The users of this software are able to have access to visualizations and intelligence and reporting tools, all which can help in providing insights that are valuable into the operations. This helps in streamlining workflow and making saving efficient. The service provider also has no concerns about piracy due to the fact that access is based on a paid subscription. Piracy may lead to damaging both the pricing and access models thus costing the supplier.

In general, this model provides many advantages that benefit both the users and the suppliers. Despite the fact that most enterprises choose to use their own services for cloud management where they orchestrate between sites and devices for controlling of their own data, most of the personal users and small businesses choose this model which helps in developing, expanding, and providing much more value to the users.

8.5.2. Infrastructure as a Service (IaaS)

Here, the infrastructure components found in the traditional data centers are hosted by the cloud provider. This is inclusive of networking hardware, storage, and servers, in addition to the hypervisor layer. The provider is also able to supply many different services for the accompaniment of the infrastructure components. This is inclusive of load balancing and clustering, security, log access, monitoring, and detailed billing, in addition to storage resiliency, such as recovery, replication, and backup (Figure 8.7).

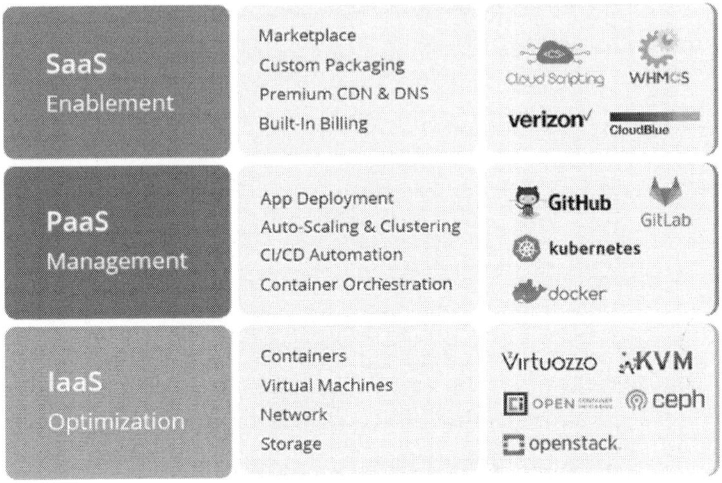

Figure 8.7. *Above are the differences in what the different models provide to their users, and the different service providers for each service.*

Source: https://jelastic.com/blog/turnkey-multi-cloud-paas-freedom/saas-paas-iaas/ (accessed on 3 April 2020).

IaaS services are policy-driven; meaning that the users are able to ensure implementation of higher levels of orchestration and automation so as to ensure that the necessary infrastructure tasks are performed. For example, it is possible for the user to perform implementation of policies for driving load balancing, so as to achieve maintenance of the applications performance and availability (Godbole, 2013).

The users of this model normally have access to the services and resources through a wide area network, for example the Internet and they are therefore able to utilize the services that are being provided, for the installation of the elements that are remaining in an application stack. For example, user is able to create virtual machines; deploy middleware, for example databases; install the workload of an enterprise into the virtual machine; create storage buckets for backups and workloads; and install operating systems (OS) in each virtual machine, just by logging into the IaaS platform. They are then able to utilize the services being provided to deal with disaster recovery, troubleshoot issues to do with the application, balance network traffic, monitor performance, and even tracking costs, among others.

The provider is expected to participate in any cloud computing model. The provider is an organization that is also referred to as a third-party, and deals with providing IaaS services. Two of the main examples of Independent IaaS providers include Google Cloud Platform and Amazon Web Services (Godbole, 2013).

- **Advantages and Disadvantages of IaaS:** IaaS is cost-efficient, faster, and easier to operate a workload without need of buying, managing, and supporting the underlying infrastructure. This model allows an enterprise to lease or rent the underlying infrastructure from other businesses (Figure 8.8).

Advantages/Disadvantages of PaaS vs IaaS

Model	Advantage	Disadvantage
PaaS	**Business:** • Low TCO • Accelerates Innovation **Technical:** • Better/Easier DevOps • Mitigates Platform Risks	**Business:** • Harder Transition to Cloud **Technical:** • Application Portability Issues • Not as mature as IaaS • Different Codebases for Cloud and On-premise
IaaS	**Business:** • Quick transition to Cloud **Technical:** • Mature ISV Ecosystem • Complete Control • Solution Portability	**Business:** • Expensive to Operate • Slows Down Innovation • Security Risks from Unpatched Servers **Technical:** • Difficult to Maintain Legacy Apps • Requires Rigorous Processes for Enabling DevOps • Requires Rigorous Server Maintenance Processes

Figure 8.8. Choosing between PaaS and IaaS can be difficult. Above is a comparison that can help make the decision. IaaS is much more commonly used because it provided a quick cloud transition

Source: https://www.slideshare.net/Manojksh/cloud-computing-opportunities-definitions-options-and-risks (accessed on 3 April 2020).

For experimental, temporary, or inconsistent workloads, this is the most effective model. For example, when a new software product is being developed by a certain enterprise, it is advisable for the business to utilize this model to test the new software product, because it is much more cost-effective and easier to host. Once the business has been able to test and refine the new software, they are then able to remove it from the IaaS model, so as to use a deployment method that is much more traditional and in-house. In the same manner, it is possible for the enterprise to use that new software with the long-term IaaS deployment, which is still considered much cheaper in long term commitment.

Generally, the users of this model normally pay on a per use basis which is either by the month, week, or even by the hour. Some of the providers of this model normally include an additional cost that the users have to pay which is based on the amount of space they use on virtual machines. Pay-as-you-go model eliminates costs associated with deployment of in-house software and hardware.

When business cannot utilize third-party providers, they still can use a private cloud that has been built on premises, which provides the same level of scalability and control that SaaS provides. However, private cloud model is much more expensive.

8.5.3. Platform as a Service (PaaS)

This is a cloud computing model whereby the provider is able to provide software and hardware tools over the internet, normally those that are required for the development of applications. The providers normally use their own infrastructure to host the software and hardware. Due to this, developers using this model are freed from the need to ensure installation of in-house software and hardware for the development or running of new applications.

It is important to note that this model does not fully replace the IT infrastructure of a business. Instead, it normally ensures the incorporation of the different components that are found in the underlying cloud infrastructure, such as storage services, networking equipment, middleware, databases, servers, and OS (Sklar, 2011).

All of the functions that are mentioned above are maintained, configured, operated, and owned by the providers of the service. This model also helps in providing some additional resources such as development tools, libraries, programming languages, and database management systems. The service provider is able to build and supply an environment that is optimized and resilient where the users are able to install data sets and applications. The users are able to pay attention on the creation and running of the applications instead of having to pay attention to the construction and maintenance that is required for the services and underlying infrastructure.

Most of the products that use this model aim at the development of software. This model helps in offering infrastructure for computing and storage, as well as testing services, compiling services, vision management, and event text editing, all which allow developers to quickly and efficiently create new software. Regardless of physical location, PaaS products can also promote the teams that are developing the software to work together and collaborate (Sklar, 2011).

The architecture of this model works to keep the underlying infrastructure away from the eyes of other developers in the users. Due to this, there is a huge similarity between this model and the server-less computing and function as a service architecture where the providers of the cloud service ensure management and running of the server, as well as controlling of resource distribution.

1. **How Does it Work:** The provider's hosted infrastructure works to provide the cloud service to the users, most frequently through access to a web browser. It is possible to ensure the delivery of this service through private, public, and hybrid clouds for the delivery of services such as Java development and application hosting (Figure 8.9).

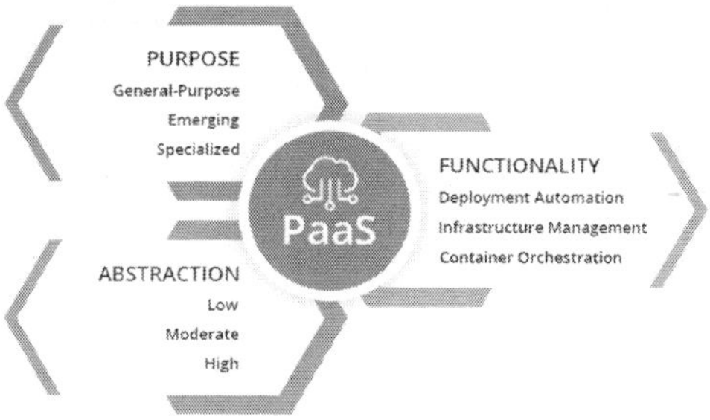

Figure 8.9. *Above is an explanation on the different types of PaaS. When it comes to its functionality, it is able to provide application deployment and container orchestration.*

Source: https://jelastic.com/blog/what-is-paas-platform-as-a-service-types-explained/ (accessed on 3 April 2020).

Some of the other PaaS services that are provided include:

- Database Integration;
- Information security;
- Web service integration;
- Application testing and deployment;
- Application development and design; and
- Collaboration of the development team.

In the same way as the other models, the users pay for these services on a per use basis. However, there are some providers of these services that normally have a flat monthly fee that the user has to pay to access the applications and the platform.

2. **Advantages and Disadvantages:** The greatest advantage of this model is its simplicity and convenience for the users. This is achieved due to the fact that the provider is able to supply most of the infrastructure as well as IT services that the users can use at any location through a web browser. The businesses are able to pay on a per use basis, thus getting rid of the extra costs that come with the software and hardware for traditional models.

Despite all the advantages, one of the disadvantages of this model is resilience or service availability. If there is a service outage on the side of the provider or even any other disruption in the infrastructure, this can greatly cause a negative effect on the user's side, and lead to lapses of productivity that are costly (Sklar, 2011).

Another disadvantage is vendor lock-in, due to the fact that users are not able to easily move most of the data produced and services available from one PaaS product to another product that is in competition. Before committing to a PaaS provider, the client needs to consider all the risks of vendor lock-in and service downtime.

Another potential issue is internal changes to products. For example, if a specific programming language is not being supported anymore by the provider, it can lead to a negative effect on the user's side which can be disruptive and difficult. The user is expected to follow the service road map that is provided by the provider so as to comprehend the plans of the provider and how these plans will affect the product's capabilities and environment (Sklar, 2011).

Developers now have access to many different types of PaaS. These will be discussed in subsections.

8.5.3.1. Public PaaS

This mainly works in the public cloud. It provides the user with the opportunity to have full control on the deployment of software, while the provider of the cloud ensures that all the other major components that are needed to host the applications are delivered, such as storage system networks, servers, databases, and OS. The providers of the public PaaS provide middleware that ensures setting up, configuration, and controlling of databases and servers without having to set up the infrastructure that is required. Due to this, IaaS and public PaaS run together, where PaaS operates on top of IaaS This is beneficial, however, it also means that the user has to use this specific option, whether or not it is the one they want.

Public PaaS has been adopted by many different small and medium size businesses, however, the bigger enterprises and organizations do not want to use it due to the fact that it is highly related to the public cloud. This is one of the main reasons why there are many compliance issues and regulations issues that come together with the development of applications within the public cloud (RichiNayak, 2008).

8.5.3.2. Private PaaS

This model mainly delivers the agility of the public PaaS, while being able to maintain the benefits, compliance, security, and sometimes even cheaper prices of the private data center. The providers normally deliver this model as software inside the firewall of the user which most of the time is maintained in the data center that is found in the company. Any type of infrastructure can be used for the development of private PaaS, and these models are able to function in the private cloud specific to the company.

This model provides an opportunity for organization to lower the high costs that many companies face, ensure improvement in the use of internal resources, and for improved service to developers. In addition, it provides developers with the opportunity for deployment and management of the applications while still being able to abide to the strict privacy and security requirements (RichiNayak, 2008) (Figure 8.10).

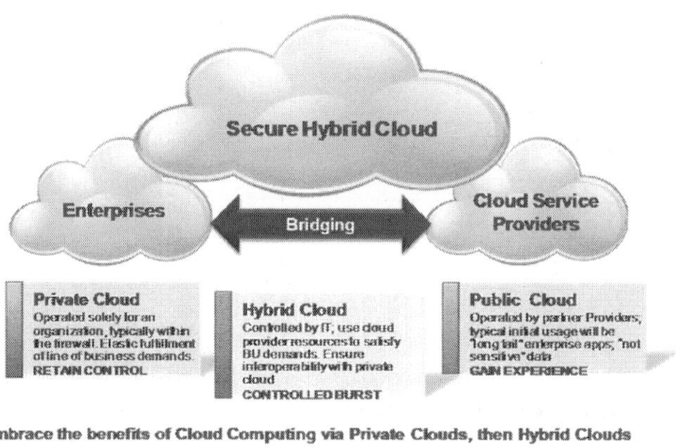

Figure 8.10. *PaaS provides different cloud computing opportunities. Hybrid PaaS provides benefits of public and private PaaS*

Source: http://knowledgeblob.com/technology/cloud-computing-levels-iaas-paas-saas-and-deployment-models-public-private-hybrid/ (accessed on 3 April 2020).

Hybrid PaaS is a combination of the private and public PaaS for provision with the flexibility of cost efficiency that the private model provides due to owning internal infrastructure and the large capacity that the public model provides. This model normally uses the hybrid cloud.

8.5.3.3. Communication PaaS

This is a cloud-based platform that provides developers with the opportunity to include real-time communications into the applications without having to invest in the back-end interfaces and infrastructure. Normally, communications in real-time only happen in applications that have specifically been built for this specific use. These include WhatsApp, FaceTime, Skype, and the traditional phone (RichiNayak, 2008).

This model ensures the provision of a development framework that is complete to create features for communications in real-time without needing a framework to be built by the developer, including sample code, prebuilt application, software tools, and standards-based application programming interfaces.

The providers of this model can help the users all through the process of development through the provision of product documentation and support. There are some providers who are also able to provide kits for developing software in addition to libraries that can make it easier for companies to build applications on various mobile and desktop platforms. This model allows the teams developing the software to save on time to market, human resources, and infrastructure (RichiNayak, 2008).

8.5.3.4. Mobile PaaS

This model helps to configure mobile applications through using an integrated development environment that is paid. One does not need to have coding skills to be able to modify mobile PaaS. A web browser can be used to deliver the service. The leasing of this service is normally done every month and the fee varies based on the number of devices and features supported.

This model normally provides an object-oriented, drag-and-drop interface. Developers can create native applications for various mobile OS (Stanek, 2014).

This model is mainly used by companies to create applications that help in providing good customer-facing an internal use. This promotes productivity and features Bring Your Own Device (BYOD) environment applications without needing the developers of mobile applications or additional IT support.

8.5.3.5. Open PaaS

Open PaaS is a business-oriented collaboration platform that is open-source, cross-platform, and free. It provides useful web applications such as mail, contacts, and calendar applications. The main reason this model was designed was to provide users with the opportunity to promote the deployment of new applications in a faster manner, with the aim of ensuring development of a PaaS technology that has a commitment to business collaborative applications, especially those that are used on hybrid clouds (Stanek, 2014).

- **Uses of PaaS:** This model is mainly used to deploy mobile applications. However, there are various companies and developers that also utilize it for building applications that can be used in many different platforms due to the fact that it is able to provide a dynamic and flexible solution that can ensure the creation of applications that can be supported by all devices.

PaaS can also be used in DevOps tools. It is able to provide features for lifecycle management of applications, in addition to certain features that help in incorporating the product development methodologies of a company. DevOps teams are able to use the model for the insertion of continuous integration tools that are cloud based, all which provide updates without the production of downtime. In addition, when following the waterfall model, companies are able to ensure the deployment of updates with the use of the same console used for employing everyday management.

The time to market of the application can be reduced with the use of this model, through the automatization or complete elimination of maintenance and housekeeping tasks. In addition, it can help in decreasing the management of infrastructure through the reduction of the stress that is present in the management of infrastructure that is scalable. It also helps in eliminating the complexities of distributing new dependent services, scaling, and load balancing. This is because the providers take responsibility of controlling these tasks instead of the developers (Figure 8.11).

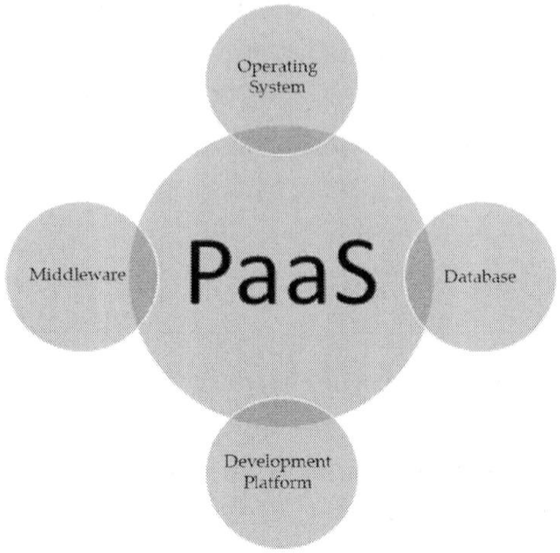

Figure 8.11. *Development platform, databases, middleware, and an operating system are some of the services that users are able to enjoy when they purchase the PaaS model.*

Source: https://www.mbaskool.com/business-concepts/it-and-systems/13294-platform-as-a-service-paas.html (accessed on 3 April 2020).

In addition, PaaS is now also able to support newer programming technologies and languages, such as server-less containers and functions, allowing the developers to now utilize this model for the introduction of newer channels of growth technically. This is considered very important for industries that have a problem with technical change due to its slow process, such as manufacturing and banking. PaaS allows for the adaption of these organizations to the new offers they provide without the need to completely change the process of business (Stanek, 2014).

8.6. DATA PRIVACY AND SECURITY

One of the greatest issues that we are forced to deal with in this modern time when it comes to the Internet, are cyber-attacks. For the longest time, they have been looming over us just like a black cloud waiting to pour at any point in time. The development of tactics for cyber security has helped in maintaining a barrier against these forms of attack. These however need to be updated constantly so as to prevent breaches that may occur to the system while still under the protection of these cyber security tactics. Systems holding sensitive data are the most susceptible to hackers and in this situation cloud, computing is one of the major targets. This is the main reason way data privacy and security in cloud computing is very important, so as to prevent susceptibility to schemes that are generated by hackers (Godbole, 2013).

8.6.1. Data Privacy

The protection of data is one of the main concerns when it to comes to privacy and security in cloud computing. There are very many users who have used the cloud to store important and sensitive data, making it much more complex to ensure that every single bit of Information is secure.

Data security has become a very huge issue in cloud computing, where there is distribution of different information to different devices and machines for storage including mobile devices such as wireless sensor networks and smart phones; servers; and PCs. If by any chance there is neglecting of the privacy and security in cloud computing, then the sensitive data of each user is put a risk, providing the opportunity to hackers for easy cyber breaching into systems, so as to use this sensitive information from malicious intent, by exploitation of users (Puntambekar, 2009).

Cloud computing provides advantages that the users enjoy almost every day and it has become part of the user's lives. This is why privacy and security in cloud computing need to work efficiently and effectively for the users to be able to invest in these services. Providers should make sure that they gain they users trust so as to have the opportunity of becoming a consistent part of the environment for cloud computing service provision.

8.6.2. Data Security

The environment for cloud computing is used for many different reasons son that involve the computing and storage of data. Being able to easily access the functions of the cloud provides users with the opportunity to effortlessly work on their tasks for computing, in addition to simply accessing the data through any connection to the Internet. The main reason why cloud computing is very popular and commonly used through its use of trust function is due to the data protection as well as its security in regards to information of specific users that is stored on the cloud (Figure 8.12).

Figure 8.12. *Above are some of the factors that cloud computing service providers should aim at when it comes to data privacy and security*

Source: https://www.quora.com/What-is-cloud-computing-security (accessed on 3 April 2020).

Large companies are also able to use cloud computing services. This provides them with the advantage of savings costs that would otherwise be spent on hardware and software infrastructure for computing services. Because of these services, large companies have been able to ensure expansion and prosperity of businesses. Actually, cloud computing has helped in decreasing labor power division and it has helped in promoting the provision of more time to the development of business plans that are strategic as well as new innovative ideas.

Due to the fact that its use is consistent and efficient, cloud computing has become a major tool for use in large scale, such as for the prosperity of companies and businesses and also for use in small scale where almost everyone globally uses cloud computing as an important part of their daily lives. Not only is it highly accessible, but cloud computing can provide high and quality performance services for computations, at rates that are much lower (Puntambekar, 2009).

This is one of the main reasons why there are so many people using cloud computing but what makes it more important is that providers are able to provide a cloud system that uses methods that are efficient and effective for ensuring data security and privacy. This is because a breach in data may lead to breaking the trust of the clients. This means that providers have to ensure the creation of a solid line of defense to prevent any of these attacks from occurring.

8.7. LIMITATIONS OF CLOUD COMPUTING

There are many companies that use cloud computing and there are also many users that use it. Despite the fact that there are many advantages, that we have been able to discuss above, these programs can also pose a couple of disadvantages. Before purchasing these services, there are a couple of things that one needs to consider. These are discussed in subsections.

8.7.1. They Depend on a Network Connection

So as to enjoy the advantages of cloud computing, an Internet connection is a requirement, in either the workplace or even at home. Sadly, this is not something that one can compromise on. So as to retrieve and send files in the cloud, one requires an Internet connection.

So as to use virtual machines, the user requires a network, whether or not they are using the infrastructure as a service model. If by any chance the user loses the Internet connection due to an outage or a storm, this may lead to experiencing downtime. However, a business continuity plan can easily be developed with the use of a good hosted service provider. The good hosted service provider can also help in promising the delivery of a service level agreement which has an uptime of more than 95%.

8.7.2. Features Are Limited

Not all the providers of cloud computing provide equal services. This means that when using cloud computing for backup and storage, it is important to be working with a provider that is able to offer the value of bandwidth that is unlimited. It is also possible to experience a limitation in accessibility and storage space. Using SaaS services may normally start with a package that is free; however, the user will have to pay for extra space and premium offerings. This can be worth it if it is at the expense of growing a business.

Partnering with hosted service providers can provide an answer to the concern of features being limited because they are able to meet back up needs, virtualization, and cloud storage that may be required for now and even later with the growing needs. Generally, it may be important to work together with providers that also include a hosted service package at the highest value for this space and features that are required by either the users or the business.

8.7.3. It Is Possible to Lose Control

Purchasing cloud computing services means having to trust a third-party to ensure security and privacy of your data. This means that you trust that they will ensure maintenance of their servers and data centers with the same care or even more than you would. The clients how to keep faith in the providers of cloud computing services that they will be able to ensure security and compliance of their data centers both online and physically (Figure 8.13).

Figure 8.13. *Cloud outage can be caused by either a power outage on the side of the provider, or by a storm.*

Source: https://www.bmc.com/blogs/cloud-outage/ (accessed on 3 April 2020).

If the business or user considers this a major concern, it is possible for them to work with a partner that has local contacts. This involves speaking with representatives one on one, who are able to address the concerns to do with access and also in learning about the methods that are being used by the Hosted services company to make sure that the safety and integrity of the cloud servers is consistent.

8.7.4. Security

Hacking cloud computing has presented very many cases in the past few years and this has shown that it is not possible to fully trust that the providers can be as secure as they say they are. Especially when it comes to businesses, they are not able to afford the leakage of sensitive information about their company or of the clients, because this can lead to many legal issues. SaaS users tend to struggle with this disadvantage more than those who are using hosted providers. Due to how popular SaaS providers are, hackers normally tend to target them more frequently and in an easier manner in comparison to hosted providers.

8.7.5. Technical Issues

When users experience technical issues, they should contact the providers of this service for technical support. It is not possible to deal with cloud computing issues in-house and there are some providers that are not able to offer technical support around the clock. This concern can be remediated in an easy way through picking hosted service providers that are able to offer 24/7-hour support to the users.

Chapter 9

How Web Technologies Are Changing Marketing?

CONTENTS

9.1. INTRODUCTION

Technology has revolutionized marketing by making the promotions more customized and immersive for users, and forming ecosystems which are more cohesive and directed for marketers. However, it's not only the interface between different brands and individuals that have undergone transformation. Emerging technologies in advertising have infiltrated the infrastructure and frameworks on which businesses are built upon, adding value to almost all marketing processes even up to procurement.

In 2013, it was estimated that roughly 47% of American-based marketers relied on creativity to influence marketing strategy. In 2012, the number stood at 29% but by 2022, it will go up to 56% of the marketers. Personal creativity combined with technology shall play a big role in deciding where and how businesses can engage with their clients (Figure 9.1).

Figure 9.1. *The internet has opened up new doors of advertising that were previously unavailable.*

Source: http://www.hitzsoft.com (accessed on 3 April 2020).

9.2. TECHNOLOGY TODAY

In many cases, technology strategic plans tend to highlight the wrong sections for improvement, very many activities within one go, or even fail to explain the reason why one form of application is more significant than the other. Ineffectual prioritization may ultimately lead to wastage of financial resources and opportunities.

Technology advances rapidly, and may change aspects of society from security to business and so on. Modern advances such as the internet, smartphones, social media, and client relationship management systems significantly affect modern marketing. Innovation helps businesses to grow and thrive, foster relationships, reinforce the effectiveness of companies, allow individuals to learn more about each other, as well as affecting how companies network with prospective clients (Benady, 2014).

Most marketers are beginning to view innovation as an important aspect in terms of progress and growth in business. Marketing is a crucial and strategic tool for increasing your company's efficiency and remaining ahead of your competitors.

While the role of advertising hasn't drastically changed because of innovation, which is the central authority in buyer-seller relationships, still the business attitudes toward the advertising function and marketing principles have all been difficult to separate apart from the change inspired by rapid progress of technology.

With the use of Web technology, consumers can now gain access to masses of data coming from all over the globe; data which is timeless, crucial, and reliable. Through a simple click of the button, clients can gain appropriate insights on businesses and their products. It's possible to compare products online, get cheaper rates, read reviews, and also communicate with others through forums concerning product quality and consumer satisfaction. Besides, the evolution of advertising from the previous year's reveals that technology began as a basic thing, then later transformed into the major marketing force it is today (Benady, 2014).

9.2.1. Product and Pricing

The Web is drastically changes the availability of product and services. For instance, web technology is allowing companies to form new 'packaged' items by offering integrated or related solutions. Through using extranets, it means that some clients may be offered access to the company's internal systems that not only add more value, but further 'lock in' clients to your brand. The growth of the Web is however creating emerging issues with respect to contract rights as well as copyright.

In terms of pricing, The Internet permits for additional information to be acquired easily by clients. Among the side effects is that its way simpler to compare prices therefore making price contests fiercer. Application of computer systems in reducing the overall time and effort needed to produce or deliver products/services simply means that, product suppliers may either improve their margins or provide the same solutions at a reduced rate (Benady, 2014).

9.2.2. Commoditization

This occurs when businesses 'package' new items and services together before offering them, through technology, at reduced rates (the top volume, reduced value approach). Virtual payment (via credit cards) makes the process more appropriate to customers plus can make money collection much quicker and affordable for suppliers-further increasing the probability of rate reductions. Still, the Web can make it quite hard to provide discriminatory pricing (that is, different rates for different client groups). In addition, improvements in database processes could mean that direct advertising is steadily coming to the frontline, therefore allowing new market sections to be effortlessly identified, and permitting the advertiser to beneficially target them.

Furthermore, though permission marketing processes are gaining momentum, they are still undergoing evolution and will become even better in the near future. The Web is also one of the top sources of information-permitting you to stay updated with your competitors' as well as clients' activities. Virtual polls and surveys may yield a considerable amount of extra information about your customers. Besides, it means that its way tougher to maintain any kind of differentiation once your solutions and approaches become clear for everyone-comprising your competitors-to view.

Additionally, the Internet permits you to access a much broader geographical scope than was formerly possible. The Web makes markets a bit more even-therefore allowing the smaller players to contest with larger players and foreign competitors to come into new marketplaces with ease. There are those who claim that the Web is just another medium that needs management, similar to other everyday mediums (such as, warehouses, retail outlets, and direct mail) (Benady, 2014).

9.2.3. Advertisement

In nearly every aspect of brand promotion-such as direct marketing, public relations and personal selling-technology such as-web sites, CD Roms and interactivity apps continue to make significant changes regarding how marketing works in general.

For example, in advertising you need to have a website, which functions as virtual brochure. It is crucial to advertise in order to drive traffic to your site. Besides, you can add a web address to your advertisements for purposes of providing additional information, or capturing client information and orders. Virtual television as well as broadcasting advancements (such as web TV) serves to make mass promotion activities both practical and reasonably priced for much smaller businesses than previously.Moreover, there are different types of fresh advertising media presently available-such as e-posters, banner ads, virtual directory entries, and information kiosks among others. Both interaction and multimedia technologies are inspiring the creative aspects of advertising and direct marketing. Plus database technology together with virtual printing of brief runs of whole color promotional content have had major impacts on direct mailing.

Furthermore, email lists can make it simpler to have systematic and focused communications alongside major customers/clients. The usage of call-centers and computer assistance voice telephony systems are revising the rules on client service and fulfillment (Benady, 2014).

Additionally, brochures, and publications have also become electronic, collaborating, and customized to the particular needs and interests that smaller markets or even individuals express. As for the WWW platform, the customer determines what information they need, plus in which order so that some amount of direct supplier control is removed.

Besides, desktop design as well as publishing is limiting the need for, as well as cost of overpriced designers and printers-nevertheless, good design is turning to be scarcer as more rookies try their hands. Customer communication systems are effortlessly maintained by using email and electronic infrastructures-factors that also minimize postage cost.

In addition, media relations may be improved by providing background details and news releases concerning websites. Not to mention, the Web environment has further created a diversity of fresh media channels that desire high quality content. Also, those who are responsible for selling may use the Web to perform quick searches into prospects. Electronic exhibitions may be simply fashioned and offered desk-side, or even remotely (through email and teleconference) (Benady, 2014).

Besides, databases have greatly transformed client and contact administration systems, apart from fielding sales staff efficiency and supervision. Additionally, the application of 3D simulations as well as virtual reality (VR) simply means that you don't have to form any real display space or showcase suites.To understand the significance of technology in modern-day marketing, it's important to check where most individuals get their information from, the preferred methods of entertainment as well as shopping preferences. Some of these factors include:

- **Connectivity:** Currently, there are more than 4 billion web-users online, which means that 50.8% of the worldwide population is fully connected. Within the coming 3 years, both China and India shall add more web users compared to what is currently in existence within the US.
- **Mobile:** Well over 5 billion individuals have smartphone devices, besides well over half of the networks are smartphones. It's projected that roughly $93 billion shall be spent on smartphone ads this year, which translates to more than $20 billion extra money, compared to what's normally spent on television. In addition, technology has fostered the emergence of e-Commerce, where it's estimated that more than 2.14 billion individuals globally are expected to purchase goods and services digitally in 2021.
- **Entertainment:** Around 1/3 of digital activity is spent viewing videos online, whereby almost half a billion individuals watch videos on Facebook almost each day.

For marketers, there are unlimited possibilities that technology provides. Nowadays, technology is becoming less of a transmission device and largely a tool for improved communication.

In a research by WBR and Monetate Group, it was found that 93% of companies with modern personalization strategies experienced a jump in overall revenue in 2018.

Technology is also ideal for experiential marketing. Unlike digital marketing, experiential strategies are perfect for creating emotional ties between clients and brands, plus they may generate 10 times the (ROI) return on investment (ROI), therefore fostering measurable loyalty (Benady, 2014).

Furthermore, technology can be useful at fostering Accountability and Transparency. Out of the approximately $63.4 billion which brands expended on programmatic within the year 2017, it's estimated that as low as 27% found its way to working media.

Moreover, up to 12% of those monies got lost to advertisement fraud, including a surprising 55% that became victim to "tech tax" which is implemented at every phase of the programmatic purchase.

9.3. THE LINK BETWEEN ADVERTISEMENT AND TECHNOLOGY

To better understand how to implement new technology, marketers require help from the firm's technology, data, and sometimes legal departments. However, the main challenge that marketers face won't be what should be done with the information they collect, instead how they utilize it. It's possible to have the most complex technology, however without marketing intelligence which combines data insights, the innovation won't deliver the return-on-investment (ROI) which you expect (Figure 9.2).

Figure 9.2. *Digital marketing is one of the fastest ways to grow your business.*

Source: https://www.standardmedia.co.ke/business/article/2001306828/five-ways-digital-marketing-can-help-grow-your-business (accessed on 3 April 2020).

9.3.1. Increased Budget for Growing Revenue

The price of investing in modern technology is a mutual concern for brand promoters, even though, just like with most technology, overall cost is estimated to lessen as the economies of scale as well as rivalry among service provider surges (Lambin, 2013).

Furthermore, marketing technology spending would likely also swell as marketing budgets continue to grow. Overall ad expenditure in America is expected to increase 24% between the years 2018 and 2022, going from $220.96 billion all the way to $274.44 billion, whereas the fraction of budget devoted to marketing innovation is predicted to remain stable throughout the same timeframe, which is 30% in 2018 as well as 32% in 2022.

The particular technology category that receives greatest investment would depend on the kind of company, as well as amount of implementation needed. There are technologies that need minimal incorporation with legacy structures, whereas others require extensive integration. Nevertheless, the investment is justifiable by the volume of revenue these innovations are estimated to generate for companies. Increased digital interactions shall create more information sets, which shall permit retailers to effectively customize promotions, rates, and products for every client, dynamically, and in real-time.

9.4. KEY TECHNOLOGIES CURRENTLY CHANGING THE MARKETING SPACE

The marketing industry is volatile, and companies are continually searching for something that can propel them ahead of any competition. So, it's simple to understand why innovation has assumed an increasingly significant role in this industry in recent years, therefore forcing businesses to conform or risk getting left behind.

As a matter of fact, it's gradually becoming obvious that computer innovation is where marketing is heading into the future. To clearly grasp this trend, one of the world's leading smartphone marketing technology designer TUNE recently performed a survey involving 350 marketers, influencers, industry stakeholders and CEOs, where they were required to provide their predictions concerning which technologies deliver the most effective impact on marketing activities in 2018 (Lambin, 2013).

Even more predictably, artificial intelligence (AI) (such as machine learning and robotics) capped the list with around 37.4%, whereas 16.8% of respondents picked big data, terming it as the year's greatest disruptive technology. This was then followed by VR, augmented reality as well as mixed-reality standing at 12.2%, messaging, and chatbots at 10.1%, as well as smartphone technology which stands at roughly 10.1%.

9.4.1. Artificial Intelligence (AI) Makes Advertising More Human

It's quite obvious why AI became such a prevalent pick. Besides if you cover technologies which need AI to work, like voice-first networking or chatbots then its reach may go even further. AI as well as machine learning (ML) are expected to have the greatest impact on marketing come 2018 and onwards, since it will essentially make 'advertising' more human. AI allows companies to better comprehend clients and their needs, customize their experience, forecast their behavior, as well as chat with them realistically.

Modern-day consumers are online natives that are media-savvy, which is what has made many to be resistant to traditional marketing techniques. Instead of attempting to sell them anything, businesses must find a means of reaching them on a much deeper and personal level.

AI will without any doubt become the technology with the greatest effect on marketing moving forward, since it gives marketers new competences to interrelate with a big number of customers from a personal level, something that wouldn't have been possible before (Lambin, 2013).

Big data allows companies to provide a more customized user experience. Same as AI, there's some considerable amount of overlap existing between big data, as well as other technologies found on the list. As a matter of fact, around 64% of every technology captured by the repliers are basically data-driven. Through big data, companies can easily keep in close contact with their clients' shopping practices through every channel, study how they react towards particular ads and offers, plus then apply this information to provide a more customized experience.

If combined with AI, then big data can grow to become a greatly powerful tool. There's absolutely no doubt that when Big Data merges with AI there shall be major progress in the sector of marketing technology. This powerful combination shall continue making big leaps in optimizing promo targeting, creative design, as well as marketing offers in which results are measured based on hard metrics such as clicks or buys (Lambin, 2013).

Case in point, Amazon uses a complex recommendation engine for developing a more customized consumer experience while also driving sales. Through examining the users' buying history, such as content that they've liked, graded, viewed, or bought in the past, including the items found in their respective shopping carts, the engine's internal systems may present them more appropriate product suggestions. Based on Amazon statistics, their recommendation engine produces well over 35% of the firm's sales.

9.4.2. Modern Ways of Marketing Communication

The increasing popularity of Siri, Alexa, and Google Assistant are clear indications that clients are progressively comfortable with this type of interaction. This attribute hasn't gone undetected by marketers, most of who are implementing intelligent talk chat bots and utilizing them to connect with customers in real-time, hence creating more intimate connections with them.

Through voice-first computing, companies can take this particular relationship to another higher level, permitting customers to buy their favorite items without even raising a finger. Roughly 39 million U.S citizens currently own the voice-assistance device, based on a report printed by Edison Research and NPR.

The smart voice systems allow marketers to link with customers from anywhere, whether they're in the car or kitchen, which happens on the go. Furthermore, Voice is regarded as the preferred technique for searching on mobile, whereby almost 40% of adults have been found to use voice-search technology at least once every day to find the products they want (Lambin, 2013).

9.4.3. The Power of Mobile Marketing

Mobile innovation might have been emphasized by just 10% of the sampled respondents, however it's possibly the most significant of the lot. Mainly because smartphones are essential to nearly everything that we do nowadays.

Billions of people accessing the internet today pre-dominantly use mobile phones, which can be seen through the meteoric growth of phone messaging, mobile payments, as well as smartphone-optimized and 'lite' sites, focusing on video, voice, as well as location-based framework, away from highly text-oriented internet. Additionally, thanks to geo-location innovation, companies shall be able to identify and target their customers with tailored, real-time promotions and suggestions depending on their past shopping habits.

Besides, VR, augmented reality, as well as mixed reality innovations also permit customers to sample their ideal products from a totally new perspective and connect with them in techniques that were just impossible in the past. Even though not everybody is convinced these technologies will form the next major breakthrough, still heavy investments coming from large companies such as Apple and Facebook show that they shall partake an increasingly significant role in the impending future.

9.4.4. Block Chain Technology-Creating a Safe and Transparent Marketplace

Both block chain and crypto currencies may have a significant effect on the direction of marketing. The technology is capable of bringing additional safety and transparency into the marketplace, thereby ending fraud, while allowing customers to safeguard their privacy, while also providing them with adequate control over their online data.

The advertising sector is sometimes filled with fraud, waste, as well as other externalities. Among this externality is the fact that individuals' privacy levels is slowly being taken away, with cash also being made selling this to the advertisers. With more businesses slowly adopting block chain technology, it's expected that the trend of security breach of online users will fall heading into the future (Benady, 2014).

Besides, technology has already revolutionized many unique aspects of present-day business, with marketing already set up to be included into this group. Through adopting technologies such as artificial-intelligence (AI) and big data, companies shall be able to deeply understand their consumers, develop stronger bonds with them, as well as offer new means of communication, apart from delivering a highly customized experience.

9.4.5. Upgrading Your Advertising

Digital platforms have transformed the marketing sector and proved to be much the game changer when it comes to product advertising. Nevertheless, marketing tools are continually evolving; therefore, it's essential for businesses to constantly update their strategies through keeping up with modern gadgets and application tools.

In order to propel the brand over to the next phase, the business must apply different marketing services which focus on diverse aspects. Conventional methods that concentrate on TV and radio commercials, including newspaper ads, or just placing marketing products in the mailbox while wishing for the best aren't effective anymore. While advertising through television may still have considerable impacts, there are various digital marketing approaches which may have a rather direct and more relatable influence on members of the public (Benady, 2014).

9.4.6. Updating Your Marketing Strategy

Marketing innovation provides unique ways for companies to be noticed on the online media. At first, it's critical to develop a website which tells your customer more about the business, which they may easily locate through the Smartphone (Figure 9.3).

Figure 9.3. *Social media is an effective channel for online advertising.*

Source: https://getsales.co.ke/tag/advertising-companies-in-kenya/ (accessed on 3 April 2020).

Nearly 50% of all smartphone searches conclude with a purchase, however you must ensure that your website shows on the top search-results page. This is the reason why you need to hire professionals or marketing firms to implement s successful search engine optimization (SEO) strategy.

In order to ensure that your product is conspicuous from the others, come up with a creative or impressive business logo apart from using visually appealing colors. Picture aids are up to 43% more effectual, since up to 90% of our everyday knowledge is determined by them in some way. Attractive images and videos can enhance the business campaign, apart from attracting more clients.

Yet another useful way to begin with virtual advertising is through posting advertisements on common social media sites. In order to develop a successful social policy, it's essential that your marketing team must be familiar with every platform and concentrate on involving your identified audience. Among the most prevalent social media, sites for marketing include:

- **Facebook:** As the largest social platform with more than a billion regular users, Facebook offers an excellent opportunity for businesses to connect with individuals from all around the globe and make significant impacts.
- **Twitter:** The platform is ideal for sharing updates, photos, videos,

and links. Besides, Twitter is among the leading 10 sites in the US with over 300,000,000 regular users.

- **Instagram and Pinterest:** They are two exceptional social media platforms used for sharing pictures and video content.
- **YouTube:** Boasting over a billion users, YouTube is a profound way of spreading your product message through video, provide tutorials and other valuable information and generate finances along the way.
- **SnapChat:** This program is specifically developed for mobile devices, whereby content disappears after around 24 hours. Besides, the application provides you the opportunity to check how many individual users have observed the post, whereas the pressure of refined content is eliminated as the post fades by day end.

9.4.7. Getting More Involved

After finishing the first steps in digital marketing, the next thing is getting more engaged with your viewers. Using modern marketing technology isn't only about sponsoring the business, but further being engaged with the customers (Figure 9.4).

Figure 9.4. *Digital advertising involves various aspects such as video marketing.*

Source: https://hostmasters.co.ke/digital-marketing-for-the-growth-of-your-business/ (accessed on 3 April 2020).

The business must be cognizant of the kind of language that it employs in its branding, including the message being sent, besides there are various steps for creating a better relationship with social media online users:

- **Not all Posts Should Cover Business Matters:** Sometimes, the message could end up being lost in case the network gets jammed with constant posts concerning your company offerings. The business must be engaged with the community, plus share meaningful content to ensure the followers' interests are covered.

- **Sharing the Expertise:** Most people like eye-openers. They provide and share relevant knowledge, including exciting facts on fascinating topics. Additionally, they offer a deeper insight on the company and its general message. Besides, encourage more visitors to vote, leave behind some feedback and inquire about the businesses' practices.
- **Virtual Reviews and Ratings:** Build a solid profile on product review sites. Depending on the digital reviews and general rating, a business may either flourish or sink. It provides increased value to established companies, including the exclusive opportunity to get insight on the visitors' demands. Additionally, in case the ratings are high, it's actually a good means of social proofing which can be posted on other social-media sites to improve your reputation.
- **Facebook Live:** By streaming live unique events about your business, this will inspire the regular customers to feel as if they're part of the business community, plus that their preferred brand truly values their say.

9.5. USEFUL TOOLS OF MARKETING INNOVATION

Though adopting the modern tools of marketing innovation might seem rather intimidating, these tools are essentially valuable commodities. Based on the company model, such as B2B (selling items/services from business-to-business) or B2C meaning (business to client), there are different software apps present in each category.

9.5.1. Marketing Automation

Monotonous tasks like social media advertising and website maintenance are easily simplified through marketing automation.

By definition, marketing automation means technology which manages marketing systems and multipurpose campaigns, across different channels, mechanically. Through marketing automation, companies can easily target clients with automated texts across email, social, online, and text.

Texts are sent automatically, based on sets of instructions known as workflows. These workflows can be outlined by templates, custom-made from nothing, or tailor-made at the center of the campaign in order to attain greater results (Benady, 2014).

Typically, marketing, and sales teams use marketing automation for purposes of automating digital marketing campaigns as well as sales activities, for purposes of maximizing revenue and overall efficiency. Whenever automation is used efficiently to handle monotonous tasks, workers are free to address higher-order issues, plus human error is greatly reduced.

Furthermore, marketing automation allows for lead generation, development, and scoring, including with measuring general ROI on campaigns. Besides, the time- and price-saving results of automation improve as the company develops in size and scope. Effective marketing automation structures are developed to run together with your business (Benady, 2014).

1. **Functions of Marketing Automation:** In its simplest form, marketing automation refers to a class of tools developed to streamline and ease up some of the core functions of present-day marketing and sales functions. Right from automation of lead qualification procedure, to the creation of a hub meant for digital campaign creation, automation involves more of simplifying the business world which is becoming way too complex, and much too fast.

Furthermore, marketing automation allows you to execute an online marketing strategy, without necessarily needing to push "send" on each email, text, campaign, or post that you make. Effective automation tools allow you to detect your audience, develop the right content then automatically trigger actions depending on the schedules and client behavior.

When your campaign is launched, you may concentrate on other tasks, and then analyze and adjust your marketing setup as results begin to show. A mechanized promotion strategy may save time as well as resources, thereby propelling revenue and ROI as you concentrate on building your business.

2. **How it Works:** The first step is collecting consumer information through different interaction platforms: such as emails, app usage and website visits, among others. The information helps to develop a 360-degree outlook on every client. Henceforth, the marketing automation program will perform all the task:

restructuring segmentation and targeting procedures to determine the appropriate audiences, rapidly, and at scale.

Customizing messaging to every customer's needs automatically can be done through technology, largely depending on the content found on their profile. Technology has allowed for the creation of useful and customized messages across mobile, email, web platforms and social media through a simple tap of the button (Lambin, 2013).

3. **How Marketing Automation Enriches the Buyer's Journey:** The client's journey consists of the collection of personal experiences they have with your product. Through marketing automation, it's possible to tailor all interactions depending on the clients' data to develop ongoing, continuous journeys through all brand touch points.

The marketing automation process develops appropriate content and messaging systems across different channels. For maximum effectiveness, send email messages having dynamic content which customizes the marketing far beyond just placing the client's name in the heading (Lambin, 2013).

Furthermore, consider incorporating mobile messaging with both email and social promotions through SMS/MMS, group messaging, as well as push notifications. Also consider generating digital ads which emerge strategically for the right individual at the appropriate time. Additionally, recommend the correct products on your site for every personal user—automatically.

Through marketing automation, it's possible to easily reach clients along their journey regardless of where they currently sit in the consumer lifecycle—from purchase to advocacy. Ideally deliver timely, appropriate content which reaches consumers when, where, as well as how they prefer—changing prospects into regular brand advocates (Lambin, 2013).

4. **Best Practices for Marketing Automation:** There are certain best practices which you must have in mind when developing your marketing automation plan. First, it's important to describe and present your objectives. While doing this use actual numbers to validate the investment made in the marketing automation system to the stakeholders (Figure 9.5).

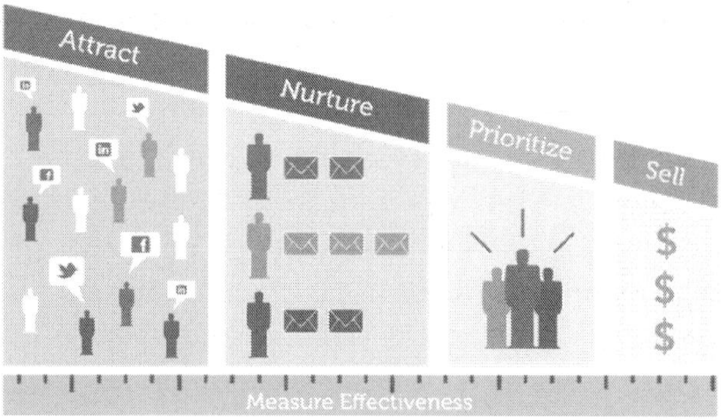

Figure 9.5. *Automation makes the marketing process much faster and efficient.*

Source: https://www.business2community.com/marketing-automation/only-22-of-businesses-use-marketing-automation-01268518 (accessed on 3 April 2020).

Also consider partnering with other team members. The marketing automation process will touch various teams in your organization. Learn their input then buy-in prior to starting. Thereafter, consider creating process visualizations. This can be done by using comprehensive maps of your marketing mechanization workflow to transmit your big picture goals to your whole business—efficiently and successfully.

Likewise, prepare for database subdivision. Consider your client data. Reflect on who you'd want to engage with the product, and why then proceed by preparing your content strategy. Also consider creating your own content library. Make interesting, engaging, and appropriate messaging intended to reach every phase of the consumer's lifecycle.

9.5.2. Tag Management

This process can amplify your digital marketing presentation by including different tags on popular websites.

Tag management can be defined as an emerging foundational platform which allows marketers to effortlessly connect, manage, and merge their online marketing applications (such as, SEO, web analytics, social technologies and advertisement) without much continuous development work. The tag, in this scenario, is just another name denoting a set of data-collection code, with a large majority of online vendors now needing their consumers to input the tag on their website pages or smartphone apps.

While these tags mostly collect visitor trend information, they can as well be applied to initiate product functionality like live chat, promotion, or surveys. Through tag management, it's possible for promoters or developers to install at least one tag onto their webpages-a master tag, kind of- and consequently apply an intuitive internet interface for adding, editing or remove any extra vendor tags within a fragment of the time it normally takes when using manual software programming methods (Lambin, 2013).

A good number of tag managerial solutions consist of a "tag marketplace" which allows marketers to choose the vendor symbol, add their account specifics and other details, determine which websites and pages are ideal for loading the tag on before final publishing.

A vendor solution would then be automatically deployed through that master-tag, without having to handle the web pages. Furthermore, tag management is compatible with mobile apps, whereby the same dexterity applies-mount the tag management system once then lessen the cycles required to alter analytics data points, or even apply mobile solutions.

Nevertheless, the actual talking point of tag management is "data layer"—which refers to behind-the-scenes information which drives consumer connections in web, smartphone, and other online channels. This data layer is found between the app levels, and consists of different mission-critical online solutions, including the experience layer which users connect with. By the formation and customization of the data level (through tag management), companies can simply standardize the data meanings used by every application, which allows them to synchronize their applications more effortlessly (Lambin, 2013).

Consider data layer to be a "control plane" which allows promoters to network and share consumer data between applications. This data level is significantly enhanced through complementary visitor segmentation as well as profile enrichment tools, like those availed by some providers which provide real-time subdivision as well as extra data distribution functions.

It's vital for developing real-time connections. Due to the reasons mentioned, the data level is a very strategic aspect of the modern online marketing technology processes, permitting these disparate implements to function amicably together for once.

- **Importance of Tag Management:** Generally, it provides numerous benefits across the business. Here are some of the primary scenarios and associated benefits of applying this technology.

- **Bringing Order to Disarray:** With promoters increasingly applying a complex range of solutions for engaging with consumers, online marketing has turned to be a disordered burden. Tag management lessens complexity for both promotion and development resources, apart from allowing promoters to move quicker and initiate campaigns much simpler than ever before. Besides, tag management might also considerably improve website performance through limiting the amount of tags coming from each page. Consequently, this allows for higher digital conversions and returns.
- **Create Your Unique Marketing Cloud:** There are marketers who believe that they must be tied to at least one promotion cloud vendor-like Adobe, Oracle or even Salesforce.com—providing both convenience as well as the promise of basic data integration. Though the truth is, there isn't any single cloud that can provide everything to everybody. Promoters need maximum flexibility to select the most ideal solutions for their exclusive business needs. The tag management system allows marketers to apply any solution that they need, be it from the marketing cloud system or even a top-class point provider, while still allowing them to function together. Moreover, this same visitor profile may effortlessly be shared throughout your whole marketing technology stack, allowing for unified messaging systems across different channels and devices.
- **Unleashing Your Marketing Prospectus:** Tag management allows promoters and their companies to leverage their marketing in more diverse methods, compared to any other online advertising solution. At a basic level, tag management allows for greater marketing agility, lower costs, and greater website performance. It helps enhance data supervision and control, marketing innovation investments, data integration procedures, and increased profitability.

In addition to the above, tag management allows for unification of internal teams by decreasing technology complexity, either via managing crucial applications or merging vital customer data.

As an industry, marketing is going into an exciting new age. Due to the rise of new technologies and ideal practices, promoters are on the grasp of attaining what some people call the marketing "Holy Grail" - ability to provide consistent, customized, real-time experiences for consumers across multiple networks and devices. However, the only factor that stands in their road is the inability to successfully manage excessive data. With tag management as well as sound technology policy, marketers can effortlessly cross over into the subsequent promotion frontier.

9.5.3. CDN (Content Distribution Network)

CDN promotes a quicker online response and downloading period for customers.

The concept refers to the transparent root of the Web responsible for content delivery. Nearly everybody works with CDNs almost daily; when going through articles found on news sites, doing online shopping, viewing YouTube videos and going through social media feeds (Lambin, 2013).

Regardless of what kind of content you consume, there are chances you'll come across CDNs in nearly all text characters, photo pixel and movie frames stored your computer or mobile device.

In order to comprehend why CDNs have become so widely popular, you must first identify the problem they solve. Latency refers to the frustrating delay which happens from the time you seek to load a website.

This delay occurs because of physical distance between you and site's hosting server. The CDN's objective is to practically reduce that physical distance, with a goal of enhancing website rendering speed as well as performance (Lambin, 2013).

1. **How CDN functions:** To decrease the overall distance between visitors and your site's server, the CDN usually keeps a cached edition of its information in several geographical locations (such as PoPs or points-of-presence). Every PoP has a certain amount of caching servers which are used for fostering content delivery to users within its proximity.

Essentially, CDN positions your content in different places at once, offering improved coverage to the users. For instance, in case someone in London gains access your US-hosted website, this would be performed through the local (UK) PoP. It is much faster than even having the guest's requests processed by travelling across the Atlantic Ocean and back. This is how the CDN system functions in a nutshell (Lambin, 2013).

2. **The Significance of CDN:** In the digital world, each second counts. Studies reveal that any second-long delay can cause a 7% drop in conversions, 11% drop in page checks, and a 16% decline in cus-

tomer satisfaction. Just about everyone uses CDN is some way or another and marketers aren't left behind in this regard.

The truth is that if whichever aspect of your company is online, then there are good reasons why you should use CDN to create more popularity. Specifically, if you are running a cross border website, with the larger majority of your visitors found in a wider geographical area, and then having a CDN will yield greater benefits (Benady, 2014). In this case, using the CDN will actually boost your website's performance through introducing another essential networking point between the site visitor, and the already adjacent server. Besides, most websites still tend to work on a wider scale, therefore making CDN use a much preferred choice in areas, such as advertising, e-commerce, and media.

Present-day CDNs are capable of handling different IT tasks, thereby allowing users to enhance page loading speed, manage high traffic loads, and stop spammers among other functions. But their primary function is reducing round-trip time through carrying the content much closer to the site's visitor. Every CDN PoP generally contains multiple caching servers (Benady, 2014).

These servers are used for storage as well as transfer of cached files. Essentially, their key role is accelerating website loading times while also minimizing bandwidth consumption. Most CDN caching servers usually hold several storage drives, including high quantities of RAM resources.

Within CDN caching servers, the cached files are kept on solid-form and hard-disk drivers (SSD and HDD), including in (RAM) or random-access memory files, where the more typically-used files are hosted within the quicker mediums. As one of the fastest mediums, RAM is commonly used for storing frequently-accessed products (Benady, 2014).

Using CDN: In order for the CDN system to work, there should be a default in-bound gateway targeting every incoming traffic. To ensure this happens, it's important to modify the root domain DNS structures (such as, domain. com) including the ones covering your sub domains.

As for the root domain, it's essential to modify its record so that it may identify to any of the available CDN's IP categories. For every sub domain, adjust its CNAME record so that it can point to the CDN-availed sub domain address.

For both cases, this causes the DNS to route all site visitors to your specific CDN, rather than being transferred to your primary server. In case any of this seems confusing, just don't worry. Modern-day CDN vendors provide detailed instructions for getting you comfortably through the activation stage. Furthermore, they help through their support team. This whole process boils down to just a couple of copy and pastes and typically takes roughly 5 minutes (Benady, 2014).

In the ideal world, CDN's would be an essential aspect of any site hosting. Nevertheless, when CDNs were originally founded during the late 90s, they became way too costly and only available to the biggest organizations.

Nowadays things have transformed and most hosting providers really do offer CDN solutions as a checkbox extra. Business-oriented CDNs have been present since the '90s. Same as any other older technology, they underwent various evolutionary stages before turning to become the strong application delivery system they are now (Benady, 2014).

The journey of CDN development mostly was influenced by market forces, such as emerging trends in content intake and vast connectivity improvements. The latter, however, has been facilitated by fiber optics technology and other modern communication technologies.

Generally, CDN evolution may be partitioned into 3 generations, with each product introducing new functionalities, technologies, and frameworks to its network model. Working in parallel, every generation saw the cost of CDN solutions trend down, ushering its transformation into the mass-market technology sector (Benady, 2014).

9.5.4. DMP (Data Managing Platform)

A brilliant software tool for safekeeping information.

The data management platform, short for DMP, refers to a form of centralized technology platform which gathers information from a variety of sources, subdivides it to pre-determined categories then further transmits it so as to reach certain objectives of the marketing campaign.

Putting it simply, the Data Management System is among the basics of Ad Tech processes. It is one large dashboard of tools which gives users the larger picture of what is happening with their efforts, plus providing the necessary instruments for reversing the tide so that it can benefit you. The DMP control panel generally is a platform where you can easily review the condition of the situation, while planning your subsequent moves.

- **How it Works in Marketing Technology:** The key function of DMP in Marketing Tech operation is maintaining a solid grasp on the activities of the campaign. Besides, application of information that's been gathered through Data Management Platform offers an extra agility towards the Ad Tech process—improving the description of the target group and consequent ad distribution (Figure 9.6).

Figure 9.6. *DMP marketing strategy mainly focuses on the consumers' needs.*

Source: https://affle.com/dmp-data-management-platform (accessed on 3 April 2020).

Ultimately, this gives promoters the agility needed to adjust their campaign while it proceeds depending on the final audience responses.

The end effect of its DMP procedure is a more effective and precise targeting for the target audience, which creates conversions which in turn improve ROI obtained from ad spending. This is a very crucial aspect of online marketing; however, gestation and hesitation still form negative approaches in marketing.

- **Forms of Data That DMP Collects:** The data management platform can easily collect data coming from the chosen source. All you must do is determine what type of data you are interested in. Essentially, Data Management Platform gets attached to the main source of data (for instance, the website) where it gathers information concerning various user activity.

This data is subsequently fused together into one large picture which can assist marketers to better.

Comprehend how to progress with their product, as well as best approaches for watching everything that the individual needs in order to progress in their daily endeavors. Otherwise, the spiritual aspect helps to reveal the information getting processed, which may be participially useful for the membership parties, whereas the original data system covers the original-, second-, or even third-party: apart from the actual data and this includes: Website/App data, CRM, Transaction structures, Audience data and subscriptions.

- **Self-Hosting or Using Third-Party:** The major difference between personalized and third-party data management platform is quite peculiar, this all depends up on the requirements of your company operation.

For the third-party service, users will get the whole package with other extra products from the provider. The program comes ready-to-use, as well as guaranteed to work adequately. Though there's one very significant thing to remember.

Upon implementing the third-party system, you'll pay for nearly all features which you may not require entirely. This is not actually cost-effective. As a matter of fact, it can profusely bleed your advertising budget if the returns will be great enough. One custom solution is the more complex yet reasonable approach. Indeed, you should be ready to perform the heavy lifting involving development of the foundation.

Nonetheless, you develop the system exactly to fitting to your goals of your AdTech set-up. This makes it way more useful and capable of creating higher rapid ROI. Nevertheless, for self-hosted DMPs you will have to find the providers of third-party data by themselves.

Chapter 10

Challenges of Web Technologies

CONTENTS

10.1. INTRODUCTION

Web applications have grown to become very reliable and simple to use. Thus, most people are confident to utilize the Internet as a medium for buying, banking, or networking with other individuals. This module inspects the architectural/design requirements and challenges faced when creating safe and scalable web systems using modern technology. It further covers a wide introduction into the flaws and restrictions of web applications plus what technical solutions may be used to overcome them.

As technology progresses at breakneck speed, ultimately it creates new prospects and challenges to network application developments. In case businesses need to create lasting, effective web applications, then they should address the existing challenges first. Of late, advanced web applications have produced quite a buzz. Even though it's a rather new concept, the technology has placed itself in a position where it would determine the direction of web development.On one hand, there are traditional apps which are smart, quick, and effectual in most cases, providing a personalized experience for users. Meanwhile, there are websites which are also relatively slow to load, they may take you places (however, not always directly providing you whatever you want) though with minimal or no possibility of personalized interaction.

Web application basically leverages the application of progressive innovation, in order to deliver the best of technology. The comparison between app and customer loyalty has been ongoing for long. However, progressive web apps move it a step further through allowing you to enjoy app-like interaction, without any need for downloading. As a matter of fact, advanced web apps are developed in a way such that they can work without the Web or in low-connectivity zones.

10.2. MODERN DAY CHALLENGES

10.2.1. Excess Simplicity

Web Apps are currently on the brink of turning into a major phenomenon, as more companies are realizing its value and many customers are reacting to it positively. Web application operators typically prefer simple and creative design that's cognizant of their navigation requirements. This is usually something that many web app developers seem to overlook, regrettably. The thing about internet users is that, patience isn't one of their merits. In case their high demands aren't fully complied with, then they just move on.

10.2.2. Impeccable User Experience

Impeccable User Experience is something that users generally look forward to. Yet, developers quite regularly fail to deliver great user experiences. This happens mainly because they're mainly involved with technical features of web app improvement; to an extent that aesthetics typically takes the backstage.

Besides, the look of the app seems as essential to users as is the work of the web application itself. Thus, it is compulsory that developers integrate the basic tenets of program design into their encryptions.

10.2.3. Selecting the Right Framework

Generally, the proper framework when combined with platform knowledge posits a direct effect on web app performance. But the challenge of selecting the appropriate framework and coming up with a remarkable product may be too much for the developer, besides they may not even realize it.

10.2.4. Determining Effective Performance

In web apps performance means speed. The loading period is an important aspect to consider in case you're seeking to drive traffic online. It is important to think about performance improvement before anything else when forming a new product. During the development of web apps, developers must be careful to avoid faults like traffic spikes, badly written programs, and un-optimized databases for ensuring that apps provide peak performance.

10.2.5. Low Scalability

Developing top scalability levels for your product may help you gain new customers and retain old ones as well. Top scalability levels of the web app are how to score points over the competitor. But scalability has got nothing to relate with bandwidth or output. It is about matching the load which you choose to place on one server, plus the best means to address it is designing the software which can operate on different servers.

10.2.6. Security Threat

It's possibly the most common matter that all businesses are faced with. Web safety is amongst the biggest challenges commonly encountered by web apps.

A few of the commonly seen threats which less secure apps must deal with are: buffer overflow, shell injection, cross-site scripting, and session hijacking. To ensure these threats are kept at bay, the website apps developer must ensure security measures are maintained throughout the development phase.

10.2.7. All-Knowing Attitude

It is tough to spot challenges faced by internet applications. Most developers responsible for developing an enticing result often feel troubled, over-worked, and pressured.

In order to conform to unrealistic deadlines, inventors sometimes ignore the most ideal practices instead of quick-repair, time-saving remedies. The developer might take to not revising codes and suppressing faults to meet with certain time limits, without comprehending that quality programming is essential to the success of the web app.

10.2.8. Getting the Appropriate Team in Place

Having the correct team of people involved in web app development is only half the journey achieved. However, very often this is easier said rather than done. Generally, a balanced team shall always include a mix of abilities relating to industry standards.

Indeed, this is an area where the majority of web app development businesses are actually struggling. Nothing makes it more obvious than the survey from 2017 confirming that only 55% of businesses are satisified with app activity.

10.2.9. Other Possible Concerns

1. **The Integration Issue:** Many business applications nowadays exist independently from the firewall. They are more varied compared to the past. For example, a contemporary business may use the SaaS-based CRM model, integral BI tools. Additionally, the business will host their site directly on the cloud. Even though this enhances flexibility, it still forms a big challenge. The problem with web-developers is not building all functions of an application, but rather developing an application which can incorporate with other apps. The largest web development setback seen in most projects nowadays is integration.

Availability of different cloud-hosted solutions is a double-sided sword. While we don't have to implement solutions for things such as storage, analytics, mail, and recurrent subscription payments. Besides, we now must incorporate cloud services which offer this functionality.
Every integration point comprises of accepting the API, programming, testing, and logging in order to troubleshoot whichever issues. Additionally, modern companies are supported by numerous cloud-hosted platforms. From assimilating with CRM solutions up to other sector-specific products, nowadays we no longer exist in our own small app universe but rather have a wide choice to pick from.

2. **The Over-Saturation Problem:** When the app store was first launched, it became a golden chance for mobile app inventors. At that time there was minimal competition. Yet presently, there are than 1.5 million apps within the store even though less than 1% of those applications are financially feasible. The same applies to web applications. As market becomes over-saturated, users are gaining more options compared to ever before.

Among the main concerns with web application invention today is over-saturation. People discovered that there was cash to be made driving social media traffic towards websites, therefore, thousands of individuals jumped into the new digital trend. It means that it watered down the market for everybody else who had strong ideas.
Now individuals come up with bizarre names, purchase a domain, and then go off. Genuine sites are currently contending with traffic. Plus, social media traffic is growing to become a pay-to-play thing. Meaning now it boils down to developing the next big thing in tech, so that a project can successfully carry off.

3. **The User-Experience Problem:** Oversaturation of web systems often produces spoiled users. Following the rise of effortlessly accessible, basic applications, user prospects have increased dramatically. Now, they expect equal levels of simplicity which they enjoy in mobile apps that they use daily. Still, the problem is that if the applications fail to meet user expectations, then they will get another option.

The test for businesses is how to deliver web applications which meet the workers' already high demands. In the past, you could easily get away with unsightly but practical web apps since it was superior to pen and paper, or some clumpy legacy app. Good app design is necessary for any website apps that intend to gain traction.

Operators are swift to judge in case your app looks ugly or even outdated. However, the problem does not stop there. Developers must not only formulate great user experiences, but also generate great experiences for other inventors. If an application obscures user or fails to offer basic integration for developers, then it is highly likely to fail.

Companies can't afford to deliver other than boundless experience, be it through mobile apps for customers or the API for designers and developers. Adoption is essential for creating revenue and interest; but bugs in production, sluggishness in the experience, and information safety concerns can all tank a corporate model depending on digital products quite fast.

Businesses shipping APIs being part of their everyday experiences or virtual product line similarly face a sharper curve for implementation and monetization, whereby their APIs must be ridiculously basic to understand and utilize by other developers, plus they must be able to distinguish from competitors by answering a problem which nobody else can do.

4. **The Speed Test:** It has scientifically been proven that people's attention spans are lessening. Over the past 13 years, the typical attention span has declined by 4 seconds. Many people now have quite short attention spans and don't have enough patience to withstand slow applications. As a matter of fact, research discovered that 40% of users will abandon any website which takes over 3-seconds to load. Digital businesses are therefore in a tight spot, where they must ensure their pages are the fastest to load once a user clicks on them.

Visitors demand feature-rich apps that typically run slower due to the extra features. But, they will mostly let go of the application in case it loads slowly. The largest web app development test facing businesses nowadays is keeping their website loading times to under one second. Many businesses want advanced media on their websites to improve design, but don't optimize them for performance. The page loading times are very important for final users to enjoy a momentous experience, but it's also significant in the context of Google. The search engine has started to account for general page loading times, as a contributor to how a website ranks within Google's online search index.

5. **The Security Concern:** Security gaps are becoming more prevalent, yet web app security is not getting better. Recent studies estimate that roughly 96% of all web apps have one or more "severe vulnerabilities." Application security is getting

more complex by the day. The test for companies is finding ways of keeping updated with emerging app security threats. Basically, how to keep every layer of the application secure.

Safeguarding your system at every possible level and continually keeping it safe as you quickly change it through swift action methodologies is considerably tough. Ask whether you're revamping your OS and model structures regularly? Doing code appraisals and auto static plus run-time code examination?

Other duties you should consider doing include; proactively gauging network traffic and program logs for peculiar behavior, using white/black listing inputs to escape any SQL inputs or scripting injection attacks, and taking time to understand every possible attack opening of your system.

6. **The Multi-Platform Test:** When smartphones apps began taking off, the main concern for businesses was, between native apps and smartphone web apps which offered the best bet for businesses. But, that is still the incorrect question. Nowadays, you require responsive web apps that address the users' needs.

Even by choosing not to produce native apps, businesses' web apps should still be able to acclimatize to the instrument on which it's watched. Moving forward, this trend would only continue growing. We're witnessing a new rise of "smart" devices, such as glasses, televisions, watches, and more.

When forming new applications, companies must consider the vast array of devices that the system can be used on. Outside cross-browser compatibility, monitor sizes, magnitudes, and pixel density also differ between devices. Without deliberate planning, the user experience can be compromised and, in some instances, functions may break.

The internet is growing rapidly with the rising number of web users all around the globe. With the increasing significance of web media, both user expectations and aspirations equally are growing. Companies now intend to get better results from their respective investments in web app development. Something that's creating new challenges when outsourcing web app development, not forgetting that the outcomes on the web tend to be more quantifiable compared to other mediums. These factors bring in new challenges especially for digital agencies, besides they are also affecting web app development patterns in a significant way.

10.3. WEB 2.0 APPLICATIONS

The Web 2.0 system symbolizes a major change in how Webpages are formed and accessed. During recent times, Web technology has grown to become vital for corporate communication. The evolution of software systems has prompted fresh user experiences by substituting older technologies. Generally, this represents the current state of technological progress, including the best models of its implementation.

There are many businesses adopting these technologies for purposes of creating richer and interactive interactions. For maximum efficacy, these applications should be more refined than conventional websites. Nowadays, Web 2.0 applications have been accepted as the new standard by many large businesses. But, with its rise, there are also some challenges that have come with its testing and implementation.

For instance, given continuous variations in web 2.0 applications, there is an increased need for automation and flexibility in the testing stage. Applications also comprise of different standalone applications rather than being single standalone programs. There are needs to update this process for testing the apps in better ways through fresh testing situations.

Moreover, it is often hard to map the end-user situations straight to the expressed requirement. User behavior shall determine whether it's necessary to create increased situations of following non-linear paths. In addition, among the most demanding aspects of the web 2.0 app is performance improvement. Besides, performance testing through conventional methodologies doesn't seem to work efficiently. Recent findings have shown that most web 2.0 apps are susceptible to security loopholes.

10.3.1. Measurement Problems of Web 2.0

The functions of measuring tools typically are categorized into subgroups, the same as development capacities and responsibilities. The different features of web 2.0 apps create multiple other challenges. Over the last few months, stakeholders in web technologies have been putting up the foundation for creating a research-fund agenda targeting the Next Generation Web initiative, which is European (EC) Commission's new flagship project seeking to develop a more comprehensive, resilient, and open future web 2.0 technologies come the next decade.

But setting out the vision for a superior, human-focused future of the internet isn't an easy task. The trials the internet experiences today are varied and complex, gradually affecting the very essence of our societies, businesses, and personal lives: from the increasing threat of cyberwar even to the monopoly of digital economies; including online harassment and compromised democracies to the "Airbnb-ification" of townships. To make sense of a field so quickly evolving, including so many varying actors and changing parts and pieces, is now becoming quite challenging to do, leave alone designing the appropriate type of solutions which may address every one of these problems effectively.

Most future goals shall by their essential nature rather limited: but we aren't in the activity of making predictions right now. It's difficult to accurately predict the future of web 2.0 technologies, or the precise impact it would have (plus unintended outcomes!) of the intercessions proposed. Creating a comprehensive vision plan and associated action plan to cater for the future web developments is further convoluted by dynamics inherent to the online community, which makes constant and well-targeted action rather hard.

10.3.2. Looking for a Panacea

If it was to be believed that tech media coverage can solve every other web problem out there, then the crux of technology is upon us. Web technologies indubitably play a significant role in creating a more human-focused internet, but there's no single solution that's a panacea. The focus on finding a "magic" solution-typically a technological fix, usually is something that we equally see in the growing climate change debate, where there's distraction from the actual matters at hand, including the political as well as economic dynamics that underpin them.

In web systems, there's the wide held belief that "fixing" the internet needs a far more inclusive approach, addressing issues across the stack, beginning at the core solid structures up to the communal interactions the web facilitates. The approach shall require technological solutions, though also regulatory involvement, culture change, and getting viable fresh business systems among others, basically: intercessions across the whole technology value chain requires action by diverse stakeholder groups.

The problem of isolated communities also arises. Getting diverse stakeholder groups operating in the web space to cooperate together, or even converse with one another, is hard. Different communities seem to function in silo-like structures, missing a mutual language for talking about problems, thereby preventing people from taking a multidisciplinary approach which is needed. Attorneys who work in data protection systems don't necessarily become involved with grassroots initiatives seeking to develop practical alternatives, and they in turn don't converse with policymakers who may execute changes on the legislative side.

However, that is still just one field: how regularly do cybersecurity experts consult with gig economy campaigners, and software engineers or digital marketers. Creating a more human-based internet space will need a sustained commitment through a wide range of groups-including developers, civil society organizations, policymakers, and private sector that all have a stake in web technologies. One main goal of Next Generation Web initiative is fostering an actual community of similar-minded actors within the web space (and beyond), those who care intensely about making the web fairer and a bit more democratic for everyone.

Moreover, too often do people treat important features of the web in isolation, even though the matters themselves are really multi-faceted and inter-linked. Developers must think more concerning how people's issues connect to as well as affect other components of the web, and how the philosophies and values we support must be embedded across different levels of the web, adopting a full-stack method.

To demonstrate, when we discuss about developing moral AI-perhaps the most hyped web technology today-we mostly focus on the rather brief slice of the entire AI development procedure, precisely decision-making, responsibility, and reducing bias. Though developing fair decision-making techniques into AI structures is of vital importance, creating truly responsible AI instruments needs us to have a much broader scope, beginning at the infrastructure layer, up to the communal and economic effects the tool produces.

If the AI system is capable of making clear and "just" decisions, though is itself applied for malicious purposes, then the question is can it still equally be considered to be ethical. And what if the device is well-developed and applied for good, though the data it depends on was obtained without any consent from its users?

10.4. EMERGING ISSUES

Keeping the above factors in mind, scholars have spent many years thinking on models for the web which can capture any possible nuances and may help to bring extra cohesion to the fragmented landscape, plus have established a set of main topics. When contemplating these cross-stack matters, the scope can be narrowed down to precisely those problems developers believe will have most effect on health of web users in few years to come.

With data-driven subject mapping activity, expert input, and individual analysis, developers have picked some key challenges which they believe must be addressed in equivalence as part of the task to create a more human-focused internet.

These topics may be subdivided in three classes: topics covering the key features contributing to the flexibility of the web, they are vital to making the internet more comprehensive, and finally aspects essential to developing a net that's more democratic. Every one of the subjects covers an extensive variety of unique sub-issues, appropriate to different stakeholder groups, and are normally tech-agnostic (with the exemption of ethical AI that is believed to be quite possibly revolutionary as a technology, and therefore merits personal attention).

10.5. SUSTAINABLE AND RATIONAL INFRASTRUCTURE CHALLENGE

One major challenge for the web going forward is guaranteeing that hardware and infrastructures which underpin it are long-term, and can significantly contribute to creating a more rounded and just economy. The tests around the web's environmental footprint are innumerable, varying from the large amounts of energy utilized by data centers to emergent technologies such as blockchain, and the expensive mining procedures behind the materials that make modern tech devices to function. Approximations indicate that come the year 2020 the universal number of connected 'objects' will hit 21 billion-normally hard to reprocess and deliberately developed not to enjoy any long lifespan.

Bibliography

1. Brian, W. J. P. D. C., (2006). How to Host Your Own Web Server (p. 92). New York: Lulu.com.
2. Miltiadis, D., & Lytras, (2009). Social Web Evolution: Integrating Semantic Applications and Web 2.0 Technologies: Integrating Semantic Applications and Web 2.0 Technologies (p. 340). Pennsylvania: IGI Global.
3. Puntambekar, A. A., (2009). Web Technologies (p. 612). New Delhi: Technical Publications.
4. Benady, D., (2014). How Technology is Changing Marketing. Retrieved from: theguardian.com: https://www.theguardian.com/media-network/media-network-blog/2014/sep/29/technology-changing-marketing-digital-media (accessed on 31 March 2020).
5. Bowen, R., (2007). What's New in Apache Web Server 2.2? (p. 32) California: O'Reilly Media, Inc.
6. Carleton, B., (2013). 10 Uses for Realtime Web Technologies. Retrieved from lostechies.com/: https://lostechies.com/chrismissal/2013/09/03/10-uses-for-realtime-web-technologies/ (accessed on 31 March 2020).
7. Christine, H., Robert, N., & Dilip, S., (2000). Applied Software Architecture (pp. 4–99). Boston: Addison-Wesley Professional.

8. Dimitris, G. A., Ilan, O., & Krsto, P., (2015). Managing Emerging Technologies for Socio-Economic Impact (pp. 1–80). Cheltenham, United Kingdom: Edward Elgar Publishing.
9. Godbole, A. S., (2013). Web Technologies: TCP/IP, Web/Java Programming, and Cloud Computing (p. 593). New York: Tata McGraw-Hill Education.
10. Gosselin, D., (2010). JavaScript: The Web Technologies Series (p. 720). New York: Cengage Learning.
11. Lambin, J. J., (2013). Changing Market Relationships in the Internet Age (pp. 11–93). Belgium: University presses of Leuven.
12. Len, B., Paul, C., & Rick, K., (2012). Software Architecture in Practice: Software Architect Practice_c3 (p. 624). Boston: Addison-Wesley.
13. Leonor, B., & Jon, H., (2000). Software Architectures: Advances and Applications (pp. 1–79). Berlin: Springer Science & Business Media.
14. Li, L., (2009). Emerging Technologies for Academic Libraries in the Digital Age (pp. 1–35). London: Elsevier.
15. Lytras, & Miltiadis, D., (2010). Progressive Concepts for Semantic Web Evolution: Applications and Developments: Applications and Developments (pp. 1–73). Pennsylvania: Idea Group Inc (IGI).
16. Gopalan, N. P., & Adikesavan, T. A., (2014). Web Technology: A Developer's Perspective (pp. 1–68). New Delhi: PHI Learning Pvt. Ltd.
17. Oliver, V., Ingo, A., Arif, C., & Timo, K., (2011). Software Architecture: A Comprehensive Framework and Guide for Practitioners (pp. 22–65). Berlin: Springer Science & Business Media.
18. Richi, N. N. I., (2008). Evolution of the Web in Artificial Intelligence Environments (pp. 1–69). Berlin: Springer Science & Business Media.
19. Silva, S., (2012). Web Server Administration (pp. 1–41). London: Cengage Learning.
20. Sklar, J., (2011). Principles of Web Design: The Web Technologies Series (pp. 1–48). New York: Cengage Learning.
21. Stanek, W., (2014). Web Server Administration: The Personal Trainer for IIS 7.0 and IIS 7.5 (p. 380). London: RP Books & Audio.
22. Vemula, R., (2017). Real-Time Web Application Development: With ASP.NET Core, SignalR, Docker, and Azure (pp. 1–87). New York: Apress.

23. Walter, B., & Schahram, D., (2009). Emerging Web Services Technology, (Vol. 3, pp. 1–105). Berlin: Springer Science & Business Media.

24. Webuters, (2018). Real-Time Web Application-Development and Technologies. Retrieved from: webuters.com/: https://www.webuters.com/real-time-web-application-development-and-technologies/ (accessed on 31 March 2020).

INDEX